Eros and Modernization

Sylvester Graham, Health Reform,
and the Origins of Victorian Sexuality
in America

Eros and Modernization

Sylvester Graham, Health Reform, and the Origins of Victorian Sexuality in America

Jayme A. Sokolow

Rutherford ● Madison ● Teaneck
Fairleigh Dickinson University Press
London and Toronto: Associated University Presses

Associated University Presses, Inc.
440 Forsgate Drive
Cranbury, NJ 08512

Associated University Presses Ltd
25 Sicilian Avenue
London W.C1A 2QH, England

Associated University Presses
2133 Royal Windsor Drive
Unit 1
Mississauga, Ontario
Canada L5J 1K5

Library of Congress Cataloging in Publication Data

Sokolow, Jayme A., 1946–
    Eros and modernization.

    Bibliography: p.
    Includes index.
    1. Sex customs—United States—History—19th century.
2. Graham, Sylvester, 1794–1851.   3. Health reformers—
United States—History—19th century.   4. Sexual ethics
—History—19th century.   5. United States—Social
conditions—to 1865.   6. United States—Social
conditions—1865–1918.   I. Title.
HQ18.U5S598   1983   306.7'0973   82-71644
ISBN 0-8386-3147-9

Printed in the United States of America

To My Parents

Contents

Acknowledgments   9

Introduction: The Origins of Victorian Sexual Ethics   11

1. Modernization and Sexuality in Europe and America   19

2. The Political Economy of Sex   40

3. From Connecticut to Physiology   55

4. The Peculiar Epidemic   77

5. The Vegetarian Persuasion   100

6. The Paradox of Victorian Free Love   127

7. Grahamite Health Reform   143

Conclusion: Victorian Sexuality and the Eclipse of
   Community   176

Bibliography   185

Index   210

Acknowledgments

The research and the writing of this book have depended heavily upon many other people. My interest in Victorian sexuality is part of a continuing fascination with the history of antebellum reform which first became apparent under the tutelage of Carl E. Prince at New York University. Irving Kristol and the late Henry Bamford Parkes also provided guidance and encouragement.

No less important are those persons who guided me in my search for primary sources. In no particular order I would like to thank Bruce Silberman, Flo Maney, Linda and Margie Hirsch, Edward Shorter, and Carroll Smith-Rosenberg for their scholarly advice. And Joan Weldon did her usually excellent work turning my handwriting into a typed manuscript. I owe, however, the greatest debt to my most insightful critics, Sara and Carl Sokolow. This book is gratefully dedicated to them.

—Jayme A. Sokolow

Introduction:
The Origins of Victorian Sexual Ethics

Ralph Waldo Emerson, in his description of New England reformers, professed amazement at "the great activity of thought and experimenting" that occurred in his society. "What a fertility of projects for the salvation of the world! . . . No doubt there was plentiful vaporing, and cases of backsliding might occur. But in each of these movements emerged a good result, a tendency to the adoption of simpler methods, and an assertion of the sufficiency of the private man." Emerson considered the "growing trust in the private self-supplied powers of the individual" to be the reigning affirmative principle of the new philosophy. Common to all these reforms, Emerson noted, was the belief in the "infinite worthiness" of man and the faith that reform would lead to perfection.[1]

Emerson defined one of the major themes of antebellum culture, the concept of romantic reform, which rejected determinism and original sin and replaced them with the conviction that individuals were not hopeless and depraved by nature, but rather were free agents possessing the ability to perfect themselves. Romantic reform broke with the Enlightenment belief in gradual progress through the careful balancing of conflicting selfish interests and passions. Instead, many antebellum reformers demanded total commitment and immediate action to regenerate American society through individual self-improvement.

The emergence of immediatism and romantic reform reaffirmed Thomas Jefferson's doctrine that the earth belonged to the living. The break with Europe, the destruction of primogeniture, the ideology of republicanism, the growth of a dynamic commercial society, and the concomitant loosening of family ties created the impression that Americans could escape the entangling influences of the past. Romantic reformers often pictured themselves and their contemporaries as the potential heroes of a new adventure; emancipated from history, fortui-

11

tously bereft of ancestry, uninfluenced by the usual inheritances of tradition and place, the antebellum American was a self-reliant and inner-directed individual, ready to sweep away the dead hand of the past and construct a more glorious future.[2] Alexis de Tocqueville commented that Americans believed "their whole destiny is in their hands." Social and cultural traditions severed the ties that usually bound the generations to each other. "The woof of time is every instant broken and the track of generations effaced. Those who went before are soon forgotten; of those who will come after, no one has any idea: the interest of man is confined to those in close propinquity to himself."[3]

Romantic reform, with its optimistic belief in the power of human conscience, altered the methods and goals of benevolent societies. The denunciation of all force and the desire to create a nation directly modeled on Jesus' precepts split the American Peace Society and led to the creation of the New England Non-Resistance Society in 1838. The doctrine of immediate emancipation discredited the schemes of the American Colonization Society; the American Anti-Slavery Society, founded in 1833, denounced slaveholding as a sin and called for repentence and purgation in the form of abolition. Pacifists, abolitionists, and many other antebellum reformers believed that immediatism and the acceptance of certain moral absolutes would lead to unlimited progress proceeding from the individual to more complex institutions. Octavius Brooks Frothingham, a sympathetic contemporary observer of romantic reform, remarked that the romantic "was less a reformer of human circumstances than a regenerator of the human spirit. . . . With movements that did not start from this primary assumption of individual dignity, and come back to that as their goal, he had nothing to do."[4]

In addition to influencing benevolent organizations, romantic reform also helped transform nineteenth-century sexual ethics and behavior. During the colonial period, sexual thought rarely achieved the coherence or dignity of an intellectual system. Both the Puritans and Enlightenment thinkers portrayed marital sex as a natural and pleasant experience while they considered celibacy unhealthy or unnatural. Sexual promiscuity was thought to be wrong because it made marital sex less satisfying. Cotton Mather, for example, who never could be accused of advocating sexual license, dealt with sexuality in a pragmatic fashion: "When your Circumstances in the world will admit of it, use the Remedy, which the Word of God has prescribed for Burning. Enter into the Married State."[5]

In the nineteenth century, however, sexual ideology became more explicit, didactic, and systematic as extreme moderation became the dominant sexual attitude, especially among the Northeastern urban middle class. By the antebellum period, medical, biological, instructional, and popular literature contained countless defenses of extreme moderation and self-control. Sexual activity before marriage was condemned and infrequent sexual relations after marriage were recommended for moral and physiological reasons. "Respectable" Americans defended sexual prudence with a frenzied intensity unique in the history of American sexual attitudes. These changes in the evaluation of sexual activities were preceded in the late eighteenth century by a rapid decline in premarital pregnancies and illegitimacy, which only began to rise in the late 1800s. Thus at least in the Northeast, there seemed to be a congruity between sexual attitudes and actual sexual behavior.

Romantic reformers helped reinforce and encourage these sexual values and prudent behavior by promoting health reform. Victorian sexual theory was first articulated by a loose alliance of Northeastern sexual reformers who advocated a variety of measures that fused bodily and social control. Voluntaristic and anti-institutional, they sided with nature against artifice in the debate over therapeutic medicine, defended the superiority of prevention to cure, directed attention to the growing hygienic hazards of urban civilization, proposed that physical circumstances shaped individual morality, and helped develop better health habits and a stricter sexual morality in America. Health reform was perfectionist because it directed science toward the social goals of romanticism and promoted physiology as the foundation of the earthly kingdom. Purity advocates condemned the alleged disorder and unhealthy habits of antebellum society, but promised sanctification through reformed diet and improved health. An exalted morality, the health reformers claimed, would naturally result from individual hygienic improvement. Like many other reformers, they shared the revivalists' and transcendentalists' faith in the perfectibility of man and the approaching millennium.[6] Proper physiology had the potential to renovate society because natural laws, in the words of William A. Alcott, were a "means of lifting us toward the Eden whence we came."[7]

The most prominent and influential antebellum sexual reformer was Sylvester Graham (1794–1851). Throughout the mid-nineteenth century, Graham's sexual and dietary theories were used, usually in a more moderate fashion, by some physicians, many health reformers, and members of the Northeastern urban middle class. For this reason, his career, lectures, and books are the surest cultural guide to the emergence of a more prudent sexuality during this era. Graham believed that Americans were suffering in unprecedented numbers from an increased incidence of debility, nervousness, and general poor health. He blamed all these problems on sexual excesses before and during marriage and concluded that uncontrolled sexuality lowered the life-force of individuals by exposing their systems to disease and hence premature death. Demanding that people radically change their diets by including foods such as unsifted wheat, rye meal, and fruits and vegetables, Graham also hoped that healthy and robust adults would limit the number of times they had sexual intercourse.

Although Graham retired prematurely from the health-reform movement in 1837, his ideas were disseminated throughout the nineteenth century in advice books, lectures, phrenology, hydropathy, and a variety of dietary and sexual practices. Graham had a remarkably logical and systematic set of physiological principles that covered virtually every aspect of life, but even many of his followers considered him too extreme or obnoxiously contentious. They often modified Graham's ideas and presented romantic health reform as a reasonable and workable solution to many American social problems. Romantic reformers were so individualistic in their activities and philosophy that cooperation was often difficult and their organizations were sometimes ephemeral. Despite these limitations, however, romantic health reform was partially successful because the purity advocates were unified by a shared intellectual discourse centered around Graham's physiological principles. He was the archetypical health reformer, and more than any other antebellum American, Graham helped establish the rationale for Victorian sexual ethics.

The transformation of American sexual ideology and behavior coincided with the modernization process. During the nineteenth century, urbanization, commercialization, industrialization, and increased geographical mobility made antebellum America appear disorderly and dangerous to many reformers. The purity advocates, in common with many antebellum Americans, left their traditional towns and farms and migrated to urban centers seeking greater opportunities. There they experienced the unsettling changes of the period and thus felt competent to advise other Americans about the perils of antebellum life. Health reformers were horrified by commercialization, the decline of Northeastern rural life, and the loosening of generational ties, but they were also confident that individual morality and proper physiology could counteract the ruinous temptations of contemporary urban civilization and lead to a moral revolution. The modernization process made Graham and the health-reform movement not only fearful and repressive, but also optimistic and perfectionist. This dual attitude had interesting results. Although the romantic health reformers were often nostalgic about the rural society they once knew, they helped modernize urban Americans by encouraging traits that led to success in an increasingly commercial and urban America.

In this study I have tried to examine some of the social, cultural, and intellectual changes which produced Victorian sexuality. To do so I have narrowed the focus of investigation to one major segment of Victorian society—the Northeastern purity advocates—and I have given particular attention to their own experiences and perceptions in determining the ideology of extreme sexual moderation. My choice of this group was governed by personal and practical considerations: the availability of sources, the inherent interest of the subject matter, their concern with a changing American society, and the strategic position of this group in Victorian America. I also wanted to test a number of hypotheses about the effects of modernization on sexual attitudes and behavior. The classic models linking modernization to certain cultural changes do not explain the Victorian American sexual experience. The health reformers' lives and ideology will help provide us with an alternative paradigm relating American modernization and Victorian sexuality to a pervasive fear of disorder and a weakening of traditional institutions which led the health reformers to place their millennial hopes in the physiological reformation of the individual. These changes and responses have affected the nature of American life down to our times.

NOTES

1. Ralph Waldo Emerson, *The Complete Works of Ralph Waldo Emerson*, ed. Edward Waldo Emerson, 10 vols. (Boston and New York: Houghton Mifflin Co., 1903–1904), 3:251–60; 10:326.

2. John L. Thomas, "Romantic Reform in America, 1815–1865," *American Quarterly* 17 (1965):656–81; Rush Welter, *The Mind of America, 1820–1860* (New York: Columbia University Press, 1975), pp. 77–104, 165–89; R. W. B. Lewis, *The American Adam* (Chicago: University of Chicago Press, 1955), pp. 1–53, 77–109; Wilson Carey McWilliams, *The Idea of Fraternity in America* (Berkeley and Los Angeles: University of California Press, 1973), pp. 229–53, 280–300; Quentin Anderson, *The Imperial Self* (New York: Alfred A. Knopf, 1971); Michael Paul Rogin, "Nature as Politics and Nature as Romance in America," *Political Theory* 5 (1977):5–30.

3. Alexis de Tocqueville, *Democracy in America*, trans. Henry Reeve, 2 vols. (New York: Random House, 1945), 2:99.

4. Octavius Brooks Frothingham, *Transcendentalism in New England*, 1876 (New York: Harper and Row, 1959), p. 155.

5. Cotton Mather, *The Pure Nazarite* (Boston: T. Fleet, 1723), p. 16.

6. For previous studies of the health reformers, see Richard H. Shyrock, "Sylvester Graham and the Popular Health Movement, 1830–1870," *Mississippi Valley Historical Review* 18 (1931):172–93; William B. Walker, "The Health Reform Movement in the United States, 1830–1870" (Ph.D. diss., Johns Hopkins University, 1955); Edith Cole, "Sylvester Graham, Lecturer on the Science of Human Life: The Rhetoric of a Dietary Reformer" (Ph.D. diss., Indiana University, 1975); Stephen W. Nissenbaum, "Careful Love: Sylvester Graham and the Emergence of Victorian Sexual Theory in America, 1830–1840" (Ph.D.

diss., University of Wisconsin, 1968). His dissertation was recently published as *Sex, Diet, and Debility in Jacksonian America: Sylvester Graham and Health Reform* (Westport, Conn.: Greenwood Press, 1980). John B. Blake, "Health Reform," in *The Rise of Adventism: Religion and Society in Mid-Nineteenth Century America*, ed. Edwin S. Gausted (New York: Harper and Row, 1974), pp. 30–49; Ronald L. Numbers, *Prophetess of Health: A Study of Ellen G. White* (New York: Harper and Row, 1976), pp. 48–76.

    7. William A. Alcott, *The Laws of Health* (Boston: J. P. Jewett, 1857), p. 187.

Eros and Modernization

Sylvester Graham, Health Reform,
and the Origins of Victorian Sexuality
in America

1

Modernization and Sexuality in Europe and America

When Graham began lecturing in the 1830s about the necessity for prudent sexual behavior, many Americans were already conforming to Victorian sexual ethics. Since the late 1700s, premarital pregnancies and illegitimacy had been declining and public sexual attitudes and behavior were becoming more constrained. Graham and his followers became influential because there was a deep-seated change in the response of their audience that made them receptive to the purity reformers' advice. They disseminated and reinforced a new morality that was a reaction to the modernization process. The result was a repressive sexual revolution, which included a decrease in premarital coitus and a growing concern about the allegedly unhealthy aspects of sexual activities.

The proportion of American women pregnant at marriage or conceiving illegitimate children has varied cyclically, with peaks in the eighteenth century and in contemporary America, and troughs in the mid-seventeenth and mid-nineteenth centuries.[1] Cyclical variations also characterize western European premarital pregnancy and illegitimacy rates. But the major decline in these European indices began in the late nineteenth century, over seventy years after the American abatement.[2]

Why did American and European sexual behavior diverge during this period? The question becomes more intriguing when we consider that western Europe and America were simultaneously modernizing. Why was western European modernization characterized by increases in premarital sex and a more liberal attitude toward sexuality while modernization in America led to a dramatic decline in premarital sex and a more repressive sexuality?

My argument for two different types of sexual revolutions in Europe and America rests upon three kinds of evidence. By themselves, any one of these sources gives an inadequate and misleading picture of changes in sexual behavior. Considered together, however, they present a coherent and plausible pattern. First, there is premarital pregnancy, the conception, before marriage, of the first postmaritally born child. Second, there is illegitimacy, a birth to any unmarried woman or the incestuous or adulterous issue of a married woman. The professional and popular literature about sex constitutes the third type of evidence.

Premarital pregnancies are an excellent index to changes in sexual behavior. This measure has the advantage of coverage, since nearly all adults marry; reliability, since legitimate births are more likely to be recorded than illegitimate births; and objectivity, since its measurement depends upon the matching of records collected for other purposes. Illegitimate births also can help determine the incidence of premarital sexual activity. Of course, not all women who are sexually active before marriage bear children. Some may practice contraception, force an abortion, spontaneously miscarry, or not be fecund. But if these intervening variables remain unchanged, we can infer from a long-term rise or fall in premarital pregnancies and illegitimacy a similar increase or decrease in premarital sexual activity.

The cultural evidence is more problematic. People have always written about sexuality, and changes in advice manuals, popular lectures, and religious tracts may only tell us about the preoccupations and values of the observers rather than any social reality. Later I will examine some of the problems associated with using antebellum cultural evidence about sexuality and propose some solutions so that this material can be studied within the broader context of American society. It is undeniable, however, that during the 1830s, there was an astronomical increase in the number of American articles and books about sexuality. These studies appeared regularly in medical and educational magazines, short tracts, and self-help manuals. They claimed their work was scientific, argued that sexual morality was primarily a problem of hygiene, and tried to prove that sexual immoderation caused a myriad of mental and physical problems. These works reflected contemporary social and demographic trends and linked changes in American sexual behavior to the disorder and rapid changes caused by modernization.

Different forms of sexual behavior in Europe and America emerged from the modernization process. Throughout western Europe, variations in sexual behavior occurred in the choice of partners, in the modes of intercourse, and in the range of psychic gratification expected from sexual activities. In America, respectable sexual behavior diverged sharply from Europe as the Northeastern urban middle class inaugurated a repressive sexual revolution.

Since World War II, modernization has been employed widely to describe the process by which nations become more advanced in the technological, political, economic, and social spheres. The core meaning of modernization deals with two ideas: economic development, and social and political change in the direction of rational, complex, secular, integrated structures. Economically, modernization is associated with the triumph of the productive ideal, rationalized production, mobilization of resources, increasing differentiation of economic functions, and an increasing scale and integration of economic operations. Industrialization and urbanization are the economic consequences of modernization. Socially, modernization implies the movement away from a traditional society based on passive and local proclivities toward the creation of one unified society characterized by secular and rational values, functional status, and a positive belief in mobility and initiative.[3] The sociologists Alex Inkeles and David M. Smith have summed up the modern personality ideal type in this way:

> The modern man's character may be summed up under four major headings. He is an informed participant citizen; he has a marked sense of personal efficacy; he is highly independent and autonomous in his relations to traditional sources of influence . . . and he is ready for new experiences and ideas, that is, he is relatively open-minded and cognitively flexible.[4]

The study of modernization, pursued comparatively, opens the possibility of general historical interpretations based upon empirical research. The concept, however, sometimes is abused.

Many analyses of modernization dramatically juxtapose the stability, cyclical sense of time, localism, kinship orientation, and deference of a traditional society with an existence based on dynamic change, a linear conception of time, literacy, specialization, and a significant drive for individual autonomy and initiative. While the dichotomy appears with startling clarity, the chronological dimensions of the transformation process and the casual forces which lead to modernity often are obscure.[5] Thus explanations of modernization can be reductive and deterministic.[5] Modernization is erroneously used interchangeably with industrialization,[6] and it is used whiggishly, implicitly assuming that the process is universal and therefore teleological, with western Europe or America being the climax of development.[7] The term is loaded, evoking a positive image of progress and prosperity based on a timeless type of yardstick. Much of Marx's most telling criticisms of classical political economy, notably its ahistoricity, can be leveled against the theory of modernization.

Yet contemporary historians have cogently discussed the modernization process.[8] They have demonstrated that modernization is not a normative, western concept and it does not imply inevitability or
improvement. Modernization is a process that is never complete and does
not necessarily generate a better, more humane, or more satisfactory
society. The concept simply is a heuristic device for organizing related
processes in different geographical areas.

The appeal of modernization models arises from their presumed ability
to demonstrate how a wide range of undeniably significant developments
have affected society over time. Mainly because modernization seems to
be such a comprehensive concept, researchers have employed it alternately as an organizational device for recounting the key points in their
narrative, as a theoretical construct for explicating and predicting social
and cultural trends over time, and as a heuristic typology to help disclose
vital questions. Throughout this study I will use the concept of modernization to organize a wide variety of historical material into common
themes and provide a perspective for evaluating the impact of Graham
and the health-reform movement on American society.

All aspects of modernization have been fraught with strife, for the
stakes are high, the pressures are powerful, and the conflicts have been
intense. Although there have been different paths to modernity, it is
possible to distinguish certain critical problems that all modernizing
societies face. First, there is the challenge of modernity, the initial con-
frontation of a society, within its traditional framework of knowledge,
with modern ideas and institutions. Second, there is the consolidation of
modernizing leadership, the transfer of power from traditional to
modernizing leaders, often in a violent or revolutionary struggle. Third,
there is an economic and social transformation from a predominantly
rural and agrarian way of life toward an urban and industrial society. And
last, there is an integration of society, which produces a fundamental
reorganization of the society's social structure.

Western Europe, led by England, began the modernization process by
the late eighteenth or early nineteenth century. Economically, local guild
economies in western Europe began disappearing and were replaced by a
commercial and mechanized agriculture and industry unfettered by traditional restrictions and customs. Regional and national systems of
transportation and communication united countries and contributed to a
dramatic urban growth.

Socially, the tightly organized, homogeneous communities that ascribed to the individual a limited role marked by forceful religious and
secular sanctions lost their ability to discipline fellow citizens. The family

lost many of its economic and communal functions as emotive responses gradually replaced more instrumental considerations in the regulation of family life. As Balzac's characters brilliantly illustrate, individual freedom and social and geographic mobility increased in an environment that was becoming more secular, rational, and oriented toward the accumulation of wealth.

During this period, there was a dramatic increase in premarital pregnancies and illegitimacy among the working and lower classes throughout western Europe. Illegitimacy accelerated around the time of the French Revolution and continued to increase until the late nineteenth century. The simultaneous rise in premarital pregnancies and illegitimacy means that the rise in illegitimacy was not merely the result of delayed marriage. If both illegitimacy and premarital pregnancies simultaneously arose, the total volume of nonmarital sex was increasing. Sexual intercourse among the unmarried was becoming more common than in the past.[9]

For example, the number of English children born within eight and a half months of marriage increased from 16.5 percent in the seventeenth century to 43.4 percent between 1750 and 1836.[10] In Elversele, Flanders, the number of children born within eight months of marriage increased from 14.8 percent at the end of the seventeenth century to 23.4 percent by 1796.[11] Sainghin-en-Melantois in the North of France experienced a premarital pregnancy explosion beginning in the late eighteenth century. Children born within eight months of marriage skyrocketed from 15.2 percent for the period 1690–1796 to 54.8 percent in the 1840s.[12] Throughout western Europe, premarital pregnancies began increasing by the late eighteenth century.

Illegitimate births followed the same trend. In Bointin in Mecklenberg, three percent of all children were illegitimate in 1800. By 1880, the figure had climbed to 29 percent. Volkhardinghausen in Hesse more than tripled its illegitimacy rate from 1800 to 1880. Illegitimacy increased 14 percent from 1800 to 1850 in Anhausen, Bavaria.[13] Rotterdam registered a sixfold increase in illegitimacy from 1720 to 1810.[14] And Stuttgart's illegitimacy rate more than doubled from 1720 to 1800.[15] Illegitimacy and premarital pregnancies simultaneously increased throughout western Europe until the late nineteenth century.[16]

A more liberal sexuality also appeared as premarital sexual activities intensified. Masturbation probably became more common during this period. Prostitution and pornography mushroomed and became more overt in the first half of the nineteenth century. Throughout western Europe there was a cacophony of complaints about immoral youths and promiscuous dating and courtship practices from doctors, administrators, ministers, and politicians. Socially, European modernization was characterized by the introduction of a less traditional, freer, and more expressive sexuality.[17]

There are three possible sources of distortion in this quantitative evidence that may vitiate my conclusions—changes in the number of unmarried females, changes in the number of legitimate births, and more efficient record keeping. First, increasing illegitimacy in large European urban centers may have resulted from internal migration; unmarried rural females may have flocked to the cities and increased the population at risk for illegitimacy. But illegitimacy was rising even in rural areas and small towns. There are places where illegitimacy did not climb in the late 1700s, but often premarital pregnancies increased in these areas, so local courtship had changed to accommodate changing sexual behavior.[18] Second, shifts in the number of legitimate births did not change illegitimacy rates. Higher proportions of women were marrying, they probably were more fecund, and more children survived both inside and outside of marriage. Changes in marriage should have lowered, not raised the illegitimacy rate.[19] And last, parish registers and local records did not dramatically improve in efficiency during this period. In many communities, accurate records had been kept since the Reformation. Thus the quantitative and cultural evidence coincide; throughout western Europe there was a permissive sexual revolution after the mid-eighteenth century.

In America, by the late eighteenth century, the social expectations and widening political participation of the colonial period, accentuated, rationalized, and extended by the Revolution and western settlement, prepared the way for economic development and political integration. Key changes had occurred in common attitudes and popular behavior. The colonial concept of deference lost its old legitimacy in political and social situations. Innovation and improvement achieved a new priority among all classes and regions. Social and geographic mobility accelerated. By the early 1800s, there emerged an American variety of the modern personality syndrome. Americans believed that the natural and social environment could be improved, believed in personal ambition for themselves and their children, were open to new experiences, were rationalizing and secularizing their economic activities, and were increasingly independent from traditional authority figures.[20] "The speculative temperament," Oscar Handlin argued, asserted itself "at every level of society."[21]

During the American modernization process, premarital pregnancies and illegitimacy plummeted until the late nineteenth century and a more prudent sexuality became the hallmark of middle-class respectability. These changes sharply contrasted with the European experience, where a more overt and liberal sexuality triumphed. The evidence, however, may be badly skewed, and perhaps sexual mores and practices on both sides of the Atlantic were not so different. Certainly the same kind of repressive sexual morality that appeared in America flourished among the middle classes in England (where the term *Victorian* developed) and on the Continent. Maybe America was not exceptional and the differences that did occur came from the greater middle-class nature of American society with a similar morality developing among the European middle class about the same time. The problems of comparison are insoluble because European and American classes and cultures were so different. The evidence that we have for antebellum America is oriented around the Northeast and may not accurately reflect other areas and especially new cities, where reporting and gathering information might have been weak. Since the health reformers came from the Northeast and confined most of their activities to that region, the biased sampling may actually benefit us by providing accurate statistics about actual sexual behavior among the middle classes in that part of America first undergoing modernization.

Inasmuch as state and national surveys during this period do not measure premarital pregnancies or illegitimacy, I am relying on the local and national studies carried out by Daniel Scott Smith and Michael S. Hindus. They have used reconstitution, genealogical, and vital records material to chart changing rates of premarital pregnancies. Their work shows that there were falling premarital pregnancy rates in the mid-seventeenth (under ten percent) and mid-nineteenth century (about ten percent) and increasing rates in the mid-eighteenth century (about thirty percent) and in contemporary America. From the late eighteenth to the late nineteenth century, there was a precipitous decline in the national premarital pregnancy rate (Figure 1).

Their work in New England towns provides local examples of this national trend (Table 1). In these communities, there was a dramatic increase in premarital pregnancies among all fecund women throughout the mid-eighteenth century. But later in the century, premarital pregnancies began declining to about one-third of the peak rate. In Hingham, Massachusetts, for example, premarital pregnancies decreased from 36.5 percent in the period from 1761–1780 to 10.2 percent by 1860. Coventry, Connecticut, registered a 20.4-percent drop in premarital pregnancies from 1800 to 1840. Throughout America, from 1761–1800 to 1841–1880 premarital pregnancies declined from 33 percent to 12.6 percent among children born under nine months.[22]

Although the proportion of pregnancies in all premaritally conceived births is not constant over time, it appears to be an international phenomena that, when the overall level of premarital conceptions in-

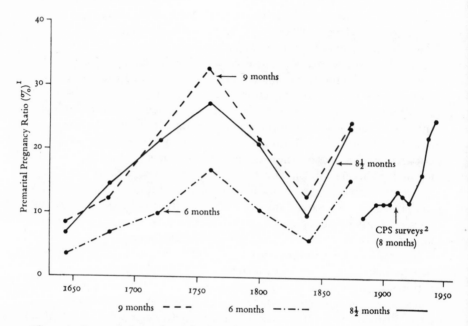

Figure 1: Premarital pregnancy in America

1. Percentage of premarital births among all births.
2. Current population survey of the United States Census Bureau. Source: Daniel Scott Smith and Michael S. Hindus, "Premarital Pregnancy in America, 1649–1971: An Overview and Interpretation," *Journal of Interdisciplinary History* 5 (1975): 538. Reprinted by permission of *The Journal of Interdisciplinary History* and the MIT Press, Cambridge, Massachusetts.

creases, the proportion of illegitimate births also rises. The higher the rate of premarital conception, the lower the chances that the premaritally conceived birth will be legitimated by marriage. The converse also holds true. Declining rates of premarital conceptions indicate a decline in the illegitimate birth rate.[23] Thus we can make the assumption, although statistics are lacking, that the decline in prebridal pregnancies was paralleled by a decline in illegitimate births.

On what grounds may we conclude that a decline in premarital sex produced a dramatic decline in premarital pregnancies and illegitimacy? Suppose we assume that illegitimacy rates were available and that the propensity of the average unmarried woman to conceive children was declining. We still would not be entitled to infer an automatic drop in sexual activity. There could be other variables that explain the decrease in premarital pregnancies and illegitimacy. We must discuss them before we are justified in claiming that changes in premarital pregnancies and illegitimacy indicate changes in sexual behavior.

Perhaps premarital pregnancies and illegitimacy declined because a greater number of unmarried women might have been less fecund, thus decreasing the likelihood that sexual activity would result in conception. This might have been caused by an increase in the average age of first menstruation, which decreased the adolescent population available for intercourse, or it might have been caused by a decline in the quality of health and nutrition, which lessened the ability of women to conceive.

We can eliminate the first possibility because unmarried women customarily did not begin engaging in sexual intercourse until long after puberty began. The second possibility—a decline in fecundity due to poor nutrition and health—is physiologically correct. Health and nutrition can affect a woman's fecundity by influencing the ages of menarche, menopause, and death, the success of each pregnancy, the duration of postpartum sterility, and fecundity during the menstrual cycle. There is no direct evidence that health or nutrition affects coital frequency or male fertility at the population level.[24] Thus the ability to conceive is partly a function of diet and general physical condition, and it has varied throughout history. During this period, however, American women were usually more fecund than western European women. The age of menarche went as high as eighteen in nineteenth-century Scandinavia; contemporary American physicians put male puberty around sixteen and female puberty

Table 1: Percent of premarital pregnancies under nine months

America		Hingham, Massachusetts (non–native-born excluded in nineteenth century)	
1721–1760	22.5%	1761–1780	36.5%
1761–1800	33.0%	1781–1800	39.1%
1801–1840	23.7%	1801–1820	28.4%
1841–1880	12.6%	1821–1840	20.3%
1881–1910	24.4%	1841–1860	10.2%
Coventry, Connecticut			
1741–1770	23.5%		
1771–1800	25.0%		
1801–1840	4.6%		

Source: Daniel Scott Smith and Michael S. Hindus, "Premarital Pregnancy in America, 1640–1971: An Overview and Interpretation," *Journal of Interdisciplinary History* 5 (1975): 561–63. Reprinted by permission of *The Journal of Interdisciplinary History* and the MIT Press, Cambridge, Massachusetts.

about a year earlier.[25] The decline in premarital pregnancies and illegitimacy was not caused by poor nutrition or health. These activities should have increased rather than declined because the American female population was healthier than their European counterparts and therefore more fecund.

If couples were using birth-control techniques and devices or using them more effectively, premarital pregnancies and illegitimacy might have decreased without a corresponding decline in premarital sexual activities. Young people may have become more adept at avoiding pregnancy. This theory is plausible but it has to be analyzed within the context of the introduction and efficiency of birth control.

The question of the acceptability and diffusion of birth control has been stated with great clarity by Norman E. Himes and Philippe Ariès. Himes, the authority on the history of contraception, has argued that the nineteenth-century decline in European and American family size was the direct result of the modernization and democratization of contraceptive use. The fertility transition was the consequence of an extensive diffusion of scientific knowledge about birth control.[26] Philippe Ariès, in contrast, believes that the desire to control fertility was not universal but fluctuated from society to society over time, depending on the permissiveness or restrictiveness of the dominant moral code. The widespread adoption of birth control was a result of a changed mentality: the fatalistic outlook that formally prevailed yielded to a rational view that distinguished between sexuality and procreation. Ariès concludes that there was no need for contraceptive innovation; coitus interruptus had only to be extended from nonmarital relations to behavior within wedlock.[27]

According to Himes, couples were always aware of the process of conception, but the means of contraception were lacking or ineffective. Ariès disagrees, and defends the position that couples simply conceived children because they could not separate sexual intercourse and procreation clearly enough. The means were available, but the goals were obscurely defined. Himes was concerned mainly with England and America, while Ariès focused primarily on France, where a fertility decline occurred at a time when no substantial improvements in contraceptive techniques had been made. In France, the new reproductive goals were defined earlier than in England and modern contraceptive technology was not needed because coitus interruptus was practiced. England was different; Malthusian restrictions on nuptiality were not easily accepted and new attitudes toward fertility had to be diffused through pressure groups.

The arguments of Himes and Ariès have both been modified over the past few decades. Although many devices and potions were used with varying degrees of effectiveness to control fertility, coitus interruptus was the principal method responsible for the nineteenth-century fertility decline. The belief that couples had the right to intervene in their fertility was connected with the dissociation of procreation from sexual gratification, the disappearance of magical and religious beliefs, rituals, and superstitions associated with sexual activities, the emergence of a value system centered around individual rights, and the growing belief that people had the right and obligation to take their own fate and that of their families into their own hands. These attitudes and forms of behavior became more widespread among the middle classes in Europe and America after the late 1700s.[28]

From the ancient world through the nineteenth century, the most common forms of birth control were infanticide, abortion, coitus interruptus, suppositories designed to form an impenetrable coating over the cervix, diaphragms, caps, intrauterine devices, internal medicine, douching, prolonged lactation, condoms, and variations of the rhythm method. Most of these were used in nineteenth-century Europe and America,[29] but their popularity can only be inferred. There are no pre–twentieth-century studies such as the Kinsey survey that would give us statistical information about birth control.

Contemporary Americans often stated that the decline in fertility within marriage (from 7.04 children in 1800 to 3.56 in 1900[30]) was the result of birth control.[31] Throughout the nineteenth century, withdrawal apparently was the most common method. One author claimed it was "a practice so universal that it may well be termed a national vice, so common that it is unblushingly acknowledged by its perpetrators, for the commission of which the husband is even eulogized by his wife."[32] Birth control begins with older, married couples and travels downward to young people.[33] It is improbable that young, unmarried couples were practicing birth control at a time (the mid-eighteenth century) when married couples were demonstrably not limiting their family size effectively. We do know that middle-class families were practicing contraceptive birth control by the 1920s. As we proceed backward from this period, the number of Americans using artificial birth control declines,[34] so it is highly unlikely that unmarried youths in the late 1700s and early 1800s used birth control effectively.

Even today, young couples do not use contraceptives often or effectively. In a 1968 West German poll, the great majority of young unmarried workers either used an ineffective contraceptive device or none at all. In a 1971 American survey, only twenty percent of unmarried adolescents contraceived consistently; half did not use any devices at all. Only in Denmark and Sweden did unmarried adolescents use contraceptive devices effectively.[35] Based on these historical practices, we can assume that effective contraception was not practiced among late–eighteenth-century unmarried couples. There is the possibility, however, that the long-term nineteenth-century decline in the birth rate was related to the decline in premarital pregnancies and illegitimacy. Extreme moderation, which the health reformers preached, may have been part of a wider emphasis on birth control.

Premarital pregnancies and illegitimacy might have declined because there were more spontaneous abortions than before. These rates could have declined without any changes in the frequency of intercourse. Even in contemporary western Europe and America, for every one hundred live births among unmarried women there are seventy fetuses that perish. Among single American black women, there are more spontaneous fetal deaths than live births.[36] In pre-modern Europe, there was a very high level of fetal loss among unmarried women. Thus, as Alain Molinier has suggested, rising western European illegitimacy rates may have been due to a decline in spontaneous abortions.[37]

An increased number of spontaneous fetal losses usually accompanies a general decline in child and maternal health conditions and a decline in a woman's physical condition.[38] Since there is no evidence that American women were less healthy during the nineteenth century than in the past, it is unlikely that there were more spontaneous abortions.

If more women were deliberating aborting themselves, premarital pregnancies and illegitimacy might have declined. In Europe, the late–nineteenth-century decline in illegitimate births was the partial result of more induced abortions.[39] Perhaps this happened in America at an earlier date. Before the nineteenth century, there were no laws against abortion in the first few months of pregnancy. Both the Catholic and Protestant churches defended the concept that abortion was possible before quickening, when the fetus gained life. Although quickening was still accepted during the first half of the nineteenth century, many states began making abortions illegal to protect the unborn fetus and the health of pregnant women. After the 1840s, however, as James Mohr has demonstrated, the overall incidence of abortion increased as growing numbers of married women used the procedure to delay childbearing or limit family size. But this recourse to abortion could not have greatly affected the downward trend in illegitimacy and premarital pregnancy which began in the late eighteenth century.[40]

A change in courtship practices may have led to a drop in illegitimacy and an increase in the percentage of children born within eight months of marriage. This did not happen too often. Both in western Europe and America, where the illegitimacy and premarital pregnancy rates are simultaneously available, they rise and fall together. During this period, fewer American women were getting pregnant before marriage and few women were having illegitimate children too.[41]

Illegitimacy might have declined because the number of illegitimate stillbirths increased. Since stillborn children were not usually recorded in church or town registers, an increase in stillbirths would lessen the number of illegitimate children registered. Stillbirths are partially attributable to poor prenatal care and childbirth procedures. Inasmuch as prenatal care and childbirth practices improved compared to the preceding period, it is unlikely that illegitimate stillbirths increased.

Last, changes in age at marriage might have led to a decline in premarital pregnancies and illegitimacy. A decline in the age of marriage should increase sexual activity among young, unmarried women because they are perceived as ready for sexual relations which are taking place among their married female peers. Other variables being constant, as the proportion of all legitimate births occurring to younger people increases, illegitimacy rates among those younger women should increase too.[42] From the colonial period to the late nineteenth century, there was a slight drop in age at marriage. Yet toward the end of the colonial era, premarital pregnancies and illegitimacy also declined. During this period, there seems to be no correlation between declining ages of American marriages and declining premarital pregnancy and illegitimacy rates.

We have examined the factors that would cause a nonpregnant, fecund, unmarried woman to become pregnant before marriage or have an illegitimate child. To summarize our evidence, there are four basic conditions that determine illegitimacy and premarital pregnancy rates:

1. *Exposure to risk of pregnancy.* This includes the proportion of unmarried women having sexual relations, the age when sexual activity begins, and the frequency of sexual activity.

2. *Control over conception by unmarried women having sexual relations.* This includes involuntary control due to an inability to conceive, and voluntary control through the use of contraceptives or birth control practices by fecund women.

3. *Control over gestation by pregnant, unmarried women.* This includes involuntary fetal loss (spontaneous abortion or stillbirth) and voluntary fetal loss (induced abortion).

4. *Legitimation of premarital pregnancies by marriage before the birth of the first child.*[43]

Premarital pregnancies and illegitimacy did not decline from the late 1700s to the late 1800s because women were less fecund, used birth control effectively, had more spontaneous or deliberate abortions, had more stillbirths, changed courtship practices, or married at earlier ages.

The fertility of unmarried women probably declined because men and women had fewer premarital sexual relations than in the preceding period. Changing sexual standards among young Europeans heralded the beginning of a sexual revolution. In America, sexual behavior became more prudent as Victorian sexual ethics became accepted by many middle-class Americans.

There is additional evidence to confirm my conclusions that a decrease in premarital sexual activity caused a decline in premarital pregnancies and illegitimacy—Victorian literature about sexuality. During the 1830s, there suddenly emerged a large body of sexual literature that ranged from scholarly monographs and earnest marriage manuals to domestic medical guides and quack physicians' pamphlets. Although these works had different attitudes toward sexual behavior, the literature directed toward the middle class usually was repressive in tone. Didactic and strident, this genre was passionately concerned with the regulation of solitary and interpersonal sexual activities.

Sexual control was described as the basic building block of personality and the foundation of civilization. Purity advocates defended regulation with an intensity alien to the tradition of the masculine ethos, which assumed that sexual energy had to be discharged to maintain health in adulthood. Though earlier writers discussed the insidious effects of passion, they also emphasized the dangers of anger, envy, or greed. Increasingly, progress was reduced to the degree of sexal continence.[44] Russell T. Trall, a Grahamite health reformer, typified this Victorian ethos when he advised his readers about the dangers of sexual intercourse:

> The frequency with which intercourse can be indulged without serious damage to one or both of the parties depends, of course, on a variety of circumstances—constitutional stamina, temperament, occupation, habits of exercise, etc. Few should exceed the limit of once a week; while many cannot safely indulge oftener than once a month. But as temperance is always the safe rule of conduct, if there must be any deviation from the strictest law of physiology, let the error be on that side.[45]

Recently, Carl Degler has challenged the opinion that sexual repression was both the norm and the reality for nineteenth-century middle-class Americans. He argues that we misread the sources if we believe that sexuality was completely condemned by Victorian popular and professional literature. In fact, a considerable number of doctors and reformers believed that sexual feelings were a natural and acceptable part of adult life. Degler believes that the literature condemning sexuality was not descriptive but normative because it was an effort to establish an ideology rather than delineate an already accepted one.[46]

He attempts to disprove the contention that a repressive sexual ideology influenced or reflected female sexual behavior by examining a unique survey of women he discovered at Stanford University. Dr. Clelia Duel Mosher (1863–1940), a physician and a pioneer in the study of female sexuality, polled forty-five middle- and upper-class women during the Progressive era. Seventeen were born before the Civil War and sixteen were born between 1860 and 1870. The survey contained detailed questions about their physiological knowledge, attitudes toward sex, and sexual experiences. According to Degler, most of the respondents accepted sexual intercourse as a natural part of womanhood and 82 percent of the women born before 1875 experienced orgasms during intercourse. He concluded that the ambivalent nature of Victorian sexual literature and the Mosher survey prove that most people apparently did not follow the prescriptions laid down by the marriage and advice manuals.[47]

Degler's study of Victorian literature and his analysis of the Mosher survey do not prove that Victorians accepted sexual desire or enjoyed sexual intercourse. Ironically, the Degler article substantiates the impact of nineteenth-century Victorian sexual ethics. First, the authors of the sexual guides agreed that a woman's sexual needs were milder than men's passions, and that sexual satisfaction could only be permitted within the framework of marriage and moderation. Any sexual behavior that violated these norms became deviant. And second, Degler badly misinterpreted the statistics in the Mosher survey, for they confirm the advice of the purity advocates. Thirty out of the forty-five women believed that conception was the primary purpose of sex. Fifteen women stated that sexual intercourse was unnecessary and nine thought it appropriate only for men. To the question, "Do you always have a venereal orgasm during intercourse,"[48] nearly twenty percent replied, "no, once, or never." If these responses are added to those who answered, "sometimes, not always or no with instances," then the total reaches 59.9 percent. The attitude of these women contrasts sharply with the more positive evaluations of sexuality expressed by women in the sexual behavior studies begun in the 1920s.[49]

Although Degler's conclusions are inaccurate and support the contentions of the moral-purity writers, he has correctly urged caution in discussing Victorian sexual morality; the values of the purity writers do not necessarily represent antebellum America. While behavior is often directly determined by attitudes, verbalized and literary attitudes also may be different from actual behavior patterns. There may be a difference between the code a society formally defends and the informal or operational code which is much closer to actual behavior. Publicly accepting the formal attitudes and norms is often more important than whether or not people follow them. This inconsistency between attitudes and behavior stems largely from the fact that behavior is subject to more rapid social change. Degler's argument about the divided nature of antebellum sexual advice is important, and there is a real danger in blindly taking sexual purism as the norm within the advice literature and among middle-class Victorian Americans.[50]

Jay Mechling's research on the impact of childrearing literature on parents can help provide us with a feasible method for meeting Degler's criticisms of Victorian purity literature. Mechling discovered that while there is evidence that official advice in childrearing literature affects parents' recall of childrearing behavior, there is no persuasive evidence that the official advice affects the parents' actual behavior. Appropriating Mechling's objections, we could argue that there are four major criticisms that can be leveled against using antebellum health-reform literature as historical evidence. First, there is some doubt about the meaning of the advice found in the purity literature. A second objection concerns the problem of sampling and analyzing a sufficiently broad range of material. The relationship between health-reform literature and the learning process constitutes another problem. Most studies indicate that behavior is not primarily learned by reading books but through social interaction. Proof that the literature reflects actual behavior inevitably depends upon other evidence of observed behavior. And last, there is the problem of the theoretical link between values and behavior. It is quite possible that the health-reform literature reflects the values of the authors and not the audience.[51]

Mechling's analysis can help us develop a more historically accurate picture of Victorian sexuality. Perhaps the solution to the problem of reconstructing the sexual values of antebellum America rests on our ability to examine sexual behavior from evidence other than the advice literature. Another solution might be to examine the conditions in American society which made the health-reform movement a plausible, acceptable activity. We could also analyze the purity literature as evidence of the authors' minds and generalize about some portion of antebellum intellectual and cultural life. I will examine romantic health reform from all three perspectives. We have already dealt with the first solution and discovered that in antebellum America when patterns of behavior developed that were contrary to accepted values, a modification of the attitudes occurred. Since the late 1700s Northeastern middle-class Americans probably had been developing more prudent forms of sexual behavior as measured by declining premarital pregnancies and illegitimacy. The amount and tone of antebellum purity literature reflects the demographic evidence and the Mosher survey. During the modernization process, European and American sexual behavior diverged as American Victorians developed more moderate sexual attitudes and forms of behavior.

NOTES

1. Daniel Scott Smith, "The Dating of the American Sexual Revolution: Evidence and Interpretation," in *The American Family in Social-Historical Perspective,* ed. Michael Gordon (New York: St. Martin's Press, 1973), pp. 321–35.

2. Edward Shorter, John Knodel, and Etienne van de Walle, "The Decline of Non-Marital Fertility in Europe, 1880–1940," *Population Studies* 24 (1971):375–93.

3. Cyril E. Black, *The Dynamics of Modernization* (Princeton, N.J.: Princeton University Press, 1966), pp. 1–34; Richard F. Jones, *Ancients and Moderns: A Study of the Rise of the Scientific Movement in Seventeenth-Century England* (Berkeley and Los Angeles: University of California Press, 1965); John Arthur Passmore, *The Perfectability of Man* (London: Scribner, 1970), pp. 212–59; J. A. Bury, *The Idea of Progress: An Inquiry Into Its Origins and Growth* (London: Macmillan & Co., 1924); Richard D. Brown, "Modernization: A Victorian Climax," in *Victorian America,* ed. Daniel Walker Howe (Philadelphia: University of Pennsylvania Press, 1976), pp. 29–46; Daniel Lerner, *The Passing of Traditional Society: Modernizing the Middle East* (Glencoe, Ill.: Free Press, 1958); W. W. Rostow, *The Stages of Economic Growth* (Cambridge, England: Cambridge University Press, 1960); Gabriel A. Almond and Sidney Verba, *The Civic Culture: Political Attitudes and Democracy in Five Nations* (Princeton, N.J.: Princeton University Press, 1963); Samuel N. Eisenstadt, *Modernization: Protest and Change* (Englewood Cliffs, N.J.: Prentice-Hall, 1966); Alex Inkeles, "Making Man Modern: On the Causes and Consequences of Individual Change in Six Developing Countries," *American Journal of Sociology* 75 (1969):208–25. The literature is so vast that the following bibliographies should be consulted: Allan A. Spitz, *Developmental Change: An Annotated Bibliography* (Lexington, Ky.: University of Kentucky Press, 1969); John Brode, *The Process of Modernization: An Annotated Bibliography on the Sociocultural Aspects of Development* (Cambridge, Mass.: Harvard University Press, 1970).

4. Alex Inkeles and David H. Smith, *Becoming Modern: Individual Change in Six Developing Countries* (Cambridge, Mass.: Harvard University Press, 1974), p. 290.

5. James A. Henretta, "Modernization: Toward a False Synthesis," *Reviews in American History* 5 (1977):445–52.

6. E. A. Wrigley, "The Process of Modernization and the Industrial Revolution," *Journal of Interdisciplinary History* 3 (1972):225–60.

7. Samuel N. Eisenstadt, "Studies of Modernization and Sociological Theory," *History and Theory* 13 (1974):225–52.

8. For example, see Knight Biggerstaff, "Modernization and Early Modern China," *Journal of Asian Studies* 25 (1966):607–19; Albert Feurerwerker, *China's Early Industrialization: Sheng Hsuan-huai and Mandarin Enterprise* (New York: Atheneum, 1970); Richard Graham, *Britain and the Onset of Modernization in Brazil, 1850–1914* (Cambridge, Mass.: Harvard University Press, 1968).

9. Edward Shorter, "Illegitimacy, Sexual Revolution, and Social Change in Modern Europe," *Journal of Interdisciplinary History* 2 (1971):237–72; "Sexual Change and Illegitimacy: The European Experience," in *Modern European Social History,* ed. Robert J. Be-

zucha (Lexington, Mass.: D. C. Heath, 1972), pp. 231–69; "Female Emancipation, Birth Control, and Fertility in European History," *American Historical Review* 78 (1973):605–40; *The Making of the Modern Family* (New York: Basic Books, 1975), pp. 79–97; Massimo Livi Bacci, *A Century of Portuguese Fertility* (Princeton, N.J.: Princeton University Press, 1971), pp. 72, 74; *A History of Italian Fertility During the Last Two Centuries* (Princeton, N.J.: Princeton University Press, 1977), pp. 74–81; Ron J. Lesthaeghe, *The Decline of Belgian Fertility, 1800–1970* (Princeton, N.J.: Princeton University Press, 1977), pp. 181–82; John E. Knodel, *The Decline of Fertility in Germany, 1871–1939* (Princeton, N.J.: Princeton University Press, 1974), pp. 39, 75–80; Lawrence Stone, *The Family, Sex and Marriage in England, 1500–1800* (New York: Harper and Row, 1977), pp. 606–15, 644–51; Jean-Louis Flandrin, *Familles: parenté, maison, sexualité dans l'ancien société* (Paris: Hachette, 1976), pp. 176–84.

10. P. E. H. Hair, "Bridal Pregnancy in Rural England in Earlier Centuries," *Population Studies* 20 (1966–1967):233–43 and "Bridal Pregnancy in Earlier Rural England, Further Examined," *Population Studies* 24 (1970):59–70.

11. P. Deprez, "The Demographic Development of Flanders in the Eighteenth Century," in *Population in History: Essays in Historical Demography*, ed. D. V. Glass and D. E. C. Eversley (London: Arnold, 1965), pp. 608–30.

12. Raymond Deniel, "La Population d'un village du Nord de la France: Sainghin-en-Mélantois, de 1665 à 1851," *Population* 20 (1965):563–602.

13. Jacques Houdaille, "Quelques résultats sur la démographie de trois villages d'Allemagne de 1750 à 1879," *Population* 25 (1970):649–54.

14. A. M. Van der Woude and G. J. Mentink, "La Population de Rotterdam au XVIIe et au XVIIIe siècle," *Population* 21 (1966):1165–90.

15. Helmut Möller, *Die Kleinbürgerliche Familie im 18 Jahrhundret: Verhalten und Gruppenkultur* (Berlin: de Gruyter, 1969), p. 290.

16. For a complete bibliography of premarital pregnancy and illegitimacy rates throughout this period, see Shorter, "Illegitimacy, Sexual Revolution," pp. 259–72; "Female Emancipation," pp. 633–40.

17. E. H. Hare, "Masturbatory Insanity: The History of an Idea," *Journal of Mental Science* 108 (1962):1–25; Robert H. MacDonald, "The Frightful Consequences of Onanism: Notes on the History of a Delusion," *Journal of the History of Ideas* 28 (1967):423–31; Steven Marcus, *The Other Victorians: A Study of Sexuality and Pornography in Mid-Nineteenth-Century England* (New York: Basic Books, 1966); Rudolf Braun, *Industrialisierung und Volksleben: Die Veränderungen der Lebensformen in einem ländlichen Industriegebiet vor 1800 (Züricher Oberland)* (Erlanbach-Zurich: Eugen Rentsch, 1960), pp. 65–72; Oscar Helmuth Werner, *The Unmarried Mother in German Literature with Special Reference to the Period 1770–1800* (New York: Columbia University Press, 1917); J. Michael Phayer, *Sexual Liberation and Religion in Nineteenth Century Europe* (London: Rowman and Littlefield, 1977); Shorter, *The Modern Family*, pp. 98–108, 120–160.

18. Alain Molinier, *Une Paroisse du bas Languedoc: Serignan, 1650–1792* (Montpellier: Imp. Déhan, 1968), p. 4.

19. Shorter, "Female Emancipation," pp. 633–35.

20. Black, *Modernization*, pp. 110–14; Richard D. Brown, "Modernization and the Modern Personality in Early America, 1600–1865: A Sketch of a Synthesis," *Journal of Interdisciplinary History* 2 (1972):201–28; *Modernization: The Transformation of American Life, 1600–1865* (New York: Hill and Wang, 1976).

21. Oscar Handlin, *The Americans* (Boston: Little, Brown & Co., 1963), p. 155.

22. Daniel Scott Smith and Michael S. Hindus, "Premarital Pregnancy in America, 1640–

1971: An Overview and Interpretation," *Journal of Interdisciplinary History* 5 (1975):537–70.

23. Shirley M. Hartley, "The Amazing Rise of Illegitimacy in Great Britain," *Social Forces* 44 (1966):540; Sidney Goldstein, "Premarital Pregnancies and Out-of-Wedlock Births in Australia, 1911–1966," *Australian and New Zealand Journal of Sociology* 4 (1968):141–45; Phillips Cutright, "Illegitimacy in the United States, 1920–1968," in *Demographic and Social Aspects of Population Growth*, ed. Charles F. Westoff and Robert Parke, Jr. (Washington, D.C.: Government Printing Office, 1972), pp. 403–5. The strong positive correlation between prebridal pregnancy and illegitimacy has been documented on an international scale by Cutright.

Table 2: Relationship between the non-marital
conceived birth rate per 1,000 unmarried (ages 15–44) women
and the percentage of non-maritally conceived births legitimated by marriage

Country	Year of Observation	Non-Marital Birth Rate	Legitimated Rate	Illegitimate Rate	Percent
Netherlands	1956	15.4	12.3	3.1	80.0
Norway	1955	29.6	21.0	8.6	71.5
England and Wales	1938	18.6	12.8	5.8	70.6
United States (white)	1964–66	28.5	17.3	11.3	60.6
Australia	1965	47.1	27.3	19.8	57.0
Denmark	1965	59.0	35.9	23.1	61.0
Sweden	1965	60.0	32.5	27.5	54.0

Source: Phillips Cutright, "Illegitimacy in the United States, 1920–1968," in *Demographic and Social Aspects of Population Growth* ed. Charles F. Westoff and Robert Parke, Jr. (Washington, D.C.: Government Printing Office, 1972), p. 405.

24. William P. Butz and Jean-Pierre Habicht, "The Effect of Nutrition and Health on Fertility: Hypotheses, Evidence, and Interventions," in *Population and Development* ed. Ronald C. Ridker (Baltimore: Johns Hopkins University Press, 1976), pp. 210–238.

25. J. M. Tanner, "Sequence, Tempo, and Individual Variation in the Growth and Development of Boys and Girls Aged Twelve to Sixteen," *Daedalus* 100 (1971):907–30; Peter Laslett, "Age at Menarche in Europe since the 18th Century," *Journal of Interdisciplinary History* 2 (1971):221–36.

26. Norman E. Himes, *Medical History of Contraception* (Baltimore: The Williams and Wilkins Co., 1936), pp. 333–94.

27. Philippe Ariès, "Interpretation pour une histoire des mentalités," *La Prévention des naissances dans la famille: ses origines dans les temps moderne,* ed. Hélène Pergues (Paris: INED, 1960), pp. 311–27; "Sur les origines de la contraception en France," *Population* 3 (1953):465–72.

28. *Popular Attitudes toward Birth Control in Pre-Industrial France and England,* ed. Orest Ranum and Patricia Ranum (New York: Harper and Row, 1972); William L. Langer, "The Origins of the Birth Control Movement in England in the Early Nineteenth Century," *Journal of Interdisciplinary History* 5 (1975):669–86; Peter Fryer, *The Birth Controllers* (New York: Stein and Day, 1966); Alfred Sauvy, *La prévention des naissances* (Paris: Presses Universitaires de France, 1965); Jean-Louis Flandrin, "Contraception, mariage, et relations amoureuses dans l'Occident chrétien," *Annales: E.S.C.* 24 (1969):1370–90; J. A. Banks, *Prosperity and Parenthood, A Study of Family Planning among the Victorian Middle Classes* (New York: Schocken Books, 1954); James Reed, *From Private Vice to Public*

Virtue: The Birth Control Movement and American Society since 1830 (New York: Basic Books, 1978).

29. Linda Gordon, *Woman's Body, Woman's Right: A Social History of Birth Control in America* (New York: Viking Press, 1977), pp. 13–71; John T. Noonan, Jr., *Contraception* (Cambridge, Mass.: Harvard University Press, 1966), pp. 387–94; Vern Bullough and Bonnie Bullough, *Sin, Sickness and Sanity: A History of Sexual Attitudes* (New York: Garland Publishing, 1977), pp. 91–117; J. Sutter, "Sur la diffusion des méthodes contraceptives," *La Prévention*, pp. 341–59.

30. Ansley J. Coale and Melvin Zelnik, *New Estimates of Fertility and Population in the United States* (Princeton, N.J.: Princeton University Press, 1963), p. 36.

31. Arthur W. Calhoun, *A Social History of the American Family from Colonial Times to the Present*, 3 vols. (Cleveland, Ohio: The Arthur H. Clark Co., 1917–1919), 2:157–59, 209–10; 3:34–35, 238–45.

32. Nicholas Francis Cooke, *Satan in Society. By a Physician* (Cincinnati and New York: C. F. Vent, 1872), p. 152.

33. Shorter, "Female Emancipation," pp. 629–30.

34. Paula S. Fass, *The Damned and the Beautiful: American Youth in the 1920's* (New York: Oxford University Press, 1977), pp. 71–78.

35. John F. Katner and Melvin Zelnik, "Contraception and Pregnancy: Experience of Young Unmarried Women in the United States," *Family Planning Perspectives* 5 (1973):21–35; Gunter Schmidt and Volkmar Sigusch, *Arbeiter-Sexualität: Eine empirische Untersuchung an jungen Industriearbeiten* (Neuwied: Luchterhand, 1971), p. 54.

36. Cutright, "Illegitimacy in the United States," pp. 395–400.

37. Molinier, *Une Paroisse*, pp. 199–202.

38. Phillips Cutright, "Illegitimacy: Myths, Causes and Cures," *Family Planning Perspectives* 3 (1971):26–47.

39. Shorter, Knodel, and van de Walle, "Decline of Non-Marital Fertility," pp. 375–93.

40. Lawrence Lader, *Abortion* (Boston: Bobbs-Merrill, 1966), pp. 75–90; Eugene Quay, "Justifiable Abortion—Medical and Legal Foundations," *The Georgetown Law Journal* 49 (1961):395–526; James C. Mohr, *Abortion in America: The Origins and Evolution of National Policy* (New York: Oxford University Press, 1978).

41. Shorter, "Illegitimacy, Sexual Revolution," pp. 266–69; Cutright, "Illegitimacy in the United States," pp. 403–5.

42. Cutright, "Illegitimacy: Myths, Causes, Cures," p. 36.

43. Kingsley Davis and Judith Blake, "Social Structure and Fertility: An Analytic Framework," *Economic Development and Cultural Change* 4 (1956):211–35.

44. Oscar Handlin, *Race and Nationality in American Life* (Boston: Little, Brown & Co., 1957), pp. 111–32; Stephen W. Nissenbaum, "Careful Love: Sylvester Graham and the Emergence of Victorian Sexual Theory in America, 1830–1840" (Ph.D. diss., University of Wisconsin, 1968), pp. 2–34; David M. Kennedy, "The Nineteenth-Century Heritage: The Family, Feminism, and Sex," *Birth Control in America: The Career of Margret Sanger* (New Haven, Conn.: Yale University Press, 1970), pp. 36–71; Michael Gordon and M. Charles Bernstein, "Mate Choice and Domestic Life in 19th Century Marriage Manuals," *Journal of Marriage and the Family* 32 (1970), 665–74; Milton Rugoff, *Prudery and Passion: Sexuality in Victorian America* (New York: Putnam, 1971), pp. 35–119; Ben Barker-Benfield, "The Spermatic Economy: A Nineteenth Century View of Sexuality," *Feminist Studies* 1 (1972):45–74; *The Horrors of the Half-Known Life: Male Attitudes Toward Women and Sexuality in 19th Century America* (New York: Harper and Row, 1976); John S. Haller and Robin Haller, *The Physician and Sexuality in Victorian America* (Urbana, Ill.: University of Illinois Press, 1973), pp. 91–103; Charles A. Rosenberg, "Sexual-

ity, Class and Role in 19th Century America," *American Quarterly* 25 (1973):131–53; Carroll Smith Rosenberg and Charles E. Rosenberg, "The Female Animal: Medical and Biological Views of Woman and Her Role in Nineteenth Century America," *Journal of American History* 60 (1973):332–56; Nancy Cott, "Passionlessness: An Interpretation of Victorian Sexual Ideology, 1790–1850," *Signs* 4 (1978–79):219–36.

45. Russell T. Trall, *Sexual Physiology: A Scientific and Popular Exposition of the Fundamental Problems in Sociology* (New York: Miller, Wood, 1866), p. 295.

46. Carl N. Degler, "What Ought to Be and What Was: Women's Sexuality in the Nineteenth Century," *American Historical Review* 79 (1974):1467–90; *At Odds: Women and the Family in America From the Revolution to the Present* (New York: Oxford University Press, 1980), pp. 249–78.

47. Degler, "What Ought to Be and What Was," p. 1489.

48. Ibid., pp. 1483–84.

49. For an interesting exchange over Degler's article, see the letter by Nathan G. Hale, Jr., and Degler's reply in the *American Historical Review* 80 (1975):1079–81.

50. For an excellent discussion of the inherent problems in studying the history of sexuality, see Ronald G. Walters, "Sexual Matters as Historical Problems: A Framework of Analysis," *Societas* 6 (1976):157–76.

51. Jay E. Mechling, "Advice to Historians on Advice to Mothers," *Journal of Social History* 9 (1975):44–63.

2

The Political Economy of Sex

Although declining rates of premarital pregnancies and illegitimacy and the rise of a strident purity literature indicate that a comprehensive sexually repressive belief system developed in antebellum America, Victorian society was very socially complex. Domesticity and the cult of true womanhood were ennobled, but Americans also supported radical communal experiments that abolished the family, created polygamy, or encouraged free love. The United States spawned the permissive sexuality of the frontier and the repressive, genteel behavior of Lydia Sigourney's Hartford. Thousands of appreciative Americans attended Victoria Woodhull's unorthodox lectures on love while other New Yorkers tried to censor allegedly pornographic books and information on birth control, eradicate prostitution, and develop a stricter urban morality. Yet there was a fairly unified nineteenth-century style of "respectable" sexual ideology and behavior. Certainly early modernists such as Sigmund Freud and Havelock Ellis were very conscious about their departures from what they considered to be Victorian sexual orthodoxy.

In America, Victorian sexual ethics were first articulated during the antebellum period by Sylvester Graham and the health-reform movement. They advocated a more moderate sexuality than their eighteenth-century predecessors because the purity crusaders perceived America as a disorderly and dangerous place. Health reformers anticipated a plausible theory of modernization to explain the extreme fragility of Jacksonian America. They blamed the lack of order on the loosening of generational ties, commercialization, urbanization, and the decline of the patriarchal agricultural family. Because traditional institutions appeared weak and unstable, the health reformers, in true romantic fashion, wanted to restore order and morality by relocating the source of authority within the individual. Proper physiology could counteract the destructive sexual and moral attitudes that resulted from modernization.

Contemporary analysts also have associated the modernization process with changes in sexual behavior. Some writers have argued that modernization leads to a more repressive sexuality while others believe that modernization is inextricably linked to an increasingly liberal sexual behavior. We will examine these models and apply them to Victorian America; perhaps they can describe the development of a restrictive sexuality.

Scholars have created different models combining the various elements of modernization, cultural cohesion, cultural breakdown, sexual liberalization, and sexual repression. Although these models differ, they commonly use the terms *capitalism* and the *subculture of sexuality*. Capitalism, which I define as a money economy in which the market dictates prices and in which ownership is private, may be traditional or promote modernization. European town-guild economies which had a regulated market were capitalistic but traditional. The attitudes that characterize a specific kind of capitalism determine whether modernization will be promoted. Of course, modernization does not have to be based on a capitalist economy. Most model builders, however, really mean modernization when they discuss capitalism, because they are not describing a static, traditional economy, but an experimental, flexible economic system involving the rationalization, specialization, and magnification of output. Thus "modernization" will be used instead of "capitalism" if the authors are discussing a dynamic type of capitalism.

The *culture of sexuality* is the set of rules and behavior prevailing between males and females. The sexual culture of popular family and social life is a standard set of social reactions followed by most people. When one group within the population has created a varient set of operating rules in the sexual sphere, a *subculture of sexuality* develops. The concepts of capitalism and a subculture of sexuality are important to the model builders, for most of them believe that modern capitalism creates a liberal sexual subculture that later becomes the dominant form of sexual behavior.

These models differ in the principal analytic concepts they employ and in the resultant changes of behavior they predict. Although they are varied, all claim to have discovered the causal factors that account for sexual changes in the modern world. Do any of the models mesh with the quantitative and cultural American evidence for the Victorian period?

The first group of writers, ranging from Max Weber to the Freudian left, have argued that repressive sexuality accompanied modernization, and that guilt over salvation and the sublimation of sexual energies into work lessened sexual gratification (Figure 1). This model of sexual subli-

Figure 2: Sexual sublimation model

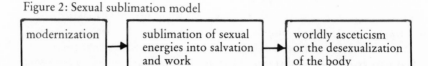

mation is distinguished by its analytic simplicity and by its linkage of sexual repression with secular industriousness.

Weber argued strenuously in *The Protestant Ethic and the Spirit of Capitalism* (1904–1905) that Calvinism created the preconditions for modernization. He contended that its members believed a person's trade or calling constituted a religious mission. The fulfillment of one's daily tasks and success in one's trade was a deed pleasing to God. These ideas promoted diligence and hard work. Weber believed that Benjamin Franklin, who hardly exemplified sexual asceticism, was the outstanding example of this outlook. The Calvinists also emphasized thrift and worldly asceticism. These habits eventually became secularized and inevitably aided the modernization process in Europe and America.[1]

Few historical arguments have aroused so much controversy as the Weber thesis.[2] Certainly in the cases of the Puritans in prerevolutionary England[3] and the Huguenots of late–sixteenth-century Languedoc, an argument could be made that the Calvinist doctrines of thrift and accumulation led to greater social repression and more attention to work at the cost of sexual pleasure. For example, in the Calvinist Cévannes in Languedoc, the consistories proscribed too long and too intimate betrothals, servants' debaucheries, premarital pregnancies, and prostitution, but never condemned usury or economic exploitation.[4] Thus there seems to be some connection between "Calvinist modernization" and the lessening of sexual gratification.

In the Calvinist countries of late–eighteenth-century Europe, however, modernization led to a break between marriage and sexual intercourse and a more liberal sexual behavior. Premarital pregnancies also boomed in mid–eighteenth-century New England, which was ostensibly Calvinist. There may be a link among Calvinism, modern capitalism, and sexual repression in Reformation Europe, but certainly changes in European and American sexual behavior cannot be correlated with the rise and fall of the Protestant ethic.

The arguments of the Freudian left have been more compelling. These European and American intellectuals denied that Freud's theories implied sexual renunciation and political conservatism. Instead, they used

Freudianism to create a radical political and sexual philosophy which challenged the dominant culture. Geza Roheim, Wilhelm Reich, Herbert Marcuse, and Norman O. Brown believed that sexual pleasure was the ultimate measure of human happiness and they vigorously attacked the supposed sexual repressiveness of modern civilization.[5] Since Reich dealt mostly with Germany and Roheim worked with anthropological evidence, Marcuse and Brown will be examined because they have greatly influenced American thinking.

During the 1950s, two books appeared which sharply challenged the prevailing interpretation of Freud, Herbert Marcuse's *Eros and Civilization* (1955) and Norman O. Brown's *Life Against Death: The Psychoanalytic Meaning of History* (1959). Both authors argued that Freud's greatest accomplishment was his emphasis on the high price we paid for civilization: they agreed with Freud that contemporary culture was built on repression because man's desire to seek sexual fulfillment and pleasure collided with the increasingly rigorous demands of civilization.[6] They rejected, however, the pessimistic conclusions of Freud and instead insisted that his work had "radical critical implications."[7] Marcuse and Brown went beyond Reich and Roheim and reached more revolutionary conclusions than those of the earlier Freudian left.

Marcuse reinterpreted Freudian theory by introducing several important historical and sociological distinctions. He transformed Freud's unhistoric concepts into historical ones so that psychoanalytic theory could be melded with Marxism. The two most important ideas Marcuse developed were surplus repression and the performance principle. Surplus repression introduced a historical dimension to Freud's equation of civilization and repression. It was the quantitative restrictions put upon sexuality from economic and political domination and was identified with Marx's concept of surplus value, which was the quantitative measure of exploitation under capitalism. The performance principle corresponded to Marx's qualitative characterization of existence under capitalism—alienation and reification.[8] The performance principle led to the nearly complete desexualization of the erotic zones so that sexual energy could be sublimated into work: "Repression from without has been supported by repression from within. . . . The unfree individual introjects his masters and their commands into his own mental apparatus."[9] The desexualization of the body, the result of modernization, led to a radical reduction in the potential for pleasure.

Marcuse concluded that the future of humanity depended on the ability to reverse the sexually repressive trend of modern civilization. In a society which had abolished material deprivation, the performance principle, and alienated labor, sexuality would be released from its exclusively genital focus and revert to its original polymorphous mode of expression. By distinguishing between repression and surplus repression, the reality principle and the performance principle, Marcuse tried to show that Freud's equation of civilization with sexual repression belonged to a stage of historical development—the modernization process. [10]

Norman O. Brown, like Marcuse, believed that people were repressed because they "refuse to recognize the realities of human nature," [11] and he attempted to demonstrate that psychoanalysis was a critical rather than a conservative philosophy. Similarly, Brown argued that modern civilization was characterized by sexual repression and uncontrolled aggression, and offered a solution to the problem of unhappiness by uncovering the promise of a nonrepressive civilization beneath Freud's historical pessimism. Brown pursued the same themes as Marcuse by defending two of Freud's psychological assumptions: the pervasive role of sexuality and the death instinct. Brown, however, differed from Marcuse in his idiosyncratic analysis of repressive sexuality and modern civilization.

More mystical and metaphorical than historical, Brown argued that the modernization process, which he dated from the Protestant Reformation, was characterized by increasing aggression and a refusal to accept death. Brown noted the Freud did not consider aggression a basic psychological fact. Aggression was a secondary manifestation of the death instinct. It was the overt expression of an impulse originally directed against the self—the desire to die or destroy oneself. Thus aggression became a problem because Eros could create life only when the death instinct was frustrated in its original enterprise. In order to live and love, people were forced to destroy by directing the energies of the death instinct away from themselves and onto others.

Brown's solution was posited on the belief that there was no necessary antagonism between Eros and Thanatos. The two instincts existed in harmony with each other—aggression was not the inevitable by-product of life as Freud had believed. Brown hoped for the development of a new accepting attitude toward death and the creation of a nonrepressive society characterized by the anarchic and total sexuality of early infancy. This polymorphous civilization would produce a "Dionysian Christian" answering to the "power of enthusiasm." [12] The destruction of repressive differentiation and the ability to learn how to die constituted Brown's solution to the general neurosis of mankind. He agreed with Heidegger and Sartre that man was a being who is aware of his mortality and must accept this fact to live authentically. Behind *Life Against Death* and *Love's Body* (1966) stands Nietzsche's dictum that man is an animal who must overcome himself. [13]

Although Marcuse and Brown wrote trenchant and disturbing studies of modern civilization, their linking of modernization and sexual repression was vitiated by an ahistorical perspective. Marcuse had taken Freud's dualism between Eros and Thanatos seriously, and suggested that aggression could be conquered by the massive accumulation of erotic energy in a nonrepressive civilization. This development involved politics and economics; it meant freeing Eros from the fetters of unnecessarily repressive work. Although Marcuse tried to put Freudian categories into a historical context, his attempt was ultimately unsuccessful. Was he suggesting that sexual relations were less repressive before modern surplus repression and the performance principle? If he had examined early modern Europe or seventeenth-century America, he would have discovered that these societies were more sexually repressive than today. *Eros and Civilization* was a brilliant but unhistorical philosophical polemic.

Despite Brown's subtitle in *Life Against Death*, his work moved exclusively on the levels of individual psychology or whole civilizations. There was no historical analysis of the social and economic factors which might have initiated a denial of death and a sexually repressive civilization. Instead, Brown offered an exclusively ontogenetic explanation which could not be applied to specific historical periods. Thus Marcuse's and Brown's studies cannot be used to explain historic changes in American sexual behavior.

The second group of writers, mostly historians and sociologists, have argued that modernization led to a more liberal sexuality by weakening the roles of established cultures. Most traditional cultures in Western society had strict rules calling for chastity before marriage, always from women and often from men. Mass violations of this rule indicate that the cultural roles are growing indistinct or that there is a growing indifference to them. These scholars explain the rise of a more liberal sexuality by referring to the social forces which destroy established norms. Changing economic structures and shifting social values (the modernization process) call into question the validity of the traditional social values. Unsettling changes disorient individuals; sexual norms lose their authority and the result is sex outside of marriage and more liberal sexual attitudes (Figure 2).[14]

Figure 3: Cultural disorganization model

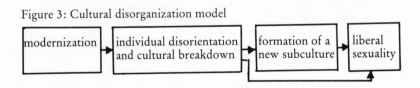

Mack Walker, for example, has used this model to explain changes in German town life from 1648 to 1871. According to Walker, after the early 1800s German states and towns were affected by the modernization process as the triumph of a free-market economy, improved transportation and communications, the erosion of local autonomy, and increased population growth and migration transformed the traditional German village.

Throughout Germany, local authorities argued that there was a link between modernization and a more liberal sexuality which was exemplified by soaring illegitimacy rates. They believed that in the past, individuals had been willing to subordinate themselves to the needs of the community. But the modernization process had encouraged egoism, the pursuit of pleasure, a taste for luxury, and a growing indifference to communal norms. In the pursuit of self-interest, increasing numbers of Germans were evading customary economic rules and were disobeying traditional mores against premarital or pre-engagement intercourse. Thus changing economic and social vaues led to a more liberal sexuality in nineteenth-century Germany.[15]

An American version of the cultural disorganization model was Daniel Moynihan's famous report, "The Negro Family: The Case for National Action." Moynihan believed a vicious cycle operated to weaken the black family. Men had no stable place in the economic system and thus were incapable of becoming strong husbands or fathers. Therefore women had to rear children without male assistance and often supported their families. Commonly, children in these families grew up in unstable homes, did poorly in school, and only qualified for low-paying jobs that could not support a family decently. The cycle then started again. The proof Moynihan offered was the fact that one-quarter of urban Negro marriages were dissolved, one-quarter of births were illegitimate, and that as a consequence, one-quarter of black families were headed by females.[16] He grimly concluded that the black community had

> been forced into a matriarchal structure, which, because it is out of line with the rest of American society, seriously retards the group as a whole, and imposes a crushing burden on the Negro male and, in consequence, on a great many Negro women as well.[17]

Although Moynihan's discussion of the destructive effects of slavery's impact on the Negro family and the migration from Southern farms to Northern cities has been effectively challenged,[18] he succeeded in highlighting the Negro's economic and social insecurity within the modern economy. A hopeless economic condition produced confusion about values and norms that persists today. In the ensuing family breakdown, premarital intercourse, marital abandonment, and female-dominated families became common. Economic change brought about cultural disorganization and libertine sexual behavior.

A variation of the cultural-disorganization model is found in Hyman Rodman's study of lower-class families in Negro Trinidad. He believes that a more liberal sexuality begins as value confusion but eventually receives official cultural sanction. Rodman's research indicates that sometimes modernization helps destroy traditional values and can lead to normlessness and antisocial behavior. People cannot operate long without valid cultural rules, however, and thus they justify their deviancy by forming a new subculture which legitimates their behavior.

According to Rodman, the family relationships of the poor in Negro Trinidad are intertwined with their position in the total society. The plantation economy made many Negro males economically marginal. This condition made husbands inadequate family providers, humiliated them and encouraged them to seek outside women to bolster their remaining self-esteem. The wife also turned to outsiders, giving sex and affection in exchange for financial support. Eventually the lower class rejected the institution of marriage for a system of monogamy out of wedlock. This system is not condemned and temporary liaisons are viewed as part of the natural order.

The values of lower-class culture in Trinidad are now transmitted from parent to child and do not depend on economic marginality anymore. Even though housing and the job situation have improved for the lower class, monogamy out of wedlock flourishes. Illegitimacy and temporary liaisons are an accepted and approved way of life. A genuine sexual and familial subculture has developed which no longer needs the conditions of social and economic marginality.[19]

The cultural-disorganization model suggests that modernization can produce a more liberal sexuality in two ways. First, modernization may destroy restrictive sexual values which are part of traditional behavioral patterns. And second, modernization may create an economically marginal group of people who create a subculture stressing immediate sexual gratification. Both these perspectives help explain changes in European sexual behavior or the sexual mores of economically marginal groups but none of them can be used to discuss the origins of Victorian sexuality. Except in a few utopian communities, frontier towns, or lower-class areas, a subculture of liberal sexuality was never formed in nineteenth-century America. During the modernization process, "respectable" Americans exhibited a more prudent rather than a more liberal form of sexual behavior. If there was cultural disorganization, it did not loosen restrictive sexual behavior but strengthened it.

A third school of analysts has created a subculture-of-gratification model that views sexual behavior within a specific cultural context. They believe that modernization creates a positive desire for a more liberal sexuality and creates a subculture in which gratification becomes legitimatized. Although modernization is responsible for these developments, the key factors within the modernization process are the mentality of the free marketplace and the separation of home and workplace (Figure 3).

Figure 4: Subculture-of-gratification model

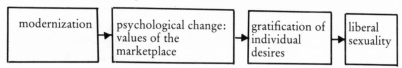

The theoretical aspects of the subculture-of-gratification model have been best explained by Fred Weinstein and Gerald M. Platt. Combining sociology, psychoanalysis, and history, they have tried to account for the growing importance of the concept of autonomy since the eighteenth century. Although they mainly discuss social and political ideas, changing concepts of sexual behavior form part of their work.

Weinstein and Platt argue that one of the most important changes in the modern Western world has been the separation of emotional and abstract functions that accompanied the movement away from traditional authority structures toward greater autonomy. In these structures, emotional and abstract obligations were not separated on a personal, social, or cultural level. Beginning in the eighteenth century, however, Enlightenment philosophes helped convince people that royal absolutism failed to provide certain emotional supports and thus people were able to challenge the authority of the state.

Aside from the civic culture, a second area of authority was embedded in the family. Children trusted and obeyed their fathers because they provided love, affection, approval, and work skills. But modernization ruptured the classical relationship between fathers and sons when the traditional agricultural and craft economy was destroyed and replaced by the bureaucracy and the factory. The separation of the home and economic life changed the psychodynamics of family life by enabling the children to distinguish clearly between paternal and maternal functions. With the father no longer nurturant, his authority was challenged as illegitimate. The modern spirit of revolt, which was exemplified by the work of Kafka and Freud, was part of the wish to be free of the father.[20]

Although Weinstein's and Platt's study is based on political and cultural evidence, their concepts can be used to explain changes in modern sexual behavior. Autonomy and self-gratification in sexual behavior could occur only when the family lost some of its nurturing functions and ceased to represent undifferentiated authority. The free marketplace, which encouraged egoistic economic behavior, weakened the family and promoted egoistic sexual behavior. The desire for sexual gratification and autonomy was partially created as a result of economic modernization.

The most vigorous and convincing proponent of the subculture-of-gratification model has been Edward Shorter. He has argued that, while the separation of home and workplace is important, the exposure of the population to the mentality of the free market is crucial. The free market generated a subculture of gratification among young workers which allowed them to violate traditional prohibitions about premarital intercourse. Those individuals involved in free-market capitalism applied the pursuit of self-interest and the maximization of individual advantage to nonmarket areas of life such as authority, the community, and sexual behavior. Capitalism encouraged economic self-interest at the cost of communal economic authority; it also promoted emotional and physical self-fulfillment at the expense of traditional community moral standards.

The second major consequence of economic modernization was the creation of a proletarian subculture with different values than the predominant culture. Economic and social changes produced a different set of sexual standards that encouraged physical gratification and a more liberal sexual behavior. Free-market capitalism also enlarged many young women's material independence. As long as women worked and lived at home, the family could extract obedience and enforce chastity before marriage. Once alternative forms of employment and living became available, women could become more independent and participate in the working class subculture of gratification.[21]

Although Shorter's analysis has been subjected to excellent criticisms,[22] his studies have a certain plausibility. It appears logical that economic self-interest would destroy communal sexual norms and lead to moral egoism and that this type of liberal sexual behavior would first appear within the context of a proletarian subculture. Shorter has added a quantitative dimension to Weinstein and Platt and convincingly argues for a link between economic modernization and more liberal sexual behavior.

The subculture-of-gratification model developed by Weinstein, Platt, and Shorter suggests that autonomy and liberal sexual behavior are linked to changes in family structure and the triumph of free-market capitalism. These concepts may cover changes in European sexuality but cannot be used to explain Victorian sexuality in America because the quantitative evidence contradicts the model. Shorter, for example, cannot include Graham's America in his analysis because sexual activities there do not fit his thesis. He uses the research of Scott and Hindus to show that premarital pregnancies rose rapidly toward the end of the nineteenth century, but he ignores the same data that indicate a drastic decline in premarital pregnancies after the late eighteenth century, which is one of the themes in their pioneering article. Shorter recognizes this part of their argument but lamely answers, "I don't believe that at all."[23] No evidence is exhibited to support his statement. He cannot explain why sexual behavior in Victorian America became more restrictive while a free-market economy developed and traditional concepts of authority and deference declined.

Another group of writers has created a model linking the decline of religiosity with the development of a more liberal sexuality. They have argued that since official Protestantism and Catholicism prohibit sexual intercourse outside of marriage, religious involvement is associated with low levels of premarital sexual activity and that the decline of religiosity associated with modernization accounts for an increase in liberal sexual behavior (Figure 4).[24]

Figure 5: Decline-in-religiosity model

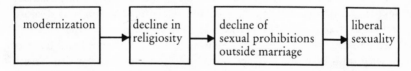

The studies on premarital sexual activities by religious background, however, are somewhat confusing and contradictory. Some research concludes that people with weak religious affiliations have higher rates of premarital sexual intercourse. In Groton, New Hampshire, 11.3 percent of all those admitted to communion between 1761 and 1775 confessed to premarital fornication while 33 percent of those who only subscribed to the baptismal covenant confessed to the same offenses.[25] The parish list of 1767 in Hingham, Massachusetts, documented that 18.4 percent of the church families had premarital pregnancies, but when neither spouse was identified as a church member, almost one-third of the women were pregnant before marriage.[26] In a more recent period, Ernest Burgess and Paul Wallin found that the rates of premarital intercourse with the person they married were highest for those couples who were nonreligious and that this group engaged most frequently in premarital intercourse.[27]

Another contemporary analysis also concluded that couples who did not attend church regularly were most apt to have intercourse before marriage.[28] And Ira Reiss, the leading authority on contemporary premarital sexual behavior, found that as church attendance decreased for whites, there was a significant increase in permissiveness.[29]

The research by Alfred Kinsey, William Masters, and Virginia Johnson supports the relationship between the degree of religiosity and sexual behavior. Religious convictions, Kinsey argued, have a powerful inhibitive influence on the sexual behavior of women. Religious women were much less likely to become involved in premarital sexual activities and when they did, their rates of sexual intercourse were almost always lower than those of nonreligious women. Kinsey also demonstrated that religious women achieved orgasms during intercourse less often than non religious women, and he blamed their frigidity on the moral restraints which led them to avoid sexual relations before marriage.[30] According to Masters and Johnson, religious indoctrination was present in the backgrounds of a high percentage of women who had orgasmic dysfunctions.[31] All these studies indicate that when age, marital status, size of hometown, father's political inclination, and religious affiliation are each held constant, the relationship between sexual attitudes and religiosity remains significant.[32]

A major limitation in these works is that the significance of religion for the behavior of individuals is very difficult to determine. One measure of any institution's significance is the degree to which its values are supported by its members. Some studies question the influence of religion on morality or sexual behavior. Will Herberg and Luther Baker believe that there is no correlation between moral concepts, behavior, and church participation.[33] Another study found that Catholic women had significantly higher rates of premarital intercourse than Protestant or Jewish women.[34] And Ira Reiss discovered that decreases in church attendance for blacks did not lead to increases in permissiveness.[35] It is unclear whether declining religiosity is the cause or effect of premarital sexual relations. Religion probably has a major impact on premarital sexual activities only when it is an encompassing and controlling force among the young rather than an option.

The American data about religion and sexual behavior is ambiguous, but we do know that religiosity increased after the late 1700s. Until the latter part of the nineteenth century, American religion was confident, vigorous, and expansive. Church attendance increased faster than population growth and evangelical Christianity had a major impact on American culture, reform, and politics.[36] The nineteenth-century American modernization experience contradicts the decline in religiosity model and besides, the relationship between religion and sexual behavior is unclear, even in contemporary America. An increase in church attendance or religiosity cannot be the principal causal factor in the triumph of Victorian sexuality.

We have examined four major models that asssociate the modernization process with changes in sexual behavior. The sexual-sublimation model certainly fits our period, but cannot be used because changes in American sexual behavior cannot be linked with the changing intensity of the Protestant ethic or the abstract and ahistorical theories of the Freudian left. The models of cultural disorganization and the subculture of gratification do not fit the quantitative evidence for Victorian America. Except for some marginal groups, American behavior often became more prudent during this period. The decline-in-religiosity model contradicts the nineteenth-century American experience and, in addition, the relationship between religion and sexual behavior is unclear. None of the accepted models explains why Graham's middle-class contemporaries championed a restrictive sexuality.

We appear to be in a difficult quandary. The quantitative cultural evidence indicates that American and European sexual behavior became dissimilar after the late 1700s; Europe became more liberal while many Americans apparently developed more repressive sexual habits. Yet no scholars have devised a model that explains the American experience. Perhaps we can find an answer by closely examining the career and influence of Sylvester Graham, the most important sexual reformer of the Victorian period. Health reform will help explain why many middle-class Americans willingly adopted a more repressive sexual behavior, why America diverged from Europe in the realm of sexuality, and will provide us with an alternative model linking modernization with a more restrictive sexuality.

NOTES

1. Max Weber, *The Protestant Ethic and the Spirit of Capitalism,* trans. Talcott Parsons (New York: Scribners, 1947).

2. For excellent summations and criticisms of the Weber thesis, see Kurt Sammuelsson, *Religion and Economic Action: A Critique of Max Weber* (New York: Harper and Row, 1961); *Calvin and Calvinism,* ed. Robert M. Kingdon and Robert D. Linder (Lexington, Mass.: D. C. Heath, 1970).

3. Christopher Hill, *Society and Puritanism in Pre-Revolutionary England* (New York: Schocken Books, 1964).

4. Emmanuel LeRoy Ladurie, *Les Paysans de Languedoc* (Paris: S.E.V.P.E.N., 1966), pp. 357–72, 391–404; "Hugenots Contre Papistes," in *Histoire du Languedoc,* ed. Phillippe Wolff (Toulouse: Edouard Privat, 1967), pp. 313–25.

5. Paul A. Robinson, *The Freudian Left* (New York: Harper and Row, 1969); Martin Jay, *The Dialectical Imagination: A History of the Frankfort School and the Institute of Social Research, 1923–1950* (Boston: Little, Brown & Co., 1973), pp. 86–112.

6. Sigmund Freud, *Civilization and Its Discontents*, trans. James Strachy (New York: W. W. Norton, 1962).

7. Herbert Marcuse, "A Reply to Erich Fromm," *Dissent* (1956):80.

8. Herbert Marcuse, *Eros and Civilization* (Boston: Beacon Press, 1955); *Negations* (Boston: Beacon Press, 1968); pp. 227–43; *Five Lectures* (Boston: Beacon Press, 1970), pp. 1–27, 44–61.

9. Marcuse, *Eros and Civilization*, pp. 15–16.

10. For intelligent evaluations of Marcuse that do not become ideological polemics, see Erich Fromm, "The Human Implications of Instinctivestic 'Radicalism,' " in *Voices of Dissent*, ed. Irving Howe (New York: Grove Press, 1958), pp. 313–20; Anthony Wilden, "Marcuse and the Freudian Model: Energy, Information, and Phantasie," *Salmagundi* 10–11 (1970):196–245; Richard King, *The Party of Eros* (Chapel Hill, N.C.: University of North Carolina Press, 1972), pp. 116–56.

11. Norman O. Brown, *Life Against Death: The Psychoanalytic Meaning of History* (Middletown, Conn.: Wesleyan University Press, 1959), p. 4.

12. Norman O. Brown, "Apocalypse: The Place of Mystery in the Life of the Mind," *Harper's* 222 (May 1961):47.

13. Norman O. Brown, *Love's Body* (New York: Random House, 1966). Because of Brown's mystical strain, his thinking is sometimes elusive and difficult to analyze. See King, *Party of Eros*, pp. 157–62; Frederick C. Crews, "Love in the Western World," *Partisan Review* 34 (1967):272–87.

14. For an excellent discussion of the relationship between cultural disorganization and changes in sexual behavior, see Edward Shorter, "Capitalism, Culture, and Sexuality: Some Competing Models," *Social Science Quarterly* 53 (1972–1973):341–56.

15. Mack Walker, *German Home Towns: Community, State, and General Estate, 1648–1871* (Ithaca, N.Y.: Cornell University Press, 1971).

16. Daniel Patrick Moynihan, "The Negro Family: The Case for National Action," in *The Moynihan Report and the Politics of Controversy*, ed. Lee Rainwater and William L. Yancy (Cambridge, Mass.: MIT Press, 1967), pp. 47–124.

17. Ibid., p. 75.

18. See Elizabeth H. Pleck, "The Two-Parent Household: Black Family Structure in Late Nineteenth-Century Boston," *Journal of Social History* 6 (1972):1–31; Herbert G. Gutman, "Persistent Myths About the Afro-American Family," *Journal of Interdisciplinary History* 5 (1975):181–210; Frank F. Furstenberg, Jr., Theodore Herschberg, and John Modell, "The Origins of the Female-Headed Black Family: The Impact of the Urban Experience," *Journal of Interdisciplinary History* 5 (1975):211–33; Leslie Howard Owens, *This Species of Property: Slave Life and Culture in the Old South* (New York: Oxford University Press, 1976), pp. 136–213; Herbert G. Gutman, *The Black Family in Slavery and Freedom, 1750–1925* (New York: Pantheon, 1976), pp. 3–44, 101–84, 432–60, 477–520.

19. Hyman Rodman, "The Lower-Class Value Stretch," *Social Forces* 42 (1963):205–15; "Illegitimacy in the Carribbean Social Structure: A Reconstruction," *American Sociological Review* 31 (1966):673–83; *Lower-Class Families: The Culture of Poverty in Negro Trinidad* (New York: Oxford University Press, 1971).

20. Fred Weinstein and Gerald M. Platt, *The Wish To Be Free: Society, Psyche, and Value Change* (Berkeley and Los Angeles: University of California Press, 1969).

21. Edward Shorter, "Illegitimacy, Sexual Revolution, and Social Change in Modern Europe," *Journal of Interdisciplinary History* 2 (1971):237–72; "Sexual Change and Illegitimacy: The European Experience," in *Modern European Social History*, ed. Robert J. Be-

zucha (Lexington, Mass.: D. C. Heath, 1972), pp. 231–69; "Capitalism, Culture, and Sexuality," pp. 348–56; "Female Emancipation, Birth Control, and Fertility in European History," *American Historical Review* 78 (1973):605–40; *The Making of the Modern Family* (New York: Basic Books, 1975).

22. See Joan W. Scott and Louise A. Tilly, "Women's Work and the Family in Nineteenth Century Europe," *Comparative Studies in Society and History* 17 (1975):36–64; Louise A. Tilly, Joan W. Scott, and Miriam Cohen, "Women's Work and European Fertility Patterns," *Journal of Interdisciplinary History* 6 (1976):447–76; Cissie Fairchilds, "Female Sexual Attitudes and the Rise of Illegitimacy: A Case Study," *Journal of Interdisciplinary History* 8 (1978):627–78. Scott's review of Shorter's *Modern Family* in *Signs* 2 (1977):692–96 is devastating.

23. Shorter, *Modern Family*, p. 334.

24. For European examples of this model, see Alva Myrdal, *Nation and Family: The Swedish Experiment in Democratic Family and Population Policy* (New York: Harper & Brothers, 1945), p. 45; Marcel Lachiver, *La Population de Meulan du XVIIIe au XIXe siècle (vers 1600–1870)* (Paris: S.E.V.P.E.N., 1969), p. 68; Alain Lottin, "Naissances illégitimes et filles-mères à Lille au XVIIIe siècle," *Revue d'histoire moderne et contemporaine* 17 (1970):278–322.

25. Henry Reed Stiles, *Bundling: Its Origins, Progress and Decline in America* (Albany, N.Y.: Knickerbocker, 1891), p. 78.

26. Daniel Scott Smith and Michael S. Hindus, "Premarital Pregnancy in America, 1640–1971: An Overview and Interpretation," *Journal of Interdisciplinary History* 5 (1975):546–47.

27. Ernest Burgess and Paul Wallin, *Engagement and Marriage* (Philadelphia: J. B. Lippincott, 1953), p. 337.

28. Eugene J. Kanin and David H. Howard, "Postmarital Consequences of Premarital Sex Adjustments," *American Sociological Review* 23 (1958):557.

29. Ira L. Reiss, "Premarital Sexual Permissiveness among Negroes and Whites," *American Sociological Review* 29 (1964):688–98.

30. Alfred Kinsey, *Sexual Behavior in the Human Female* (Philadelphia: Saunders, 1953), pp. 247–48, 304–6, 424, 463, 515–16, 521–24.

31. William Masters and Virginia Johnson, *Human Sexual Inadequacy* (Boston: Little, Brown & Co., 1970), pp. 229–33.

32. Jean Dedman, "The Relationship Between Religious Attitude and Attitude Toward Premarital Sexual Relations," *Marriage and Family Living* 21 (1959):175.

33. Will Herberg, *Protestant, Catholic, Jew* (Garden City, N.Y.: Doubleday, 1955), p. 2; Luther G. Baker, Jr., "Changing Religious Norms and Family Values," *Journal of Marriage and the Family* 27 (1965):6.

34. Robert R. Bell and Leonard Blumberg, "Courtship Intimacy and Religious Background," *Marriage and Family Living* 21 (1959):357.

35. Reiss, "Premarital Sexual Permissiveness," p. 692.

36. Edwin Scott Gaustad, *Historical Atlas of Religion in America* (New York: Harper and Row, 1976), pp. 37–56.

3

From Connecticut to Physiology

When Sylvester Graham was born in West Suffield, Connecticut, on July 4, 1794, the modernization process had transformed eighteenth-century Connecticut life cycles. Until the early eighteenth century, the Connecticut social order was patriarchal and hierarchical. Local towns acted as corporate entities, and community welfare took precedence over individual self-fulfillment. The hallmarks of the community were law, authority, order, and clearly defined aims. Such a society molded the character of its members by producing personalities who had rigorous moral standards and who exercised strong religious and civil authority. The Puritans believed in the superiority of husbands over wives, parents over children, masters over family servants, ministers and elders over congregation in the church, and rulers over subjects in the state.

During the eighteenth century, Connecticut Puritans became New England Yankees as the population increased rapidly, as religious dogma shifted away from the church toward the individual, and as the original convenanted communities were weakened and dispersed. As mid-eighteenth-century families became more mobile and independent than their seventeenth-century predecessors, they also became uprooted, anxious, and dislocated, and thus were susceptible to religious revivals or reform movements. The sheer growth of a tight, hierarchical society produced a looser and more open polity in which many people became independent, avaricious, and shrewd, and felt guilty about their declension from their forefathers' standards.[1]

Graham was born and raised in a society that recently had shifted from a traditional toward a modern structure. There are no primary sources about Graham's emotional and intellectual development before he became a temperance lecturer, and so we cannot create a convincingly balanced picture of his pre-reform years. We do know, however, that his unstable family life and his difficulty in establishing a career and an

55

ensitized him to important changes occurring in the American
 structure. Graham struggled to reconcile a natural, orderly exis-
with the increasing demands of an untraditional, dynamic country
generalizing from his own experiences and by assuming that many
Americans were victimized by similar environmental and social problems. Graham, unsure of his personal identity or his place in the American social order, was in search of an ideology, as Erik Erikson uses the
term:

> The tendency at a given time to make facts amenable to ideas, and
> ideas to facts, in order to create a world image convincing enough to
> support the collective and individual sense of identity. Far from being
> arbitrary or consciously manageable . . . the total perspective created
> by ideological simplification reveals its strength by the dominance it
> exerts on the seeming logic of historical events, and by its influence on
> the identity-formation of individuals.[2]

By the early 1830s, Graham had achieved a satisfying identity, ideology, and career when he became a professional health reformer. He
believed that a prior social harmony had been shattered when America
ceased to be a balanced, traditional society. Ambivalent about commercialism and hostile toward the city, Graham and his followers supported
physiological reform to preserve the social and moral characteristics they
thought existed at an earlier period. But the health reformers were not
merely representatives of a disintegrating social order who reacted to a
new America fearfully and defensively. In the early 1830s they began
developing a comprehensive and positive program based on proper sexual
and nutritional habits which supposedly helped regenerate individuals by
fusing bodily and social controls. While the purity advocates heavily
criticized contemporary American culture and behavior, they also
confidently expected that their crusade would lead to the renovation of
American society.

Sylvester Graham's roots penetrated deeply into Connecticut. Two
generations of his forebears were New England ministers and both his
parents were born and raised there too. Graham's family had the characteristics traditionally attributed to early new Englanders: they were industrious, self-reliant, independent thinkers, puritanical in their conduct,
and deeply pious. His paternal grandfather, the Reverend John Graham,
was a graduate of the University of Glasgow who emigrated to America
in 1718 and held different pulpits in western New England. Sylvester's
father, John, Jr., was born in 1722 and, after graduating from Yale College in 1740, became a minister and an enthusiastic supporter of the New

Lights in the Great Awakening. In 1746 he became the pastor of a new congregation in West Suffield, Connecticut, where he preached for fifty years. During his life John, Jr., married twice and his wives produced seventeen children; Sylvester, the youngest child, was two years old when his father died at the age of seventy-four.[3]

Ruth Graham, widowed at forty-one, was unable to care for the seven children by John's second marriage who still lived at home. In 1801 the probate court of Hartford County appointed a guardian for the three youngest children because their mother was "in a deranged state of mind." According to one account, Sylvester continued to live in the community parsonage, for he and his mother were counted together in the 1810 census. Another historian suggested that Graham lived in his guardian's home and later boarded with an older sister in Middlebury, Vermont, where he trained to become a schoolteacher until recurring illnesses forced him to retire prematurely. We do know that Sylvester was an unhappy, emotionally deprived child who suffered from dyspepsia and consumption.[4] Throughout his life Graham believed that his childhood had been stunted and melancholy:

> In gloom, in sadness and in tears,
> Thro' childhood's period thou dids't languish,
> And up thro' manhood's early years,
> Thy every pulse was beat in anguish.[5]

When Ruth left West Suffield in 1817 to live with a son in Newark, New Jersey, Sylvester moved there too because he had neither learned any marketable skills nor married. For a while he ran a small country store in Parsippany. A local resident, Isaac Lyons, remembered him as an "eccentric and wayward genius from first to last." Graham was foppish in manners and appearance and spent most of his leisure time giving poetry recitals, acting in plays, writing articles for local newspapers, unsuccessfully wooing women, and pathetically attempting to court the town's influential citizens.[6]

At the age of twenty-nine Graham entered Amherst Academy, a preparatory school run by Amherst College. He left the academy after only one semester, however, because his arrogant and forceful personality alienated the younger students who got him expelled on a false charge of criminal assault. The private educational institutions in antebellum Amherst were tumultuous and dangerous places. During the 1830–1831 academic year, for example, the Amherst College faculty acted on eighty-nine cases of student discipline at its regular meetings. The influx of older and poorer students transformed preparatory and collegiate life and put new kinds of stresses on the traditional system of tutorial watchfulness and petty rules. Graham probably was the victim of disruptive students whom the school could not control. After leaving Amherst, he traveled to Compton, Rhode Island, where he had a nervous breakdown because of his academic failure. Graham recovered with the help of two daughters of a sea captain, Oliver Potter Earl, and, on September 19, 1824 he married Sarah, the older of the two women.[7]

After his marriage, Graham decided to become a minister, but inasmuch as he did not want to pursue a formal education he studied privately with Emerson Paine, the minister who had officiated at his wedding. On November 18, 1828, Graham was licensed at the age of thirty-two as an evangelist at Rehoboth, Massachusetts, by the Mendon Association. Graham returned to New Jersey and preached in a succession of local towns as an itinerant Presbyterian minister. On November 15, 1827, he was paid ten dollars for preaching in Belvidere and proudly noted in his journal that the occasion was "my first regular compensation." In February of 1829 the congregation in Bound Brook asked Graham to remain as the regular pastor, and six months of preaching netted him three hundred dollars and the ability to rent a ten-room house. He remained in New Jersey until he moved to Philadelphia, after being hired in June of 1830 as a lecturer by the Pennsylvania Society for Discouraging the Use of Ardent Spirits.[8]

Graham experienced great difficulty in developing a satisfactory adult life. Most antebellum youths were finished with their schooling, apprenticeship, and parental tutelage by their early twenties. The failure of Graham's family to prepare him for adult responsibilities becomes obvious when we compare the ten children of John Graham's first marriage, born between 1749 and 1768, with the seven children of his second marriage born between 1780 and 1794. The four daughters born to his first wife all contracted successful and prosperous marriages. Five of the six sons became wealthy and highly respected. Two of John, Jr.'s sons became prominent physicians while two others were affluent land speculators and merchants. One son died before his business venture returned a profit.

All of John, Jr.'s children by his first marriage had left the Suffield area by their father's death and were solidly established in their careers. While Sylvester's mother was desperately attempting to raise seven children, her family had no contact with the children from their father's first marriage and were wards of the community.

The seven children from the second marriage were greatly affected by the death of their father and their mother's inability to raise them. Two of the four girls never married and another remained single until she was almost forty. The two most successful boys had reached adolescence when their father died. Isaac King remained in Suffield and lived a se-cluded and respectable life; Charles worked as an accountant in New York City and in 1817 he moved to Newark, where he married a moder-ately wealthy woman and lived in comfortable circumstances. He valiantly tried to bolster the disintegrating Graham family by lodging and helping support his mother, three sisters, and Sylvester. In West Suffield the Grahams had led a prosperous and honorable existence; after John Graham's death, the family collapsed and never recovered their lost posi-tion or respect.

Sylvester keenly remembered his family's previously high position and later in life he became quite interested in the Graham genealogy. But his letters to surviving brothers and sisters indicate that he was uninterested in reuniting his family. Graham only wanted to be remembered and respected.[9] The Graham family certainly had changed from Puritans to Yankees. The children from the first marriage used their industrious, self-reliant attributes to carve prosperous commercial careers in an increas-ingly materialistic environment. The five younger children from the second marriage had been raised in an unstable family without strong father and mother figures and floundered in a competitive, open society. Like many of their Connecticut breathren, they were free but rootless and dispirited.

Of all the children from the second marriage, Sylvester became the most famous and influential. When he was thirty-six, he created a new identity for himself that first became available in the turbulent, dynamic, melioristic atmosphere of antebellum America—he became a professional reformer. Graham took full advantage of his one-year stay in Philadel-phia. He seriously studied science and physiology, assimilated the medi-cal theories of the Paris school, and became part of a growing health-reform movement.

When Graham became a temperance lecturer in Philadelphia during the summer of 1830, the city dominated American medicine. Since the mid-eighteenth century, Philadelphia had been famous for its hospital and medical school, the distinguished College of Physicians, its unsurpassed libraries and clinical facilities, and its fine institutional equipment. Novel developments in physiology and the latest methods of surgery were pur-sued enthusiastically in the city that had sustained the work of Benjamin Rush and John Bartram. Although Graham had studied physiology and diet while ministering in New Jersey, he had not formulated a systematic medical philosophy. During his Philadelphia residence, however, he rapidly assimilated highly technical medical works, combined them with his own inclinations, and emerged as a health-reform lecturer. Graham accomplished this feat because of medical developments in Philadelphia and his role in the temperance movement. Medical research provided a scientific underpinning to his ideas, and the temperance movement enabled him to articulate and develop his theories.

Philadelphia was an important center of the temperance movement and the city retained its preeminence in this area until the end of the 1830s. During the colonial period, there was little sentiment in Pennsylvania against the consumption of alcohol; protest centered around the sale of liquor to the Indians and the dangers of alcohol to certain types of industrial workers. But by the early national period, evangelical and medical reformers began preaching the concept of moderate drinking, although they shied away from complete abstinence. Only during the antebellum period did Pennsylvanians defend prohibition, and there developed 150 local temperance societies throughout the state by the early 1830s. In Washington County, for example, one-ninth of the population belonged to thirty-six temperance societies and many local stores and hotels sold no liquor. After 1834, the state legislature succeeded in progressively raising the minimum amount of liquor that could be sold without a dealer's license.[10]

In New England, clergymen such as Lyman Beecher promoted the temperance movement. By contrast, the Philadelphia medical profession dominated the crusade against alcohol. Eleven of the thirty-six members of the state temperance governing board were physicians. When the Philadelphia Medical Society commissioned an investigation into the effects of liquor, they concluded that many deaths were caused by intemperance. And in 1830 a group of eighty Philadelphia physicians argued that alcohol had no medical value and sometimes causes diseases. Even a Medical Student's Temperance society was founded at the University of Pennsylvania. Doctors played prominent roles in the Philadelphia temperance movement because of their high status and the medical opinions of Rush, who had condemned distilled liquor.[11]

Philadelphia's most famous physician wrote the first important American temperance work, the *Inquiry into the Effects of Ardent Spirits on the Human Body and Mind* (1785), which became the authoritative study on the subject for many decades. Although Rush believed intemperance caused the debilitation of the organism through disease, he did not support abstinence and believed that wine, beer, and cider were acceptable substitutes for distilled spirits. The early temperance movement followed Rush's suggestions and tried to promote moderate drinking, especially at social events. One temperance society was organized at a tavern and celebrated their new constitution by bolting a shot of hard liquor! Evidently moderation was subject to different interpretations. Although

Beecher's popular *Six Sermons on Intemperance* (1826) challenged Rush's concepts by arguing that moderate drinking often led to disease and alcoholism, a movement toward total abstinence was slow in gaining followers.[12]

Graham had been an ardent temperance man and vegetarian for at least a year before he gave his Philadelphia lectures. While he lived in Bound Brook he purchased no butcher's meat or white bread and allowed his wife wine and gin only while she was ill and nursing her infant. Graham also studied physiology, anatomy, and diet from contemporary medical texts and so his innovative perspective on temperance flowed from his dietary habits and medical studies in New Jersey and Philadelphia. His advice was attractive, for he began drawing enthusiastic crowds to his lectures. By the fall of 1830 audiences in Kensington had applauded his efforts and Graham became a popular speaker at local churches.[13]

Graham used his newly learned chemical and physiological principles to prove that alcoholic beverages were "foreign and deleterious principles, which disturb the play of chemical and vital affinities within us." Although spirits temporarily excited the body, Graham believed they left the drinker feeble and languorous. The stomach became heated and irritated and so large amounts of blood rushed to the inflamed area and normal circulatory operations were inhibited. As the body malfunctioned, the skin did not perspire, the muscles contracted irregularly, and the gastro-intestinal membranes became inflamed.[14]

These temperance lectures departed from the venerable ideas of Rush and the contemporary principles of Beecher. Rush condemned only hard liquor and immoderate drinking while Beecher considered distilled alcohol an addictive substance which inevitably led to intemperance. Alcohol was an artificial stimulant that the human body could not control. Graham never discussed the addictive properties of alcohol or the results of immoderate drinking. Instead, he emphasized its immediate effects on normal physiological processes. Rush and Beecher highlighted the habitual qualities of alcohol; Graham believed that pain and irritation, not alcoholism, were the most serious consequences of drinking. The consumption of any liquid stronger than water was dangerous because stimulants disturbed the body and ruined the drinker's health.[15]

Graham's arguments were unique; the temperance societies of Pennsylvania only began advocating abstinence a few years later. His perspective was unusual because he rejected the physiology of Rush, who believed that all fevers resulted from a predisposing debility, a stimulus which was the immediate, inciting cause, and a convulsive excitement in the walls of the blood vessels. This last condition, which constituted his theory of pathological physiology, was the essence of the fevers. The physician's duty was to relieve the excitement and allow the underlying debility to dissipate. Since all illnesses were caused by "excessive action" in the arterial walls, purging and bleeding, not vegetarianism and abstinence, could treat the problem. Although Rush's medical principles were an improvement over eighteenth-century humoral physiology, by the early national period medical attention slowly began to shift from concepts of fevers to visceral and nervous disorders.[16]

Rush's doctrines were challenged and transformed by the Paris school of medicine, which gradually influenced the Philadelphia medical profession during the antebellum period. The Parisian physicians endorsed the concept of underlying debility that predisposed the organism to disease, but they emphasized the principle of vitalism, studied histology, and concentrated on the gastrointestinal tract. Graham read the works of the school's two famous physicians, François J. V. Broussais and Xavier Bichat, and used their medical principles to erect a coherent physiology that radically departed from Rush while encompassing almost all human activities.

There is overwhelming evidence that Graham developed his physiological principles from the Paris school of medicine. First, while in Philadelphia he purchased a copy of Broussais's *Physiology*.[17] This book probably led him to Bichat because the two doctors were considered important and complementary vitalists. And second, throughout Graham's published works, the basic principles of Broussais and Bichat formed the underlying foundations for his physiology and diet. Graham's beliefs in vitalism, in an organic-animal dichotomy in man, in the importance of the gastrointestinal tract, and in the necessity for healthy food, exercise, fresh air, and the control of the passions all were garnered from early–nineteenth-century French medicine. His major organizing principle was the concept of vitalistic laws, which hindered the organism's unavoidable susceptibility to disease.

The Paris school of medicine was the product of the French revolution's administrative changes, which created more efficient hospitals and better schools for physicians. Under the leadership of such medical luminaries as Philippe Pinel, Broussais, Bichat, R. T. H. Laennec, and Jean Baptiste Bouillard, medicine became reoriented around new concepts—physical examination by hand and ear, microscopic pathological anatomy, statistics, and the concept of the lesion. They also developed specialties such as psychiatry, pediatrics, dermatology, orthopedics, urology, otology, and legal medicine.[18]

Broussais (1772–1838) was an influential professor of medicine and a prolific writer who helped shift attention from symptoms and essentialism toward lesions and localism. His entire system was related to his doctrine of vitalism. According to this concept, living tissues could not be analyzed by chemical and physical formulas; organic and inorganic substances were governed by totally different laws. Unknown vital forces changed inanimate matter due to the singular laws of vital chemistry.

In the case of disease, organs could be stimulated by modifiers (especially cold air), the "ingesta" (food, drugs, noxious atmospheric substances), and the "percepta" (moral or physiological influences). Since diseases usually were caused by the surface inflammation of internal membranes, Broussais believed that the pulmonary and the gastrointestinal tracts often were infected and so he argued that all diseases could be traced to an irritation of the gastrointestinal system because its ganglionic nerves were the single most important area of organic life. Thus Broussais denied, like Rush, the existence of all specific diseases: cancer, syphilis, tuberculosis, and malaria were all the result of neglected alimentary inflammations.[19]

Broussais became acceptable to Philadelphia physicians not just because he was a famous doctor but also because his pathologies and therapeutics were similar to Rush's practice. Both men believed that disease was produced by inflammation and cured by bleeding. Broussais modified Rush's concepts by using a nineteenth-century terminology and by replacing fevers with nervous and visceral disorders. Although Broussais's physiology was discredited by the middle of the century, he had a salutary effect on the European and American medical professions through his emphasis on physical examinations, localism, and the importance of tissues.

Bichat (1771–1802), a contemporary of Pinel, was less influential in America than Broussais because of his premature death. Like Broussais, Bichat studied pathological anatomy, was interested in the properties of living tissues, and made important physiological contributions to the doctrine of vitalism. He believed organic matter was perpetually striving against the inanimate laws governing inorganic matter. In nature, Bichat believed, there were two classes of sciences: organic and inorganic, vital and nonvital properties, and the physiological and physical sciences. "Life is the sum total of those functions which resist death" and so the primary purpose of vitalistic laws was to defend or resist destruction.

Bichat distinguished between animal and organic functions. Organic life centered around respiration, circulation, and the digestive processes. Animal functions helped adapt the organism to its environment and included the five senses, voluntary motion, and thinking. Organic life was directed around the network of nerves in the different viscera, including the lungs and the gastrointestinal tract. Animal life was contained in the nervous tissue of the brain and the spinal column. Bichat believed that these organic and animal systems were separate and autonomous.[20]

The Paris school of medicine helped convince many Philadelphia physicians that Rush's system was based on conjecture and that no enlightened medicine could ignore tissues and local pathology. In the *Journal of Foreign Medical Science & Literature,* which had been founded at Philadelphia in 1810, French articles replaced Scottish and English extracts after 1820. For example, in 1821 there appeared articles on "Laennec's New System of Diagnosis," "Exposition of the Doctrines of Broussais," and "Medical Letters from Paris."[21] Local physicians also praised the new doctrines and soon medical students began migrating to Paris.[22] French medicine helped Philadelphia physicians master new ideas and techniques and promoted the construction of more hospitals and medical libraries.

The doctrines of Broussais and Bichat provided Graham with a respectable and convincing physiological theory while they encouraged him to broaden his temperance principles. The involvement of physicians in the Philadelphia temperance movement probably reinforced Graham's reliance on the two French doctors. John Bell, a prominent Philadelphia physician who printed Graham's temperance lectures, also helped the young reformer use Broussais and Bichat to construct new physiological principles in America. Bell taught at the Philadelphia Medical Institute and was on the governing board of the Pennsylvania Society for Discouraging the Use of Ardent Spirits. He also aided in publishing the English translation of Broussais's *Physiology* in 1826. In a glowing introduction, Bell claimed that Broussais's physiological medicine appealed to nature and offered "the strongest support to sound morality." He had proven that disease and death occurred "when the rules of hygiene are neglected, and the laws of sound physiology broken by perpetual stimulation of the gastric surface." Bell concluded that there could be no health for the sensualist and no pleasurable emotions for the person who indulged his appetites.[23] This was a perfect summation of Graham's future philosophy of health.

Bell's interest in temperance and the Paris school of medicine continued to develop as he and Dr. Charles Condie began publishing in 1829 the first popular American medical magazine, the *Journal of Health.* The editors based their temperance principles on the existence of "vital or organic laws" which governed the behavior of all organisms. Although they first admitted that the moderate consumption of malt liquor was healthy, by 1831 the *Journal* condemned all alcoholic beverages because they contained "noxious, and, at times, directly poisonous ingredients." Alcohol fermented food in the stomach and therefore replaced organic laws with chemical or inorganic laws.[24]

Bell and Condie rapidly moved from temperance to general health. They attacked the popular idea that disease was caused by weakness or

exhaustion because this fear encouraged people to ingest stimulating foods and alcohol which actually increased debility. Only "temperance, pure air, exercise, and the subjection of the animal passions" could prevent disease. Bell and Condie believed that diet was the key to good health. Because urban civilization destroyed instinctive dietary regulations, nutritional habits had to be reconstructed in an artificial and dangerous environment. Although these doctors never clearly and systematically explained their food regimen, they did recommend moderate amounts of vegetables and meat, but admitted that vegetables were "fully sufficient of themselves for maintaining a healthy existence."[25]

John Bell provided Graham with new arguments against alcohol and the study of French medicine also encouraged him to analyze general principles of health. Once pain and irritation replaced addiction and drunkenness as the harmful consequences of drinking, Graham discussed other stimulants that supposedly irritated the gastrointestinal tract. On November 8, 1830, he lectured on the "health, happiness and long life of man." In January of 1831 he gave a series of talks on the "organic structure of man." Graham became so popular that when he gave his last series of lectures at the Franklin Institute in late May, series tickets were sold "to prevent too great a crowd." Throughout this period he combined Broussais, Bichat, and Bell with his own theories to deliver addresses on such varied topics as chastity, courtship and marriage, the intellectual and moral faculties, the treatment and prevention of cholera, and dietary reform. Finally Graham became a free-lance speaker because temperance was no longer his sole concern; in his last Philadelphia lectures he talked about "the Science of Human Life." During the summer of 1831 Graham "received an urgent invitation from New York" to repeat his Franklin Institute lectures and so for the next year he spoke in America's largest and most important city.[26]

Graham rapidly established a career during his one-year sojourn in Philadelphia. He had systematized the temperance and vegetarian principles he first developed in New Jersey by combining his own inclinations with contemporary medical research. The large and enthusiastic crowds that flocked to hear his lectures increased his confidence in his message and mission. In the next year, his New York lectures on the cholera epidemic made him a national figure and part of a diverse health-reform movement.

During the nineteenth century, cholera epidemics, which formerly had been confined to the Far East, spread throughout the world. When cholera appeared in America during 1832, the colonial epidemic diseases of yellow fever and smallpox no longer were national problems. This Asiatic disease became the most dreaded epidemic killer of the nineteenth century when it appeared in 1832, 1848, and 1873, where it was limited to the Mississippi Valley. Only in 1883 did Robert Koch, who was directing a German scientific commission in Egypt, isolate the organism that causes cholera. Once the *vibrio comma* reach the human intestine, they can produce a serious disease that kills almost half of those who contract it if they are untreated. Cholera is spread through pathways leading to the human digestive tract; unwashed hands, uncooked fruits and vegetables, and sewage-contaminated water supplies have caused the most severe epidemics. The devastation of the cholera epidemic encouraged Americans closely to examine their hygiene principles, the medical profession, and the quality of urban life. In 1832 and 1833 hundreds of works were published about the disease that usually advised people to fortify themselves by consuming large amounts of meat, spices, and brandy.[27] Graham's lectures on cholera departed from these other works not in his use of the epidemic to criticize contemporary American health habits, but because he recommended a radical change in American nutrition and sexual behavior as the most effective antidote to the disease. These ideas later became the foundation of the health-reform movement.

When Graham came to New York, he first lectured on diet and physiology, but in March of 1832 he spoke before 2,000 people on a topic of considerable interest—the approaching cholera epidemic.[28] The next month Graham gave a second series of fifteen well-attended and received lectures that discussed cholera and

> the effect of diet on the size, symmetry, and beauty of the human form, features, and complexion; the importance of correct diet in assisting the renovating powers of the system in recovering from disease; a correct system of diet for man in the various circumstances of civil life . . . ; the effect of various causes in society on health and longevity . . . ; [and] the effect of artificial stimuli on the human system, such as pepper, mustard, tea, coffee, opium, tobacco, malt liquors, cider, wine, distilled liquors.[29]

On July 4 he gave the same presentations in Albany and then retreated to Rhode Island until the epidemic subsided. Graham's addresses provoked both interest and scepticism, for his preventive and therapeutic recommendations were considered extreme by some physicians and lay people while his followers claimed that Grahamism had preserved them during the epidemic and afterwards restored the health of those who had been affected by the disease.

Graham's analysis of cholera, like his temperance lectures, extended far beyond the particular problem. When discussing the epidemic, he indicated that his concepts were a specific application of the principles contained in the "Science of Human Life." Graham, however, did conceal the influence of Broussais and Bichat. He admitted that after delivering his first talk, Broussais's lectures on cholera appeared in New York. As Graham read Broussais, he "was not a little surprised to find a very striking resemblance . . . between them and mine,"[30] especially as Graham claimed he had read no specific studies on cholera but had synthesized material from newspapers and his own physiological views. He was only partially correct; his cholera lecture had been delivered before Broussais's book was published, but Graham copied passages directly from Broussais's and Bichat's earlier works. In the opening section of his major speech, he boldly announced his vitalistic theme that "life is a temporary victory over the causes which induce death."[31] Perhaps Graham incorrectly attributed this quotation to Rush so his audience would not realize the real sources of his ideas.

The first ten pages of his lecture never mentioned cholera, but instead discussed the nature of human life, which Graham defined as a "continued, antagonistic conflict between vitality and the more primitive affinities of inorganic chemistry."[32] Following the Paris school, he sharply distinguished between animal and organic life, which was centered in the gastrointestinal tract. Because the digestive process was connected with all other parts of the body, it insured the maintenance of life. This was especially true of the stomach lining, which was "brought into distinct and special relations with the brain, heart, lungs, liver, skin, and indeed with all the organs of the system."[33] Thus when the stomach became irritated, the entire organic system suffered. If the stomach remained irritated and weak, the body could not create its own substances from foreign sources and so the ultimate result was disease and death. Graham blamed the artificial habits stemming from urbanism for the common ailment of "preternatural irritability and diseased sensibility," and implied that this unhealthy condition led to the cholera epidemic:

> All undue excitements and exercises of the mind and of the passions; all excessive indulgences of the appetites; improper qualities and quantities of feed; the debilitating habits of indolence and effeminacy; the various customs and circumstances of artificial life . . . and worst of all, the habitual use of artificial stimulants . . . all act upon the stomach to disturb its functions, and to impair the health of its nervous and muscular tissues.[34]

In such a state of dependence and weakness, the human body lost its natural awareness of external stimuli and was powerless to resist disease. Thus cholera was not the cause but the consequence of poor health.

When the stomach was debilitated, the heart was less vigorous, circulation was feeble, the entire capillary system suffered a loss of vital power, and the body was unable to endure "noxious and pestilential causes." When a healthy gastrointestinal tract became irritated, the body relieved the irritation by a mild form of diarrhea. The response to cholera— vomiting and diarrhea—was similar because the body was attempting to purge itself of poisonous impurities. Cholera was deadly to many people, Graham argued, because their health had been impaired by such prolonged exposure to artificial stimulation that their bodies could not respond naturally to a stomach irritation. Since they were in such a weakened condition, an "adscititious cause" which scarcely would affect a healthy system became fatal.[35]

Because Graham considered cholera a massive irritation of the alimentary canal, he prescribed a thorough regulation of diet and personal hygiene. Graham denied that meat, condiments, and liquor cured cholera because he thought they irritated the stomach and weakened the organism. Instead, he recommended strict hygiene and a simple vegetarian diet based on unsifted bread because it was not overstimulating and allowed the body to repel the cholera.[36] Diet, however, was not the only form of temperance Graham required; he blamed the cholera epidemic on sexual dissipation too. Graham used contemporary newspaper accounts to prove that the Hindus suffered enormously from the cholera because they were enervated by indolence, sensuality, and licentiousness. Promiscuity and homosexuality negated the effects of their vegetarian diet and caused them to succumb rapidly to the ravages of the dreaded disease. The same fate befell Parisian prostitutes; in one area, 1,300 out of 1,400 promiscuous women died of cholera.[37]

Graham considered diet and sexual behavior the major causes of organic debilitation: "[In] the whole career of the Epidemic Cholera, dietetic intemperance and lewdness have been the grand purveyors to its devastating rage."[38] Like stimulating food, unnatural sexual desire and too frequent sexual activity resulted in irritation and disease. No laws or institutions, he believed, could save people from the violation of the natural order. All excesses were dangerous to mental and bodily health and thus Graham concluded his startling lecture with a plea for dietary and sexual temperance as the most effective cure for cholera and any other diseases.

Graham's analysis of cholera represented both traditional and novel attitudes toward the disease. Many physicians and citizens believed that overindulgence in diet and sexual behavior were important predisposing causes of cholera. This concept provided a satisfying explanation for the high mortality rate among the poor, the Irish, and blacks. Throughout the entire epidemic many middle-class New Yorkers thought that only the imprudent succumbed to cholera. Sexual excesses left individuals weakened and artificially stimulated and so their systems were defenseless against the disease. Contagion, before the germ theory, was visualized as the direct passage of some chemical or physical influence through the atmosphere. Until the theory of inanimate contagion was replaced by a theory of germs that could be transmitted by water, food, and living carriers, most Americans believed that there was a direct relationship among poverty, vice, and cholera.[39]

This perspective probably was reinforced by Graham's address because he repeatedly emphasized the debilitating nature of stimulating food and overstimulating sexual activity. Although Graham did not attribute these characteristics just to the lower classes, his audience might have considered themselves immune to cholera because they led respectable lives. But Graham's cholera lecture also represented a fresh approach to the disease because he used the epidemic to castigate contemporary American dietary, health, and sexual habits. Cholera was symptomatic of a deeper problem: Americans were abusing their bodies so regularly that they were expiring from diseases which would not unduly harm healthy individuals. His cure was as radical as his diagnosis. Only a complete reformation in diet and sexual behavior could counteract the debilitating tendencies of modern civilization.

Graham's cholera lecture linked him with the concept of health reform and produced disciples and opponents who rejected his physiology and believed that a Grahamite regimen weakened the body. One angry letter to the editor in a New York newspaper agreed with Graham that dietary intemperance might cause cholera, but scoffed at the idea that "arrowroot and barley water" could prevent disease. The writer accused Graham of intemperance because his extreme doctrines were the "result of a most unruly passion for temperance."[40] These kinds of criticisms did not deter Graham; an appendix was attached to his published lecture which contained written testimonials proving the effectiveness of his treatment. The next year he collected a large number of enthusiastic recommendations from Philadelphia and New York and published them under the title *Aesculapian Tablets of the Nineteenth Century* (1834).[41]

Graham's growing popularity was partly predicated on revolutionary changes in printing, publishing, and the rise of the lecture as a major form of American entertainment and instruction. During the antebellum period, printing was transformed by the development of the cylinder press, the increased use of type-casting and composing machines, and the technique of converting colored rags into usable paper. The advent of the industrial revolution simultaneously occurred with the triumph of popular literacy. Throughout the Jacksonian era, literacy and the amount of printed material both dramatically burgeoned. From 1840 to 1860, literate Americans increased from 6,440,000 to 15,300,000 while the value of manufactured books rose from $2,850,000 to $9,5000,000. The number of daily and weekly newspapers more than doubled and the average circulation of monthly magazines reached about 12,000 subscribers by the Civil War. Not only did the printing revolution help create a mass audience, but it also shifted the centers of opinion making from county seats and capital cities to metropolitan centers. Reduced costs and the accessibility of steam presses enabled writers such as Graham to expand their market by publishing and selling their books in places such as New York, Philadelphia, and Boston. Graham and his fellow health reformers adroitly capitalized on these publishing opportunities to reach millions of Americans through their pamphlets and books.[42]

In addition to changes in printing and publishing, antebellum culture was also transformed by the lecture. Throughout New England and the Middle Atlantic states, lyceums and professional lecturers were popular because many people believed they would diffuse education more generally, convey practical information, entertain in an instructional fashion, and help develop an intelligent electorate. With the rise of paid lyceum speakers and professional lecturers, literature and public speaking became enmeshed. Lecturing offered the writer a means of making money and an opportunity to try his shorter works on a captive audience. As Ralph Waldo Emerson appreciated, lectures represented an important intermediate step in the process of composition because they were a place for experimentation and revision. Graham's four major works on the cholera epidemic, young male sexual behavior, the art of making bread, and human physiology were all first delivered as lectures.

Within both the publishing industry and the lecture circuit, earnest advice manuals and conduct-of-life talks predominated. Some of these themes were the secular derivatives of American Protestantism, where the sermon rather than the service was the main vehicle of instruction. The organization, length, style, and subject of the manuals and lectures closely resembled the religious homily. The emphasis on the conduct of life was also related to fundamental changes taking place in American society. As Jacksonian America became more commercial, mobile, and materialistic, the traditional religious doctrines of election and reprobation became discredited. Instead, during the first half of the nineteenth century proper behavior was heavily emphasized as the counterpart to faith and good works. Americans were searching for stabilizing values and habits in an unsettling era and consequently lecturers and writers often assured their audiences that good behavior would lead, to good works, which were open to all since everyone enjoyed the blessings of free will. Many of the most popular manual writers and lecturers such as William A. Alcott and Emerson tried to assist their readers and listeners in improving their minds and bodies, making them sharper, stronger instruments for the service of God and Mammon as well.[43] The increased interest in antebellum health reform was partially related to the purity advocates' ability to exploit these new ways of addressing Americans.

Graham's sudden rise to regional prominence was probably augmented by his unusual platform style. On the stage he exuded sincerity as he vividly illustrated his jeremiads by discussing physiology, science, health reform, the Bible, and his own personal experiences. For example, in one of his lectures Graham regretted that he would

> not be able to do myself justice this evening, for I acknowledge with shame and sorrow that I have disgraced and abused my vital functions. I have reduced myself to a level with brutes—and now I pay the penalty. . . . I yielded to temptation . . . and ate a slice too much of [Graham] bread! Look at me—at my exhilaration—all arising, let me assure you, from one extra slice of bread. I should have known better—I did know better.[44]

This part of his speech was accompanied by dramatic gestures and sudden outbursts of emotion. Later in the lecture, Graham calmed down as the alleged effects of the bread wore off and he finished his address with an examination of vegetarianism. His audiences must have been alternately stunned and amused by the content and delivery of these talks, which apparently touched a responsive chord, for they were often well attended and considered provocative.

After he left New York, Graham capitalized on his fame by moving to Northampton, Massachusetts, so he could lecture throughout the Northeast. Every spring and summer he embarked on long lecture tours. Following a short vacation in the fall, he traveled west and then ended the year with a series of speeches in Boston. In 1836, for example, he appeared in Nantucket, Lowell, Worcester, and Millbury, Massachusetts, and Albany, New York. The next year, he visited Portland, Maine, New Bedford, Massachusetts, Providence, Rhode Island, New York, Newark, and Philadelphia. When Graham visited Boston in 1837 he gave three talks on diet and regimen, four lectures to young men, four speeches to mothers, one course on comparative anatomy and physiology, and Sabbath evening talks on biblical attitudes toward meat and wine. He even delivered "two lectures to the colored people, besides all his other labors in the vincity of Boston."[45]

Graham had rapidly emerged as the spokesman for a provocative set of ideas that included medicine, physiology, diet, and sexual behavior. His popular publications and controversial lectures brought him a wide reputation. "No man can travel by stage or steamboat," Graham claimed, "or go into any part of our country . . . and begin to advocate a vegetable diet . . . without being immediately asked—'What. Are you a Grahamite?' "[46] He owed his meteoric rise to a number of favorable circumstances and personal traits: Graham was persistent, able to synthesize existing scientific concepts, and utilized the principles of Broussais and Bichat to create a comprehensive and convincing world view during a period of cultural and medical ferment. In Philadelphia and New York, Graham moved quickly from alcohol and cholera toward sexuality and diet—the two subjects which became the main concerns of romantic physiological reformers. During the next five years, he further developed these two topics and helped launch the American health movement.

Graham and his fellow health reformers, whom we will examine later, had similar backgrounds and experiences that led them into this new field. All of the leaders were natives of New England and western New York who left their fathers' farms and towns and migrated to urban centers where they participated in the new tertiary sector as lecturers, editors, publishers, and professional reformers. In their own lives they experienced the rapid changes and instability of their era and thus they could address other young men who had left home for new and frequently marginal urban careers. They also could articulate the fears of rural and urban fathers whose sons had adopted new behaviors and values. Because of the inevitable shock of transition from country to city, the romantics developed advice literature that counseled their young readers to "control your appetites, subdue your passions, firmly and rigidly practice right principles, [and] form habits of purity, propriety, sobriety, and diligence."[47]

These health reformers came from diverse rural and small-town backgrounds in the Northeast and pursued careers that required broadly applicable skills not dependent on traditionally determined local status. Because mobility characterized the careers of Graham and the other leaders of the health-reform movement, they believed that the gap between traditional values and tumultuous new conditions could be bridged by character building, a form of inner control that was self-regulating. Their physiological theories and migratory experiences led them to believe that Jacksonian America was a hostile environment which was external, inorganic, and threatened the individual with destruction. Therefore they concluded that the healthiest form of behavior was living in a wholly internalized manner, using the animal senses to protect the vital organic functions. By retreating into sexual and dietary temperance, Graham and his followers could jettison the problematic aspects of life and become human fortresses. Throughout the mid-nineteenth century, the purity advocates preached an extreme form of self-control because they believed that only constant prudence could minimize the impact of an unreliable world. Simultaneously, however, their pessimistic analysis of contemporary America was tempered by romantic perfectionism, for the health reformers fervently believed that their society was not decadent and hopelessly depraved but capable of infinite improvement through the adoption of correct physiology. The modernization process propelled the health reformers into a commercial, urban environment where they developed an ideology and appropriate behavior to cope with the unsettling changes they experienced. Health reformers were people with modern sensibilities, whose awareness of life was rooted in radical doubt and anxiety. Throughout their lives Graham and his followers were afflicted by a sense of loneliness, emptiness, and the precariousness of their personal beings. It is no wonder that they channeled these feelings into a searching critique of American life that led to more restrictive forms of behavior.

NOTES

1. Edmund Morgan, *The Puritan Family: Religious and Domestic Relations in Seventeenth-Century New England,* 1944 (Westport, Conn.: Greenwood Press, 1966); Richard L. Bushman, *From Puritan to Yankee: Character and Social Order in Connecticut, 1690–1765* (Cambridge, Mass.: Harvard University Press, 1967); Richard J. Purcell, *Connecticut in Transition, 1775–1818* (Washington, D.C.: American Historical Association, 1918), pp. 1–30. For an excellent discussion of the major themes of modernization and family history, see Tamara K. Hareven, "Modernization and Family History: Perspectives on Social Change," *Signs* 2 (1976):190–206. Changes in late-eighteenth and early-nineteenth-century life cycles are ably discussed in Tamara K. Hareven, "Family Time and Historical Time," *The Family,* ed. Alice Rossi, Jerome Kagen, Tamara K. Hareven (New York: W. W. Norton, 1978), pp. 55–70; Joseph F. Kett, "Growing up in Rural New England, 1800–1840," *Anonymous Americans: Explorations in Nineteenth-Century Social History,* ed. Tamara K. Hareven (Englewood Cliffs, N.J.: Prentice Hall, 1971), pp. 1–16; Joseph F. Kett, *Rites of Passage: Adolescence in America, 1790 to the Present* (New York: Basic Books, 1977), pp. 3–50.
2. Erik Erikson, *Young Man Luther* (New York: W. W. Norton, 1958), p. 22.
3. Helen Graham Carpenter, *The Rev. John Graham of Woodbury, Connecticut, and His Descendants* (Chicago: The Monastery Hill Press, 1942), pp. 6–90.
4. Carpenter, *John Graham,* p. 184; Mildred V. Naylor, "Sylvester Graham, 1794–1851," *Annals of Medical History* 4 (1942):236; *Water Cure Journal* 12 (1851):110.
5. *Hampshire Gazette,* 17 September 1850.
6. Carpenter, *John Graham,* p. 184; Naylor, "Graham," p. 236; *Palladium of Liberty,* 18 April 1822; *Newark Journal* (1872):33–36. On April 17, 1822, Graham charged twenty-five cents admission for a public recitation of poetry by Aikinside, Campbell, Byron, Collins, and himself.

7. Carpenter, *John Graham*, p. 184; Naylor, "Graham," p. 236; David F. Allmendinger, "The Dangers of Antebellum Student Life," *Journal of Social History* 7 (1973):75–85.

8. Rev. Mortimer Blake, *A Centennial History of the Mendon Association of Congregational Ministers* (Boston: S. Harding, 1853), pp. 78, 309; Joseph H. Kler, *God's Happy Cluster: 1688–1963, History of the Bound Brook Presbyterian Church* (n.p., 1963), pp. 64, 73; Carpenter, *John Graham*, p. 184; Naylor, "Graham," pp. 237–39. Naylor refers to Graham's account book, which unfortunately disappeared in 1941 from the library of the Middlebury Chapter of the Daughters of the American Revolution at Bound Brook, New Jersey.

9. Carpenter, *John Graham*, pp. 5–6, 123–90.

10. Asa Earl Martin, "The Temperance Movement in Pennsylvania Prior to the Civil War," *Pennsylvania Magazine of History and Biography* 99 (1925):195–230; Harry M. Chalfant, *Father Penn and John Barleycorn* (Harrisburg, Pa.: The Evangelical Press, 1920), pp. 38–39, 62–75.

11. *Poulson's American Daily Advertiser*, 5 March 1831; John A. Krout, *The Origins of Prohibition* (New York: Alfred A. Knopf, 1925), pp. 88–92; Joseph R. Gusfield, *Symbolic Crusade: Status Politics and the American Temperance Movement* (Urbana, Ill.: University of Illinois Press, 1963), pp. 44–57.

12. Benjamin Rush, *Medical Inquiries and Observations*, 5 vols. (Philadelphia: Thomas Dodson, 1794–1798), 4:59–62, 70–72; John Kobler, *Ardent Spirits: The Rise and Fall of Prohibition*(New York: Putnam, 1973), pp. 42–47, 52–58; August F. Fehlandt, *A Century of Drink Reform in the United States* (Cincinnati, Ohio: Jennings and Graham, 1904), pp. 25–30, 36–37.

13. Naylor, "Graham," pp. 237–38; *Poulson's American Daily Advertiser*, 5 November, 27 November 1830.

14. *Journal of Health* 2 (1831):113–114.

15. Lyman Beecher, *Six Sermons on Intemperance* (Boston: T. R. Marvin, 1827), pp. 92–96; *Journal of Health* 2 (1831):114.

16. Rush, *Medical Inquiries*, 4:123–29, 181–258; Richard H. Shryock, "The Advent of Modern Medicine in Philadelphia, 1800–1850," *Medicine in America: Historical Essays* (Baltimore, Johns Hopkins University Press, 1966), pp. 203–32.

17. Naylor, "Graham," p. 238.

18. Erwin H. Ackerknecht, *Medicine at the Paris Hospital, 1794–1848* (Baltimore: Johns Hopkins University Press, 1967), pp. 3–47; Michel J. P. Foucault, *Naissance de clinique* (Paris: Presses Universitaires de France, 1963); George Rosen, "The Philosophy of Ideology and the Emergence of Modern Medicine in France," *Bulletin of the History of Medicine* 20 (1946):328–39; Owesi Temkin, "The Role of Surgery in the Rise of Modern Medical Thought," *Bulletin of the History of Medicine* 25 (1951):248–59.

19. François J. V. Broussais, *A Treatise on Physiology Applied to Psychology* (Philadelphia: H. C. Carey and I. Lea, 1826), pp. xvii–xx, 42–45, 52; J. D. Rolleston, "F. J. V. Broussais: His Life and Doctrines," *Proceedings of the Royal Society of Medicine* 32 (1939):405–13; Ackerknecht, *Paris Medicine*, pp. 61–83.

20. Xavier Bichat, *Physiological Researches upon Life and Death* (Philadelphia: Smith and Maxwell, 1809), pp. 1–4, 94–134; Xavier Bichat, *General Anatomy, Applied to Physiology and Medicine*, 2 vols. (Boston: Richardson and Lord, 1822), 1:249–53; Pedro Lair Entralgo, "Sensualism and Vitalism in Bichat's 'Anatomie Générale,'" *Journal of the History of Medicine and Allied Sciences* 3 (1948):47–64; Ackerknecht, *Paris Medicine*, pp. 51–58.

21. *Journal of Foreign Medical Science & Literature* 1 (1821):40, 365, 516.

22. Russell Jones, "American Doctors and the Parisian Medical World, 1830–1840," *Bulletin of the History of Medicine* 47 (1973):40–65, 117–204.

23. *Poulson's American Daily Advertiser,* 31 May 1831; Broussais, *Treatise in Physiology,* p. viii; *The Philadelphia Journal of the Medical and Physical Sciences* 4 (1822):72–113.

24. *Journal of Health* 1 (1830):41, 212, 2 (1831):42–51, 209–222, 272, 281; Frank Luther Mott, *A History of American Magazines, 1741–1850* (New York: D. Appleton, 1930), p. 440.

25. *Journal of Health* 1 (1829):3–7, 32–24, 277–78. Later in Bell's career, he became an enthusiastic supporter of Graham and claimed that anyone would "derive gratification and instruction from an attentive perusal" of Graham's books. See Joel Shew, *Hydropathy; or The Water-Cure: Its Principles, Modes of Treatment &c.* (New York: Wiley and Putnam, 1844), pp. 276–77.

26. *Poulson's American Daily Advertiser,* 8 November, 10 December 1830, 24 January, 29 January, 1 February, 18 March, 7 May, 26 May 1831; Sylvester Graham, *Lectures on the Science of Human Life,* 2 vols. (Boston: Marsh, Capon, Lyon, and Webb, 1839), l:vi; Naylor, "Graham," p. 239.

27. Charles E. Rosenberg, *The Cholera Years* (Chicago: University of Chicago Press, 1962), pp. 1–39; George Rosen, "Public Health Problems in New York City during the Nineteenth Century," *New York State Journal of Medicine* 50 (1950):73–79; R. E. McGrew, "The First Cholera Epidemic and Social History," *Bulletin of the History of Medicine* 34 (1960):61–73; J. S. Chambers, *The Conquest of Cholera: America's Greatest Scourge* (New York: Macmillan Co., 1938), pp. 24–84; R. Pollitzer, *Cholera* (Geneva, Switzerland: UNESCO, 1959), pp. 17–38, 97–101.

28. Sylvester Graham, *A Lecture on Epidemic Diseases generally, and particularly the Spasmodic Cholera* (New York: M. Day, 1833), pp. iii–iv; *New York Daily Advertiser,* 25 April 1832.

29. *New York Evening Post,* 24 April 1832.

30. Graham, *Lecture on Epidemic Diseases,* p. iv.

31. Ibid., p. 2.

32. Ibid.

33. Ibid., p. 9.

34. Ibid., pp. 10–11.

35. Ibid., pp. 14–19.

36. Ibid., pp. 20–36, 43–47, 52; *New York Evening Post,* 27 July 1832.

37. Graham, *Lecture on Epidemic Diseases,* pp. 48–49.

38. Ibid., p. 40.

39. Rosenberg, *Cholera Years,* pp. 40–81; "The Cause of Cholera: Aspects of Etiological Thought in Nineteenth Century America," *Bulletin of the History of Medicine* 34 (1960): 331–54; Erwin H. Ackerknecht, "Anticontagionism Between 1821 and 1867," *Bulletin of the History of Medicine* 22 (1948): 562–93; Phyllis Allen, "Etiological Theory in America Prior to the Civil War," *Journal of the History of Medicine and Allied Sciences* 2 (1947):489–520.

40. *New York Evening Post,* 12 June, 28 July 1832.

41. Graham, *Lecture on Epidemic Diseases,* pp. 66–77; *Aesculapian Tablets of the Nineteenth Century* (Providence, R.I.: Weeden and Cory, 1834).

42. Carl Bode, *Antebellum Culture* (Berkeley and Los Angeles: University of California Press, 1959), pp. 109–32; Frank Luther Mott, *American Journalism: A History, 1690–1960* (New York: Macmillan Co., 1962), pp. 200–207; Charles A. Levermore, "Rise of Metropolitan Journalism," *American Historical Review* 6 (1901):446–65; James L. Crouthamel, "The Newspaper Revolution in New York, 1830–1840," *New York History* 45 (1964):91–113.

43. Carl Bode, *The American Lyceum: Town Meeting of the Mind* (New York: Oxford University Press, 1956).

44. *New Experiments: Means without Living* (Boston: Weeks, Jordan, 1837), p. 62.

45. *Health Journal and Advocate of Physiological Reform* 1 (1840–1841):78–79; *Graham Journal of Health and Longevity* 1 (1837):6, 8.

46. *Boston Medical and Surgical Journal* 14 (1836):25.

47. Daniel Wise, *The Young Man's Counsellor* (New York: Carlton and Phillips, 1853), p. 17.

4

The Peculiar Epidemic

Ralph Waldo Emerson claimed that the antebellum period was "bewailed as the Age of Introversion" and he suggested that young people became highly self-conscious during this time because there were fewer traditions and greater choices than in the preceding era. These "young men were born with knives in their brains, a tendency to introversion, self-dissection, anatomizing of motives." The key "to the period appeared to be that the mind had become aware of itself." Emerson believed that, as a result, many youths were "infected with Hamlet's unhappiness— 'Sicklied o'er with the pale cast of thought.' "[1]

The sage of Concord's characterization aptly described the health reformers, who were frightened by the lack of order and structure in Jacksonian America. The fear of losing control dominated their books, speeches, and reform activities. Reaffirming traditional values, they contrasted the alleged virtues of rural society to the dangers of urban civilization, the purity of the rural economy to new speculative and commercial values, and the patriarchal family to the stress on individual rights. Ultimately a symbolic figure emerged who represented the forces of disorder and change—the young male. The purity reformers addressed their tracts on sexuality, diet, and personal hygiene to recent male migrants to urban centers because they embodied the reformers' deepest hopes and fears about America's future. The conduct and values of these young citizens, according to the purity reformers, would determine the fate of the republican experiment.

Graham had argued in his cholera lectures that there was an inexorable connection between sexual excesses and poor health, but he had not described the relationship in detail. This topic later was discussed by Graham before an enthusiastic audience of a few hundred at the American Lyceum in New York in May of 1832. Because the subject was so important, he decided to publish the lecture a year later:

77

When I commenced my public career . . . it did not, in any degree,
enter into my plan to treat upon this delicate subject: but the continual
entreaties and importunities, and heart-touching . . . appeals which I
received from young men, constrained me to dare to do that which I
was fully convinced ought to be done; and the result has entirely
justified my decision and conduct. . . . Hundreds who have listened to
the following lecture, have thereby been saved from the most calamit-
ous evils: and great numbers, among whom are many physicians and
clergymen, have asked me to publish it.[2]

Graham confessed it was difficult to discuss openly the problem of
sexual excesses, but young men desperately needed sound information.
In a revealing metaphor, he claimed that, while parents had been
confident of their children's innocence and purity, their sons had been
"clandestinely drinking in the most corrupt and depraving knowledge
from mercenary and polluted hands."[3] In his temperance and cholera
lectures Graham had espoused the physiological principles of Broussais
and Bichat; after 1832 he incorporated these theories into a bold analysis
of normal and abnormal manifestations of sexuality, especially male masturbation.

The published lecture on masturbation by Graham was the first
nineteenth-century work on a new genre in American literature—medical
tracts on self-abuse. Before the 1830s, there were few British or American
monographs about masturbation except for some medical treatises,
pseudoscientific works, and didactic religious sermons. Most seven-
teenth- and eighteenth-century writers regarded sex as a healthy passion
and condemned masturbation because it hindered marital sexual satisfaction. Self-abuse was treated as merely another sexual problem, like impotence, infertility, and other sexual malfunctions.[4]

But during the antebellum period, there was an astronomical increase
in the number of American articles and books on sexual excesses and
masturbation. The growing popularity of these works was not just due to
increased literacy and improved marketing techniques, for material on
masturbation appeared regularly in literary forms that formerly had not
examined sexual excesses closely—medical and educational journals,
scientific treatises, and male self-help manuals. Graham's Lecture to
Young Men (1834) was the first and most influential of these anti-
masturbation tracts; it rapidly went through ten editions in fifteen years
and was translated into a number of languages.

The sexual studies of Graham and his fellow health reformers were
strident, didactic, and obsessively concerned with the regulation and
rationalization of sexual activities. Claiming to be based on scientific

observation, these books presented sexual morality as a problem of hygiene and attempted to prove that masturbation caused insufferable mental and physical problems. Significantly, the purity reformers associated masturbation with rootless male migrants like themselves who were flooding America's commercial and urban centers.

Although sexual overindulgence generally has been considered debilitating since the time of Hippocrates, masturbation was not widely accepted as a disease until the nineteenth century. The Judeo-Christian tradition pictured masturbation as an evil because it denied the normal function of sexuality, which was procreation. Masturbation often was declared a venial or mortal sin, but the practice rarely was viewed as a medical problem. Medical references about the harmful effects of masturbation were quite rare before 1700.[5]

In the eighteenth century, two works appeared which signified the emergence of a new attitude toward masturbation. Around 1710 an anonymous work was published in England entitled *Onania: or The Heinous Sin of Self-Pollution, And all its Frightful Consequences . . . ;* by 1750 the book had sold 38,000 copies in nineteen editions. The author condemned masturbation as a sin, but stressed the harmful marital consequences of the act. His mild treatment involved meditation, a careful diet, avoidance of violent exercise and the handling of the genitals, and early marriage.[6]

The new concern about masturbation as a health problem was illustrated by the publication of Samuel Tissot's *L'Onanisme, ou Dissertation physique sur les maladies produites par la masturbation* (1758). The Swiss physician condemned the British *Onania* for its irrelevant moral and theological reflections and, instead, emphasized the harmful physiological consequences of masturbation. According to Tissot, semen was a precious substance and its loss under any conditions caused health hazards. Seminal discharge was necessary for procreation, but any other sexual activities were harmful because they caused insanity, impotence, and bodily decay. Semen was

> the Essential Oil of the animal liquors . . . the rectified spirit, the dissipation whereof leaves the other humours weak, and in some degree vapid. . . . [The] loss of an ounce of this humour would weaken more than [the loss of] forty ounces of blood.[7]

These concepts became widely accepted by physicians and lay people throughout nineteenth-century Europe and America. Although American writers disagreed about the causes of self-abuse, they believed masturbators were easy to recognize because the symptoms were so clear. They were usually shy and suspicious. As the vital semen drained from their bodies, they became dull, languid, and unconcerned with personal hygiene. Eventually their memories and senses became defective as they slowly succumbed to self-abuse. Their muscles became flabby, and the victims often contracted diabetes, jaundice, blood diseases, or consumption. Because many British and American physicians believed that somatic disorders caused mental problems, it was relatively easy to trace "masturbatory insanity" to the exhaustion of the brain and nervous system from self-abuse. A Midwestern doctor, R. N. Barr, summarized this medical perspective when he warned about the mortal dangers of masturbation:

> In vain we scan the springs of human woe,
> To find a deadlier or more cruel foe
> To erring man, than this sad self-pollution,
> This damning wrecker of his constitution.
>
> In its foul march it tramples vigor down,
> Darkens the soul, usurps the mental throne,
> Preys upon the vitals of its filthy slave,
> And drags him early to a hopeless grave.[8]

Thus a broad and heterogeneous class of signs and symptoms were recognized in the nineteenth century as part of a syndrome or disease called masturbation. An explanation of this phenomenon entails a reexamination of the concept of disease because masturbation has been evaluated differently over the past three centuries. A number of scholars have tried to explain why masturbation was perceived as a serious medical problem by examining the psychological aspects of the disease. René Spitz argued that the anti-masturbation literature was a phobic defense against sexualilty which became accepted as Protestant notions of sin and sexual repression spread throughout Europe.[9] Robert MacDonald suggested that the new concern about masturbation "catered to the general neurosis of the period."[10] The masturbation phobia as a modern paranoid form of witch hunting and scapegoating was defended by Alex Comfort and Thomas Szasz.[11] And E. H. Hare believed that self-abuse probably increased during the nineteenth century because sexual repression became normative and there was a great fear of venereal infection.[12]

These studies are original and insightful, but explanations such as phobic defense, neurosis, repression, and paranoia explain little about the growing concern over masturbation. Of course, without statistics on the prevalence of self-abuse, it is impossible to confirm or refute any of these arguments.[13] Some European historians, however, have provided us with a possible explanation for the hysteria over masturbation. John R. Gillis, Robert P. Neuman, and Sterling Fishman have suggested that the late–nineteenth-century European interest in youthful sexuality and masturbation was related to the creation of adolescence. Attitudes toward masturbation reflected and influenced the modern concepts of childhood and adolescence which were probably part of a confused response to the earlier onset of puberty in western Europe.[14] These interpretations are important because they have linked the nineteenth-century interest in masturbation to concrete social-historical changes.

In America, similar intellectual and cultural modifications occurred. Although adolescence was not accepted until the late nineteenth century, antebellum Americans did believe that a new period of life called youth was developing as a critical transition between childhood and adulthood. This stage was sometimes a lengthy period of semidependence between the ages of ten and twenty-one or a time of indecision and identity formation between ages fifteen and twenty-five. The concept of youth was related to the disintegration of traditional Northeastern rural life and the rise of urban centers which created discontinuities between parents and children. Concurrently, a new tolerance for youthful activities emerged as adults recognized that age specific behaviors were developing.[15] The purity advocates perceptively linked their concern about masturbation to contemporary demographic changes and the migration of male youths to commercial and urban centers. Self-abuse symbolized the larger problems of control, authority, and change in nineteenth-century America.

During the antebellum period, a large number of youths and young adults in their late teens and early twenties appeared in the population. This was in sharp contrast to the colonial period, when the population had been very young, with half the people in the late eighteenth century below the age of fifteen and a median age for white males around sixteen. In 1790 there were almost two children for every white female and nearly 40 percent of American families contained between four and seven children.[16]

But in the pre–Civil War years, youths and young adults became a larger portion of the total population. The ratio between adults over twenty and children below sixteen grew even during the 1830s and throughout the rest of the century the ratio favored the adults. By 1840, the median age for white males had climbed to 17.9 and by 1860 to 19.7. More than two-thirds of the population was below the age of thirty and nearly 30 percent of the population belonged to the categories of youths and young adults. This percentage remained steady throughout the century even though there was a sharp decline in younger ages and increases among the older ones.[17]

Physical mobility complemented the effects of demographic changes. Most migrants to the cities were unmarried youths or young married couples. Compared with rural areas, antebellum cities contained low proportions both of children and adults in their thirties. In 1840, for example, white people aged twenty to twenty-nine formed about 45 percent of the white population aged twenty or more in large American cities.[18] This large scale migration had been set in motion by the modernization process, which began disrupting Northeastern rural society during the eighteenth century.

With abundant land for themselves and their offspring, colonial Northeastern settlers established patriarchal families in which fathers often maintained their authority over mature sons by withholding control over land from them until late in their lives. Delayed marriages indicated a prolonged attachment to paternal families while the sons' residences in houses built upon their fathers' lands sustained close relationships with parents and siblings. Most people lived in areas that had a low population density, a wide distribution of wealth, and were relatively removed from dependency on the market economy. The family, church, and community trained youths, educated the young, distributed property, and provided a sense of economic and social continuity through a complex kin and community network.[19]

Yet eighteenth-century America was not a static society. The population doubled every twenty or thirty years. In 1700 there were 250,000 Americans; around 1815, the population reached 8.5 million. By the late eighteenth century population density and land shortages had increased significantly. Men coming of age in 1720 could expect to live like their fathers as semisubsistence farmers. In 1770 men faced the choice of migrating, trying to penetrate more deeply into the market economy, or remaining home and subsisting at lower standards of living than their fathers.

By the Revolution, America was a society in flux. Probably 40 percent of the population moved during a few years' time, usually for economic reasons. Significant numbers of young men were not restrained by family, church, community, and apprenticeship, for American society had not developed new institutions to control and discipline them. At the same time, economic inequality increased because a commercial society was replacing a primarily subsistence economy.[20]

Economic and social changes accelerated in the nineteenth century.

About five percent of the American population lived in cities between 1730 and 1820, but during the antebellum era the percentage of the urban population began to rise from 8.5 in 1840 to 22.6 by 1880. Cities grew rapidly and chaotically; from 1820 to 1870 Philadelphia's population increased from 65,000 to 674,000 while New York expanded from 152,000 to 1,478,000.[21] The growth of commercial exports after the War of 1812 stimulated the establishment of banks, warehouses, insurance companies, and businesses and so young people, especially men, deserted the countryside and moved to the cities. Urban commercial opportunities had a devastating effect on country life. In the Northeast, agriculture declined in status throughout the nineteenth century. Youths left the farms because they were unconvinced that farming was the avenue to wealth, honor, and happiness. The traditional rural and Calvinist concept of calling became synonymous with occupational mobility and thus rural life appeared uninspiring and provincial. The patriarchal, hierarchical colonial order dissolved and was replaced by the first stages of commercial and industrial capitalism. Although most Americans continued to live in rural communities, urban centers became the cultural and economic meccas of America. Henry James complained that there was a "terrible paucity of alternatives"[22] in antebellum rural New England and Emerson commented that "the cities drain the country of the best part of its population: the flower of the youth, of both sexes, goes to the towns, and the country is cultivated by a so much inferior class."[23]

The large-scale migration of young men to urban areas drastically affected urban mobility, city life, and the American family. Although contemporary orators or distinguished foreign visitors such as Alexis de Tocqueville believed that upward mobility and democracy were increasing during the antebellum period, the evidence tells another story. Population concentration and commercial differentiation brought increased inequality and lower rates of upward mobility. In Brooklyn, 12 percent of the population held 83 percent of the total wealth in 1841. The New York City figures were similar; 4 percent of the population controlled 81 percent of the wealth by 1845. Inequality in Southern and Western cities was similar to the maldistribution in Eastern cities. Even in rural areas, economic disparities were increasing rapidly. A massive internal migration of younger, marginal persons of low economic status in and out of cities probably enlarged the power and the share of wealth commanded by the more stable elements. For example, in Boston there was an annual population turnover of about 30 percent from 1830 to 1840 and 40 percent from 1850 to 1860. Geographical movement involved the improvement of the migrants' economic status less often in the antebellum era than at any time after the period.[24]

Phenomenal geographic mobility and urban growth transformed the antebellum city. Class and ethnic divisions multiplied. Unattached and marginal young men became involved in business enterprises, peer associations, political machines, and volunteer fire companies. Traditional rural or urban institutional structures were unable to contain and discipline them because antebellum cities contained many more rootless and violent youths than the smaller towns of the eighteenth century.

Commercialization and urbanization also had a drastic effect on the rural and urban family. As subsistence farming and rural crafts declined in relative importance, the family lost many of its traditional economic and social functions. Institutional differentiation and the demise of the apprenticeship system weakened the integrity of rural families. Fathers no longer had the power to determine their sons' occupational choices and values. Young men spent their adolescent years within their families, but they had to plan for a future outside the traditional familial and communal network. They were becoming more marginal to their fathers' social and economic arrangements.

Urban families also were disrupted by the modernization process. Master craftsmen lost control over traditional trades and their sons could not inherit their positions. As American society became more dynamic and less traditional, the skills and values of artisan families became obsolete. Both urban and rural fathers were alarmed and distressed by the uncertain futures their sons faced. Fears of uncontrolled young men combined with father-son conflicts to produce a great anxiety about the lives of young men in antebellum cities.

As more youths pursued commercial and urban occupations, purity reformers began writing advice manuals that answered the question, "How is the stranger youth armed to meet the attack of worldly excitement and sensual allurement?"[26] The health reformers, who had experienced the unsettling transition from rural to urban America, displayed a genuine alarm over the moral perils that faced the new migrants. Because cities contained no apparent role models or reliable guides, the purity writers emphasized character building as a substitute moral gyroscope for earnest young urbanites. The reformers condemned idleness, disobedience, vanity, and dissipation and tried to instill what they considered traditional rural virtues in the city. Although they tolerated and sometimes promoted self-assertion, the antebellum advice manual writers also attempted to temper aggressive behavior with a strong sense of self-restraint.

Many of these recent male migrants also were frightened by urban life and their new autonomy. A young clerk wrote Samuel B. Woodward about the perils of urban life and plaintively told the following story:

I am alone in this city—away from home, and in fact I am aloı
the world—none to whom I dare to communicate the cause of
distress. . . . I am without funds, except for a small salary . . . and am in
debt for my academic education which I completed not long since at
one of the New England colleges.[26]

The health reformers tried to help these insecure youths by creat-
ing a respectable sexual ideology. This cluster of ideas stressed the importance of sublimation, submissiveness, and continence before marriage and
sexual moderation within marriage. Using an economic analogy, self-
control, self-denial, and the postponement of sexual gratification were
the biological and physiological equivalents of economic savings and
capital accumulation. The reckless "spending" of sperm led to moral and
physical bankruptcy.[27] The lack of sexual activity before marriage was
perceived as normal and socially necessary. The anti-masturbation literature was the cutting edge of the new respectable sexual ideology; these
warnings were an attempt to defend the medical veracity of the new
sexual concepts while warning against transgressions, which threatened
the individual and the society. Graham's popular *Lecture* and the other
purity literature articulated middle-class urban society's fears about masturbation and linked self-abuse with demographic and social changes.

According to the purity reformers, the stability and happiness of
American society rested on the moral education and physical health of
young males:

The wisest and best men, of every age, have manifested a deep interest in the welfare of youth; and have considered their intellectual,
moral, and physical education, character, and condition, of the utmost
importance to the individual, social, and civil welfare of mankind. . . .
[T]he proper education of youth . . . constitutes the foundation and
efficiency of all our civil and political institutions.[28]

By combining temperance, vegetarianism, and the Paris school of
medicine with their own fears and aspirations, the romantic reformers
constructed a model of the American male that centered around the gastrointestinal tract and the genitals. They condemned sexual activity, except for reproductive purposes, because its intensity had disastrous social
and physiological consequences. The male orgasm was pictured as uncontrollable, raging, and destructive, for it threatened the body's hierarchy
of functions. The purity reformers visualized the body as a closed energy
system; sexual excitation and orgasm disrupted the natural functions and
resulted in moral, intellectual, and physical degeneracy:

The convulsive paroxysms attending venereal indulgence, are connected with the most intense excitement, and cause the most powerful agitation to the whole system, that it is ever subject to. The brain, stomach, heart, lungs, liver, skin—and the other organs—feel it sweeping over them, with the tremendous violence of a tornado. . . . [This] violent paroxysm is generally succeeded by a great exhaustion, relaxation, lassitude, and even prostration.[29]

Because the male orgasm had only one justifiable purpose, the purity advocates believed that youths should be continent until they married in their late twenties or thirties.[30] But most importantly, young men must not masturbate. One writer suggested that the discharge of sperm "obliterated" and "prostrated" the body's energy and so the masturbator concentrated his energies on a "loathsome and beastly habit."[31] John Ellis argued that male overindulgence caused "general debility, weakness and lameness of the back, dyspepsia, [and] impotency."[32] And Elizabeth Willard claimed that "we must stop this waste through the sexual organs, if we would have health and strength of body."[33] Masturbation was the "worst form of excessive and perverted amativeness,"[34] complained Orson S. Fowler, and John B. Neuman summed up the whole purity attitude when he condemned self-abuse as "a crime wholly unnatural and . . . pernicious. It is worthy only of brutes, like the dog-faced monkey."[35]

According to Graham, masturbation was the worst form of venereal indulgence; it was an unhealthy expression of an unhealthy urge that could not be cured by marriage. The institution of marriage was not designed to satisfy sexual urges but to blunt them. When the husband and wife became accustomed to each other's bodies, sexual excitement waned and sexual intercourse seldom occurred. Graham recommended that healthy and robust individuals should have intercourse no more than twelve times a year. Anything beyond this would impair a person's physiological powers, shorten life, and increase the possibility of disease and suffering.[36]

Masturbation also was an unnatural act that harmed the mind and the body because it overstimulated the nervous system. This heinous practice usually began early in life when the human organs were not fully developed and hence subject to permanent injury. Here Graham departed radically from earlier writers because he linked youthful masturbation to antebellum demographic and social changes.

Graham believed there was an epidemic of masturbatory activity throughout America and estimated that 70 percent of American boys were acquainted with the activity by the age of twelve. He blamed this

epidemic on the lack of parental vigilance, the debasing character of n
servants and the lower classes, and the growing popularity of pu
schools, boarding schools, and colleges.

Parents, Graham demanded, should watch their children closely and
give them proper hygienic instructions. Anything less would be a "most
culpable neglect of parental duty."[47] Lorenzo Fowler, an influential
phrenologist and avid purity reformer, echoed Graham when he warned
that "in the unformed condition of the physical system . . . an unbridled
indulgence could not fail to prove destructive to the perfection of the
bodily powers."[38] Although servants and the lower classes sometimes
initiated children in self-abuse, Graham and his followers believed that
most boys learned to masturbate from their peers, especially in schools:

> [T]he extent to which it prevails in our public schools and colleges is
> shocking, beyond measure! I have known boys to leave some of these
> institutions at the age of twelve and thirteen, almost completely ruined
> in health and constitution by this destructive practice; and they have
> assured me, that, to their certain knowledge, almost everybody in the
> school practiced the filthy vice; and many of them went to the still
> more loathsome and criminal extent of an unnatural commerce with
> each other![39]

Graham's accusations about servants, the lower classes, and schools
also were repeated by European writers. Some people believed that
nurses and servants fondled infants' genitals to quiet them and this led to
self-abuse. It is impossible to determine whether this was common or
whether this encouraged masturbation among children. Perhaps the middle classes feared that nurses, servants, and the lower classes did not
follow the respectable sexual ideology and thus could not be trusted with
middle-class children.

Complaints about schools were common too. Samuel Tissot wanted
his book about masturbation to "become familiar to these persons who
are appointed to supervise the education of children"[40] because he believed that many children were learning to masturbate in schools. Hermann Rohleder, a late–nineteenth-century medical expert on
masturbation, begged Latin and Greek teachers to make their lessons
more interesting to prevent self-abuse! He argued that schools encouraged the habit with their boring courses.[41] By blaming masturbation
on schools, servants, and peers, Europeans and Americans could continue to believe that masturbation was a learned rather than an innate
response.

Graham went beyond these standard nineteenth-century arguments, however, and linked the supposed increase in masturbation to changing experiences among children and youths. He carefully divided young people into children and youths. The difference between the two involved the onset of puberty, which he estimated began around fourteen or fifteen in boys. Graham created this division to make two arguments about masturbation. First, he believed that before fourteen or fifteen, boys were not yet sexually mature. Thus masturbation could cause lasting damage. For boys above the age of puberty, masturbation was an ever-present danger because they were sexually more mature.[42] Graham's call for increased vigilance and intervention in childrearing reflected his recognition of physiological and social changes in growth and it fit new conceptions of childrearing which downplayed a stern Calvinism and instead emphasized the importance of environment, example, and responsible adult supervision. Importantly, his unwillingness to blame masturbation on the young masturbator reinforced the idea that children were fragile, innocent, asexual creatures who could be easily corrupted.

Not only was masturbation unnatural and unhealthy, it was a secret and solitary vice. Thus it was antisocial and promoted a destructive form of individualism. Self-abuse also debased the mind and impaired the intellectual and moral faculties. Masturbators felt an instinctual shame and self-loathing which could not be hidden from others. Such a deep and abiding sense of abasement seared the sinner with "the hot iron of iniquity" and produced a "most sickening and withering influence." Suicide often followed this overwhelming anguish and despair.[43]

Graham's description of the heinous consequences of masturbation was vivid, convincing, and appealed to other purity writers. Continued self-abuse led to physical and mental decay until the "wretched transgressor" sank into a "miserable fatuity."[44] According to Graham,

> Among the hapless inmates of the lunatic asylum, none is more incorrigible nor more incurable than the wretched victim of this odious vice! What of the fragments of his shattered reason he is still capable of gathering up from the general wreck, he craftily exercises in devising means and securing opportunities to elude the vigilance of his keepers, and to indulge his despotic lust![45]

This was a popular analysis of an illness that persisted into the twentieth century, "masturbatory insanity." For example, William A. Alcott, an antebellum educator and author of many advice manuals, argued that after continual self-abuse, "signs of mental aberration" appeared and the transgressor was "sent to the hospital for the insane; and very properly too."[46]Russell T. Trall, Woodward, and Neuman also suggested that degeneration was the inevitable consequence of masturbation.[47] Even

Charles Knowlton, an influential antebellum physician who believed that natural sexual urges should be properly gratified, suggested that masturbation impaired the mental and bodily powers and frequently led to insanity.[48]

The concept of "masturbatory insanity" gained credence from the reports of the State Lunatic Hospital in Worcester, Massachusetts. The superintendents there, especially the prestigious psychiatrist Samuel B. Woodward, who was a follower of Graham, claimed that over 30 percent of the admissions to the hospital were insane due to masturbation. In 1861, the superintendent of the Eastern Lunatic Asylum in Lexington, Kentucky, also believed many of the insane masturbated, which further deranged them. Other reputable physicians agreed that many masturbators had been driven insane by their unfortunate habits.[49] The insane asylums played a strategic role in labeling and controlling nineteenth-century deviants. Caretaker institutions had been erected during the antebellum period because some Americans believed that their society was becoming more disorderly, chaotic, and caused individuals to go insane. Insane asylums, like prisons, schools, and benevolent institutions, were partly designed to inculcate discipline and traditional morality.[50] The masturbatory activities of the insane thus appeared to reinforce the need for corrective institutions and also validated the health reformers' contentions.

Heredity, along with disease and insanity, was another sanction used by the purity advocates. Throughout the century, the basic assumptions of heredity were not controversial but widely accepted. Physicians and lay people assumed that acquired characteristics were inherited. They also believed heredity was a dynamic process that began with conception and ended with weaning. Most Americans thought the inheritance of personality or disease was not specific, but a matter of tendency and predisposition. And last, contemporaries agreed the sexes played a different role in heredity.[51] The health reformers appropriated these popular beliefs to prove that there were universal physiological laws that could not be violated without punishment.

What I would do is to impress upon the minds of the young, that punishment, however long deferred, must certainly come. . . . [T]he punishment will come just as certainly when we sin in ignorance as with our eyes open. . . . Nor is there any atonement for physical transgression. May we not be thankful—ought we not to be—that provisions of this sort are made anywhere?[52]

Thus young men had important responsibilities because sexual excesses threatened the continuation of the family and society. Alcott recounted stories of fathers begetting weak children because they had masturbated before marriage.[53] And Orson Fowler asked his readers to think about "how many parents . . . entail . . . even loathsome diseases and sensual propensities upon the fruit of their own bodies" because they failed to realize that "PARENTAGE is EVERYTHING."[54] Graham and his followers tried to remind young men of generational continuity, which was rooted in the past and broken in the present by their migration to urban centers. The state, the church, and society might not be able to control young men, but their own behavior provided a bridge between themselves and their progeny.

Although the health reformers were most repressive when they discussed the evils of masturbation and sexual excesses, their perfectionist impulses appeared while analyzing the influence of heredity. The purity advocates and many other romantic antebellum thinkers used hereditarian language in an optimistic fashion even though the implications of hereditarianism were not inherently optimistic. The health reformers interpreted heredity positively because it was a mechanism that could be manipulated to improve American society. Although the purity advocates thundered admonitions about the transmission of physiological sins, they were basically optimistic because heredity proved that people had the power to improve the nation's health. "There is a bright side to this view," Alcott assured his readers. "Few persons are so much affected by inheritance as to render their condition necessarily one of misery."[55] Thomas L. Nichols also agreed that "we must not despair, but try to improve by culture and education."[56] The virtuous male youth could usher in the physiological millennium by preserving his health and passing on his acquired characteristics to his children. "Lay it up in your memories," said Lorenzo Fowler, "that *we* give to our *children* their bad heads and bodies."[57] If young men and parents obeyed the laws of heredity, they would help perfect the human race and rid the world of vice and immorality.

Vitalistic arguments tied the health reformers' discussions of sexual excesses together and gave their analyses a common direction. While the purity advocates quoted Tissot, they did not rely on his pangenesis argument, which stated that the genitals converted a portion of arterial blood into semen, and thus the ejaculation of sperm diminished and exhausted the body's energy. This belief in pangenesis was an accepted scientific theory and was popularized by Georges Buffon, Charles Lyell, Herbert Spencer, and Charles Darwin.[58] Graham, in contrast, declared there was no evidence that the mere loss of semen was the source of bodily injury. Using the concepts of vitalism and physiology that he had learned from Broussais and Bichat, Graham argued that "the peculiar excitement, and the violence of the convulsive paroxysms," and the "actions of the mind"⁵⁹ made masturbation the worst form of venereal abuse. Inasmuch as the genitals were connected to the brain through the nervous system, masturbation inevitably led to mental and physical problems. Because sexual desire became unnatural and debilitating when it was irresistible or overpowering, the reformers recommended moderation and self-restraint as the cure for all physical and mental afflictions.

The health reformers urged males to control their sexual activities through a rigid system of prohibitions. They constantly referred to the human body as a balanced constitution subject to inviolable physiological laws. Among the lower animals, all behavior was determined by instinctual processes. But man had the power to violate his natural physiological laws because commercialization and urbanism had created effete and unhealthy habits. Underlying romantic health reform was a desire to discover or erect absolutes that were beyond human volition. Because they believed that artificial and overstimulating food, which was associated with the new urban environment, irritated the digestive system and hence the genitals, they advocated a strict regimen of diet and personal health to remove people from too great a dependence on their unhealthy surroundings. Sound personal hygiene, a moderate amount of unstimulating food, and chaste behavior would keep the fragile body from becoming overirritated and subject to debility. Masturbation, sexual excesses, or overstimulating food destroyed manhood:

> The man lays down his nobleness, dignity, honor and manhood and is no longer bold, resolute, determined, aspiring, dignified, but becomes deprecated, irresolute, undetermined, tamed . . . disheartened, uncertain in his plans . . . a drone to himself and society.⁶⁰

The purity advocates' belief system, which centered around bodily controls, purity regulations, and a hierarchical order within the human body, was not unique to Victorian America. Both primitive and advanced societies have evolved similar beliefs because symbolic behavior works through the human body. Natural symbols always have been derived from bodily structure, from the blood, and from bodily excretions and exhalations. These symbolic systems express social changes and cultural tensions. Society constrains the way the physical body is perceived and the physical experience of the body, which always is modified by social categories, sustains a particular view of the world. Societies which develop strong physiological ideologies share a deep concern for social control and a fear of familial and institutional disintegration. Their regulations fuse the moral and the physical because there is an emotional and symbolic logic that connects an individual's perception of his relation to society, to his family, and to his body. Thus all symbols are, in a sense, both sensory and sociological. The physical body serves both as a microcosm and counterpoint to the social structure and to social arrangements.

If the body serves as a symbol for society, then a desire to control bodily functions rigidly indicates a determination to protect specific groups or institutions within the society. If the body is supposedly threatened by uncontrollable forces, then the society is visualized simultaneously as beyond control. The body symbolizes the struggle between order and disorder in all societies.[61]

For the health reformers, urban male youths represented the struggle between order and formlessness. They devoted little attention to female sexual excesses or the problems of young females in the cities even though young women were less valuable on farms than men and hence were more likely to leave agricultural communities at earlier ages. Significantly, usually the female reformers examined women's sexuality. The male purity reformers chose the rootless urban male youth as the symbol for disorder because he was a newly emerging figure in the commercial world of antebellum America. The sexual and social temptations that endangered his body threatened the order and structure of society.

> It is not, then, a matter of course . . . [that] young concupiscence should kindle into a passion of despotic power, and compel the unwary youth, either to break through the restraints of civil and moral law, to find indulgence in illicit commerce—or more clandestinely to yield to the more degrading and destructive vice of self-pollution?
>
> To what avail, then, are moral laws, and civil legislation . . . in the cause of chastity—while all the elements combine to give invincible efficiency to the work of ruin?[62]

But not all male youths were dangers to the American social order. Rural sons who worked on the family farm or who were apprenticed in traditional trades posed no threat to the home or community. Only males who lived outside the more traditional patriarchal structure were perceived as marginal figures. Their reckless autonomy and precocious maturity frightened the reformers because they appeared beyond the bounds of organized society. Woodward, for example, believed that "students, merchants, clerks, printers and shoemakers" were more likely to masturbate than "young men who labor at agricultural employments."[63] Urban life enticed and corrupted young men; the cities offered an alternative ethos to the natural economic and moral economy of the countryside.

Although these reformers idealized an arcadian America that was vanishing, they were not reactionary. The purity advocates did not advise young men to abandon commercial occupations in the cities and return to the villages. Because they were cautiously optimistic about the future, the purity reformers accepted the inevitability of cities and instead tried to modify individual behavior within an urban context. Since city life threatened the integrity and proper functioning of the body, the re- formers wanted urbanites to internalize their environment by using the animal senses to protect the vital organic system, which alone insured life. Paradoxically, the purity advocates condemned the decline of a social and communal spirit while they jettisoned any institutional structures that might restore order and morality. They were both the quintessential critics and creatures of their time.

The metaphors and symbols of the reformers expressed eternal fears of Oedipal conflict and the potentially destructive power of sexuality. But they also provided an ideal sexual and moral regimen for the newly urbanized Northeastern middle class, some of whom listened to their lectures, read their books, and participated in health-reform organiza- tions. The purity advocates' belief in a closed energy system and their insistence that work and energy be directed toward socially acceptable goals helped industrialize and bureaucratize a once agricultural people. The purity reformers stressed the values of deferred gratification, hard work, sobriety, seriousness, individualism, and good health. In the pre- carious world of antebellum urban America, these habits were valuable attributes, for too early a marriage, too many children, or too dissipated a life could mean financial and social ruin. Health reform promoted social and personal order and provided Americans with satisfying goals stress- ing a continuity with the past.

During the beginning of the modernization process in America, there was individual disorientation and cultural breakdown, but sexual at- titudes and behavior became more restrictive as premarital pregnancy and illegitimacy rates drastically declined and deferred sexual gratification became normative among the "respectable" classes. Rapid change helped destroy the status and power of the rural patriarchal family and loosened generational ties as America became more commercial and urban. These disconcerting transformations led to a fear of disorder which was sym- bolized by the plight of male youths in the city. This fear engendered a more prudent sexuality because chaste behavior was perceived as an anti- dote to a new and frightening environment.

The sexual attitudes of the purity reformers were not just a nineteenth- century expression of a perennial condemnation of sexual excesses which substituted physiological arguments for Enlightenment philosophy and biblical threats. Their criticisms and a complimentary decline in pre-marital sexual activity signified major change in sexual ethics. They articulated a growing belief that most sexual activities were antisocial and debilitating expressions. Except for reproductive purposes, sex was a depraved drive that emanated from the breakdown of the countryside and the dangerous allurements of urban life.

The purity reformers helped redefine the American male. They rejected previous evaluations of sexuality and role models and, instead, reduced males to the functioning of their genitals. Some historians already have claimed that nineteenth-century physicians perceived women as the products and prisoners of their reproductive systems. Doctors, who derived support from traditional male attitudes, tried to deny women autonomy by arguing that a woman's uterus and ovaries controlled her body and behavior from puberty through menopause. The uterus, many males assumed, was connected to the central nervous system; shocks to it might alter the reproductive cycle while changes in this cycle shaped emotional states. Women were the creatures of their internal organs, of forces beyond their control.

The image of women drawn by respectable medical opinion was remarkably consistent with traditional female social roles. The instincts connected with ovulation made them by nature gentle, affectionate, and nurturant. Weaker in body and confined by menstruation and pregnancy, they were both physically and economically dependent upon stronger, more forceful males. Some physicians were handicapped by an acquired hostility toward women that was reflected in their brutal therapies.[64]

But if male physicians defined women as sexual objects, health reformers and the orthodox medical profession also considered males as extensions and victims of their reproductive organs. Too much sexual excitement, purity reformers and physicians agreed, upset the delicate equilibrium of the body. Because they believed that the body was a closed energy system, physicians blamed many male ailments on overactive genital stimulation. While doctors debated the health of women, they also pondered male medical issues such as seminal loss, masturbation, frequency of intercourse, venereal disease, and the proper age for fatherhood. Although they treated their male patients with punitive surgery, painful medicines, and dehumanizing therapies, most physicians thought that sexual moderation and a moral, industrious life would cure most male and female diseases. Self-denial eliminated sex-related disorders as well as the susceptibility to other diseases.[65] Paradoxically, while orthodox physicians condemned the romantics for their unscientific beliefs, both groups had strikingly similar medical goals. Purity reformers and nineteenth-century doctors reinforced each other's doctrines and helped popularize the belief that many American problems had sexual causes and cures.

They helped created a pollution and taboo system by affirming the relationship between continence, health, and social order. Although their medical theories are considered inaccurate today, their diagnosis and therapeutics had an emotional and symbolic truth which helped guide Americans through an unstable and unsettling era. The purity reformers' theories demonstrate, as Michel Foucault has enigmatically argued, that sex is not an autonomous force.[66] It is an intellectual construction which reduces the body and its often chaotic sensations to a meaningful system. Graham and his followers delineated sexual activity as problematic and unhealthy, and thus with physicians they helped establish the basic propositions of Victorian sexual ethics.

NOTES

1. Ralph Waldo Emerson, *The Complete Works of Ralph Waldo Emerson*, ed. Edward Waldo Emerson, 10 vols. (Boston and New York: Houghton Mifflin Co., 1904), 1:109; 10:326, 329.

2. Sylvester Graham, *A Lecture to Young Men* (Providence, R.I.: Weeden and Cory, 1834), p. iv.

3. Ibid., p. iii.

4. John S. Haller and Robin Haller, *The Physician and Sexuality in Victorian America* (Urbana, Ill.: University of Illinois Press, 1974), pp. 92–96; Otho T. Beall, Jr., "Aristotle's Master Piece in America: A Landmark in the Folklore of Medicine," *William and Mary Quarterly* 20 (1963):207–22; Edmund S. Morgan, "The Puritans and Sex," *New England Quarterly* 15 (1942):591–607; Vern Bullough, "An Early American Sex Manual, Or, Aristotle Who?" *Early American Literature* 8 (1973):236–46.

5. René Spitz, "Authority and Masturbation: Some Remarks on a Bibliographical Investigation," *Psychoanalytic Quarterly* 21 (1952):490–527; E. H. Hare, "Masturbatory Insanity: The History of an Idea," *Journal of Mental Science* 108 (1962):1–21; Robert H. MacDonald, "The Frightful Consequences of Onanism: Notes on the History of a Delusion," *Journal of the History of Ideas* 28 (1967):423–31.

6. Hare, "Masturbatory Insanity," p. 19; MacDonald, "Frightful Consequences," pp. 423–25. Onan's sin was not masturbation, but his refusal to marry his brother's widow, which was required by Levirate law. By the nineteenth century, most American writers believed Onan's act was *coitus interruptus* rather than masturbation. See Genesis 38:8–10.

7. Samuel Tissot, *Onanism: Or, a Treatise Upon the Disorders Produced by Masturbation; or, the Dangerous Effects of Secret and Excessive Venery* (London: D. Bell, R. Gray, and W. Thompson, 1871), pp. 51, 8.

8. *Ohio Medical and Surgical Journal* 8 (1855):174–75.

9. Spitz, "Authority and Masturbation," pp. 490–94.

10. MacDonald, "Frightful Consequences," pp. 430–31.

11. Alex Comfort, *The Anxiety Makers* (London: Nelson, 1967), pp. 69–113; Thomas Szasz, *The Manufacture of Madness* (New York: Harper and Row, 1970), pp. 180–260.

12. Hare, "Masturbatory Insanity," pp. 1–21. Arthus Gilbert supports Hare's argument and has argued that status anomaly—the gap between prestige and skill level—encouraged physicians to explain masturbation and other diseases in terms of the moral failings of their patients. See Gilbert, "Doctor, Patient, and Onanist Diseases in the Nineteenth Century," *Journal of the History of Medicine and Allied Sciences* 30 (1975):217–34. For an excellent overview of the whole concept of masturbation, see H. Tristam Engelhardt, Jr., "The Disease of Masturbation: Values and the Concept of Disease," *Bulletin of the History of Medicine* 48 (1974):234–48.

13. There have been few studies about the prevalence of male masturbation. Jean-Louis Flandrin has argued that early modern French youths used masturbation and homerotic sexual contacts to satisfy sexual urges before marriage. Recently, Edward Shorter has suggested that until the late eighteenth century masturbation was not practiced widely in Europe. He believed that it first became common among urbanites, the middle classes, and secondary-school youths, and was connected with a premarital sexual revolution. See Jean-Louis Flandrin, "Mariage tardif et vie sexuelle: discussions et hypothèses de recherche," *Annales, E.S.C.* 27 (1972):1351–78; Edward Shorter, *The Making of the Modern Family* (New York: Basic Books, 1975), pp. 98–102.

14. Robert P. Neuman, "Masturbation, Madness, and the Modern Concepts of Childhood and Adolescence," *Journal of Social History* 8 (1975):1–27; John R. Gillis, *Youth and History: Tradition and Change in European Age Relations, 1770–Present* (New York: Academic Press, 1974), pp. 95–132; Sterling Fishman, "Suicide, Sex, and the Discovery of the German Adolescent," *History of Education Quarterly* 10 (1970):170–88. For dissenting view of European adolescence dating the concept to an earlier period, see Natalie Zemon Davis, "The Reasons for Misrule: Youth Groups and Charivaris in Sixteenth-Century France," *Past and Present* 50 (1971):41–75; Steven R. Smith, "The London Apprentices as Seventeenth-Century Adolescents," *Past and Present* 61 (1973):149–61; "Religion and Conceptions of Youth in Seventeenth-Century England," *History of Childhood Quarterly* 2 (1975):493–516.

15. Kenneth Keniston, "Social Change and Youth in America," *Daedalus* 91 (1962):145–71; John Demos and Virginia Demos, "Adolescence in Historical Perspective," *Journal of Marriage and the Family* 31 (1969):632–38; Joseph F. Kett, "Adolescence and Youth in Nineteenth-Century America," *Journal of Interdisciplinary History* 2 (1971):283–98; *Rites of Passage: Adolescence in America, 1790 to the Present* (New York: Basic Books, 1977), pp. 11–108. For dissenting views dating concepts of childhood and adolescence back to the colonial period, see Ross W. Beales, Jr., "In Search of the Historical Child: Miniature Adulthood and Youth in Colonial New England," *American Quarterly* 27 (1975):379–98; N. Ray Hiner, "Adolescence in Eighteenth-Century America," *History of Childhood Quarterly* 3 (1975):253–80; Peter G. Slater, *Children in the New England Mind* (Hamden, Conn.: Archon Books, 1977).

16. W. S. Rossiter, *A Century of Population Growth: From the First Census of the United States to the Twelfth, 1790–1900* (Washington, D.C.: Government Printing Office, 1909), p. 94; U.S. Bureau of the Census, *Historical Statistics of the United States: Colonial Times to 1957* (Washington, D.C.: Government Printing Office, 1960), p. 10.

17. Rossiter, *Century of Population*, pp. 98, 103–5; U.S. Bureau of the Census, *Historical Statistics*, p. 11; J. Potter, "The Growth of Population in America, 1700–1860," in *Population in History: Essays in Historical Demography*, ed. D. V. Glass and D. E. C. Eversley (London: Arnold, 1965), p. 670.

18. Warren S. Thompson and P. F. Whelpton, *Population Trends in the United States* (New York and London: McGraw-Hill Book Company, 1933), pp. 128–38.

19. Philip Greven, Jr., *Four Generations: Population, Land and Family in Colonial*

Andover, Massachusetts (Ithaca, N.Y.: Cornell University Press, 1970), pp. 261–89; "Historical Demography and Colonial America," *William and Mary Quarterly* 24 (1967):438–54; Richard L. Bushman, *From Puritan to Yankee: Character and Social Order in Connecticut, 1680–1765* (Cambridge, Mass.: Harvard University Press, 1967), pp. 3–40; James Henretta, *The Evolution of American Society, 1700–1815: An Interdisciplinary Analysis* (Lexington, Mass.: D. C. Heath, 1973), pp. 5–39; Michael Zuckerman, *Peaceable Kingdoms: New England Towns in the Eighteenth Century* (New York: Alfred A. Knopf, 1970).

20. Jackson Turner Main, *The Social Structure of Revolutionary America* (Princeton, N.J.: Princeton University Press, 1965), pp. 164–96, 270–87; Allan Kulikoff, "The Progress of Inequality in Revolutionary Boston," *William and Mary Quarterly* 28 (1971):375–412; James Henretta, "Economic Development and Social Structure in Colonial Boston," *William and Mary Quarterly* 22 (1965):79–82; James T. Lemon and Gary B. Nash, "The Distribution of Wealth in Eighteenth Century America: A Century of Changes in Chester County, Pennsylvania, 1693–1802," *Journal of Social History* 2 (1968):1–24; Kenneth A. Lockridge, "Social Change and the Meaning of the American Revolution," *Journal of Social History* 6 (1973):403–39; John K. Alexander, "Poverty, Fear and Continuity: An Analysis of the Poor in Late Eighteenth-Century Philadelphia," in *The People of Philadelphia: A History of Ethnic Groups and Lower-Class Life, 1790–1940*, ed. Allen F. Davis and Mark H. Haller (Philadelphia: Temple University Press, 1973), pp. 13–36; Gloria L. Main, "Inequality in Early America: The Evidence from Probate Records of Massachusetts and Maryland," *Journal of Interdisciplinary History* 7 (1977):559–82.

21. Rossiter, *Century of Population*, p. 15; U.S. Bureau of the Census, *Historical Statistics*, p. 14; Sam Bass Warner, Jr., *The Urban Wilderness: A History of the American City* (New York: Harper and Row, 1972), p. 70.

22. Henry James, *Partial Portraits* (London: Macmillan & Co., 1911), p. 7.

23. Ralph Waldo Emerson, *Collected Works of Ralph Waldo Emerson*, ed. Robert E. Spiller and Alfred R. Ferguson, 3 vols. (Cambridge, Mass.: Harvard University Press, 1971), 1:228.

24. Edward Pessen, "The Egalitarian Myth and the American Social Reality: Wealth, Mobility, and Equality in the 'Era of the Common Man,'" *American Historical Review* 79 (1971):989–1034; *Riches, Class and Power Before the Civil War* (Lexington, Mass.: D. C. Heath, 1973); Lee Soltow, "Economic Inequality in the United States in the Period from 1790 to 1860," *Journal of Economic History* 31 (1971):822–39; Stuart Mack Blumin, "Mobility and Change in Ante-Bellum Philadelphia," in *Nineteenth-Century Cities: Essays in the New Urban History*, ed. Stephen Thernstrom and Richard Sennett (New Haven, Conn.: Yale University Press, 1969), pp. 165–208; Stephen Thernstrom and Peter R. Knights, "Men in Motion: Some Data and Speculations about Urban Population Mobility in Nineteenth-Century America," *Journal of Interdisciplinary History* 1 (1970):7–36; Robert E. Gallman, "Trends in the Size Distribution of Wealth in the Nineteenth Century," in *Six Papers on the Size Distribution of Wealth and Income*, ed. Lee Soltow (New York: Columbia University Press, 1969), pp. 1–25; Peter R. Knights, *The Plain People of Boston, 1830–1860: A Study of City Growth* (New York: Oxford University Press, 1971), pp. 19–32, 48–118; George Blackburn and Sherman L. Richards, Jr., "A Demographic History of the West: Mainstee County, Michigan, 1860," *Journal of American History* 57 (1970):613–18; Gavin Wright, "'Economic Democracy' and the Concentration of Agricultural Wealth in the Cotton South, 1850–1860," *Agricultural History* 44 (1970):63–94; Randolph B. Campbell and Richard G. Lowe, *Wealth and Power in Antebellum Texas* (College Station, Tex.: Texas A & M Press, 1977); Robert Doherty, *Society and Power: Five New England Towns, 1800–1860* (Amherst, Mass.: University of Massachusetts Press, 1977).

25. 1852 quotation of Daniel Lord in Laurence L. Doggett, *Life of Robert McBurney* (Cleveland: F. M. Barton, 1902), p. 28.

26. Samuel B. Woodward, *Hints for the Young in Relation to the Health of Body and Mind* (Boston: Light, 1856), p. 12.

27. For perceptive studies of the respectable sexual ideology, see Peter Cominos, "Late Victorian Sex Respectability and the Social System," *International Review of Social History* 8 (1963):18–48, 216–50; Ben Barker-Benfield, "The Spermatic Economy: A Nineteenth-Century View of Sexuality," *Feminist Studies* 1 (1972):45–74; Stephen Kern, "Explosive Intimacy: Psychodynamics of the Victorian Family," *History of Childhood Quarterly* 1 (1974):353–66.

28. Graham, *Lecture*, p. 7.

29. Ibid., p. 20.

30. Orson S. Fowler, *Amativeness: or Evils and Remedies of Excessive and Perverted Sexuality* (New York: Fowler and Wells, 1846), pp. 43, 48; William A. Alcott, *The Young Man's Guide* (Boston: Lilly, Wait, Colman, & Holden, 1833), pp. 325–26; George R. Calhoun, *Report of the Consulting Surgeon, on Spermatorrhoea, or Seminal Weakness* (Philadelphia: Howard Association, 1859).

31. *Boston Medical and Surgical Journal* 12 (1835):109.

32. John Ellis, *Marriage and Its Violations, Licentiousness and Vice* (New York: John Ellis, 1860), p. 21.

33. Elizabeth O. G. Willard, *Sexology as the Philosophy of Life* (Chicago: J. R. Walsh, 1867), p. 307.

34. Fowler, *Amativeness*, p. 48.

35. John B. Newman, *Philosophy of Generation; its Abuses, with their Causes, Prevention and Cure* (New York: n.p., 1853), p. 56.

36. Graham, *Lecture*, pp. 33–37.

37. Ibid., p. 43.

38. Lorenzo N. Fowler, *The Principles of Phrenology and Physiology Applied to Man's Social Relations; together with an Analysis of the Domestic Feelings* (New York: Fowler and Wells, 1842), p. 18.

39. Graham, *Lecture*, p. 43.

40. Tissot, *Onanism*, p. iv.

41. Hermann Rohleder, *Die Masturbation: Eine Monographie für Aerzte und Pädagogen* (Berlin: Kornfeld, 1899), pp. 54, 260.

42. Graham, *Lecture*, pp. 41–42.

43. Ibid., pp. 45–47.

44. Ibid., p. 58.

45. Ibid., p. 62.

46. William A. Alcott, *The Physiology of Marriage* (Boston: Dinsmoor and Co., 1866), p. 78.

47. Russell T. Trall, *Home-Treatment for Sexual Abuses. A Practical Treatise* (New York: Fowler and Wells, 1853), p. xvi; Woodward, *Hints for the Young*, p. 7; Neuman, *Philosophy of Generation*, pp. 44, 57.

48. Charles Knowlton, *Fruits of Philosophy, An Essay on the Population Question, 1842* (London: Freethought Publishing Co., 1877), pp. 55–56.

49. C. Bigelow, *Sexual Pathology; A Practical and Popular Review of the Principal Diseases of the Reproductive Organs* (Chicago: Ottaway and Colbert, 1875), p. 50; W. S. Chipley, *A Warning to Fathers, Teachers and Young Men, in Relation to a Frightful Cause of Insanity and Other Series Disorders of Youth* (Cincinnati: n.p., 1866), p. 117; *Boston Medical and Sugrical Journal* 18 (1838):124–26, 30 (1844):228; State Lunatic Hospital at

Worcester, *Annual Report of the Trustees,* 5th (Boston: n.p., 1837), pp. 45–46; *Annual Report of the Trustees,* 9th (Boston: n.p., 1841), p. 50.

50. David J. Rothman, *The Discovery of the Asylum: Social Order and Disorder in the New Republic* (Boston: Little, Brown & Co., 1971). Michael B. Katz, *The Irony of Early School Reform: Educational Innovation in Mid-Nineteenth Century Massachusetts* (Cambridge, Mass.: Harvard University Press, 1968); Allen Stanley Horlick, *Country Boys and Merchant Princes: The Social Control of Young Men in New York* (Lewisburg, Pa.: Associated University Presses, 1975).

51. Charles E. Rosenberg, "The Bitter Fruit: Heredity, Disease, and Social Thought," *Perspectives in American History* 8 (1974):189–235.

52. Alcott, *Physiology of Marriage,* pp. 61–63.

53. Ibid., pp. 140–142.

54. Orson S. Fowler, *Love and Parentage* (New York: Fowler and Wells, 1844), pp. xii, ix.

55. William A. Alcott, *The Laws of Health* (Boston: J. P. Jewett, 1857), p. 12.

56. Thomas L. Nichols, *Esoteric Anthropology* (New York: Thomas L. Nichols, 1853), p. 150.

57. Fowler, *Principles of Phrenology,* p. 89.

58. Conway Zirkle, "The Early History of the Inheritance of Acquired Characters and Pangenesis," *Transactions of the American Philosophical Society* 35 (1946):141–46; Elizabeth Gasking, *Investigations into Generation, 1651–1828* (Baltimore: Johns Hopkins University Press, 1966).

59. Graham, *Lecture,* p. 32.

60. Fowler, *Amativeness,* pp. 28–29.

61. Mary Douglas, *Natural Symbols; Explorations in Cosmology* (London: Barrie and Jenkins, 1973), pp. vii–18, 156–68; *Purity and Danger: An Analysis of Concepts of Pollution and Taboo* (New York: Basic Books, 1966), pp. 1–28, 140–79; Victor Turner, *The Forest of Symbols* (Ithaca, N.Y.: Cornell University Press, 1967), pp. 28–47. I am indebted to Caroll Smith-Rosenberg's unpublished paper, "Sex as Symbol in Victorian Purity: An Ethnohistorical Analysis of Jacksonian America," for these references and for her provocative analysis of the male-purity reformers. A modified version of this paper has been published in *Turning Points: Historical and Sociological Essays on the Family,* ed. John Demos and Sarane Spence Boocock (Chicago: University of Chicago Press, 1978), pp. 212–47.

62. Graham, *Lecture,* pp. 27–28.

63. Woodward, *Hints for the Young,* p. 63.

64. Regina Morantz, "The Lady and Her Physician," in *Clio's Conciousness Raised: New Perspectives on the History of Women,* ed. Mary Hartman and Lois W. Banner (New York: Harper and Row, 1974), pp. 38–53; Anne D. Wood, "The Fashionable Diseases: Women's Complaints and Their Treatment in Nineteenth-Century America," *Journal of Interdisciplinary History* 4 (1973):25–52; Carroll Smith Rosenberg and Charles E. Rosenberg, "The Female Animal: Medical and Biological Views of Woman and Her Role in Nineteenth-Century America," *Journal of American History* 60 (1973):332–56.

65. Haller and Haller, *Physician and Sexuality,* pp. 89–139, 189–270; Gail Pat Parson, "Equal Treatment for All: American Medical Remedies for Male Sexual Problems, 1850–1900," *Journal of the History of Medicine and Allied Sciences* 32 (1977):55–71.

66. Michel Foucault, *The History of Sexuality,* vol. I: *An Introduction,* trans. Robert Hurley (New York: Random House, 1978).

5

The Vegetarian Persuasion

Graham's lectures on cholera and masturbation had emphasized the crucial role of sexuality as the key to survival in a dangerous and hostile environment. After 1834, however, he stopped lecturing about sexuality because it became controversial and divisive; instead, Graham began promoting sound nutrition and personal hygiene. Although he shifted his emphasis, the principles of vitalism still dominated his ideology. Throughout his reformist career, Graham had dismissed the possibility that traditional sources of authority such as civil law, government, the Bible, churches, and the family could mediate effectively between the individual and the environment. For example, he had argued in 1829 that "civil legislation may exhaust itself adding statute after statute,"[1] but no government could control human behavior. He repeated this analysis in his New York City cholera epidemic lectures and in his study of masturbation. In common with other romantic reformers and perfectionists, Graham discounted institutional controls and, instead, believed that the only legitimate and effective order resided within the individual.

In his *Lectures on the Science of Human Life* (1839), Graham examined a danger that was as pervasive as sexual desire, the sensation of hunger. Although hunger was necessary for self-preservation just as sexuality was necessary for the preservation of the species, both impulses were internal irritations which could harm the body. Normal sexual desire was possible only when it reflected the "natural excitements of the organs themselves rather than the unnatural needs of habit or artificial irritation."[2] Similarly, hunger was a "true, instinctive indication of the alimentary wants of the system" only when the stomach was in a "perfectly normal, healthy and undepraved state."[3] Graham warned that this "morbid appetite is always the more despotic and imperious in proportion as it is removed from the original integrity of the function."[4] The rules and priorities he established to control hunger closely resembled his ascetic strictures regarding sexuality.

100

EVERY INDIVIDUAL SHOULD, AS A GENERAL RULE, RE-
STRAIN HIMSELF TO THE SMALLEST QUANTITY, WHICH
HE FINDS FROM CAREFUL INVESTIGATION AND EN-
LIGHTENED EXPERIENCE AND OBSERVATION, WILL
FULLY MEET THE ALIMENTARY WANTS OF THE VITAL
ECONOMY OF HIS SYSTEM—KNOWING THAT WHAT-
SOEVER IS MORE THAN THIS IS EVIL.[5]

Graham's massive study of nutrition and health helped establish a
physiological defense of vegetarianism[6] that became an influential aspect
of the health-reform movement. The purity advocates used vitalistic principles to prove that a vegetarian diet was healthier and more gentle than
one based on meat. They also believed that dietary reform would lead to
the social and moral elevation of the nation. Like their writings on sexuality, the vegetarian studies of the health reformers were strident, didactic,
and obsessively concerned with the regulation and rationalization of nutrition. Although they based many of their dietary principles on religion
and morality, the purity advocates claimed their conclusions were
founded on scientific evidence, argued that the craving for meat, like the
craving for sex, was a depraved habit, and tried to show that a diet based
primarily on meat caused overstimulation and debilitation. While their
extreme suggestions were not heeded, they did encourage Americans to
modify their food habits in ways that are considered quite healthy today.

The health reformers' physiological vegetarianism was an integral part
of their program and it served the same functions as their anti-
masturbation tracts. They associated an unhealthy diet with the breakdown of the rural community and the rise of a disorderly commercial and
urban existence. Proper vegetarianism was the romantic reformers' answer to the problem of sexual excesses and a dependence on unhealthy
surroundings. "A Vegetable Diet," Alcott argued, "lies at the basis of all
Reform, whether Civil, Social, Moral, or Religious."[7] Ideally, physiological vegetarianism was supposed naturally to modify destructive sexual
urges by depriving the body of overstimulating foods and also help counteract a dangerous new environment. Paradoxically though, the purity
advocates accomplished the opposite goal; they helped modernize Americans by developing traits which acclimated them to the new commercial
order. Preaching dietary moderation and sexual self-control, the health
reformers helped provide men and women with a coherent mode of
adjustment in an uncertain urban setting.

When Graham developed his dietary principles in the early 1830s, he
became the second public advocate of vegetarianism in America. The first
was William Metcalfe, a Manchester, England, clergyman and

homeopath, who defended vegetarianism for moral and religious reasons. In 1817, he and his followers established the Bible Christian Church in Philadelphia, where Metcalfe created the first American vegetarian society, edited its magazine, and publicized the benefits of asparagus seed as a coffee substitute. Graham might have met Metcalfe or discussed his doctrines when he worked in Philadelphia, but Graham's vegetarianism did not stem from Metcalfe's biblical arguments. In fact, Alcott and Graham helped Metcalfe develop a physiological defense of vegetarianism that deemphasized the scriptural foundations for a healthy diet.[8] This was a complete departure from the classical explanations of vegetarianism.

The traditional Western belief that meat was nutritionally superior to vegetables explains why a scientific or physiological vegetarianism developed slowly in Europe and America.[9] Alcott, a vigorous defender of the new doctrines, recognized that romantic health reform represented a major ideological alteration in traditional vegetarianism. He perceptively remarked that classical vegetarianism was designed to make men "better rationals, more truly noble and godlike," while Graham intended to produce "better, or more healthy, or longer-lived *animals* [people]."[10] The health reformers' analysis of Luigi Cornaro's *Discourses on a Sober and Temperate Life* (1558) illustrates this transformation of vegetarianism into a physiological doctrine.

Cornaro was a Renaissance Venetian nobleman whose ruinous habits and dissipated court life almost killed him by the age of forty. But an improved diet restored his health and allowed him to live to the age of ninety-eight. Cornaro based his dietary rules on Galen's concept that the healthy human body mirrored the harmonious relationship of the four elements. Since immoderation created an imbalance in the body, the cure was moderation: "Whoever leads a sober and regular life, and commits no excess in diet, can suffer very little from disorders of any other kind."[11]

Although Cornaro's dietary rules were restrictive, they concerned the quantity rather than the kind of food consumed, and so his diet included veal, mutton, poultry, partridge, fish, and thrushes. Because he believed that people should eat only as much as they could digest easily, Cornaro consumed twelve ounces of solid food and fourteen ounces of wine daily. He rejected vegetarianism since meat agreed with his digestion and Cornaro believed too many vegetables would lead to immoderation.[12]

Graham completely rejected the traditional concept that meat was more nourishing than vegetables and that mere quantitative changes in diet could improve health. In his edition of Cornaro's *Discourses*, he complimented the Venetian for his moderate habits, but Graham also printed two testimonials which contradicted Cornaro's principles by stressing the importance of vegetarianism.[13] John Burdell, another health reformer who also edited the *Discourses,* apologized for some of the courtier's dietary rules and argued that many of Cornaro's ostensibly healthy foods were actually harmful.[14] Graham's preface neatly summarized the philosophy of physiological vegetarianism when he stated:

> One important fact, however, is very prominent in the matter before us, namely: those who have by any means, impaired their constitution and become diseased in body, never recover their health and live to be old by irregularity of habits and intemperance of diet;—but when such people do recover their health, and attain to old age, it is invariably, by the virtues of a temperate and correct regimen.[15]

Graham and his followers developed this philosophy by analyzing vegetarianism as a religious-moral tradition, as a body of medical-dietetic knowledge, and as a schema of classification. Physiological vegetarianism utilized a bewildering variety of arguments, but the conclusions were always the same: the craving for meat was a habit that symbolized the depravity of modern civilization which only a strict vegetarian diet could cure.

The health reformers contrasted their dietary theories to the supposedly unnatural environment of mid-nineteenth-century America. This was not an unusual tactic; throughout the period reformers criticized America by referring to other allegedly natural and moral societies or periods of history. This was the romantic version of the Puritan jeremiad, which Perry Miller and Sacvan Bercovitch closely identified with the idea of a nineteenth-century American "chosen people."[16] George Ripley, for example, a transcendentalist and Fourierist, warned that "modern society, though it creates a superfluety of wealth . . . also produces a state of unmitigated poverty and physical and moral wretchedness." Significantly, Ripley considered poor diet a leading example of how Americans substituted "for the law of Eternal Providence their own miserable contrivances and projects."[17] And John H. Griscom, an influential New York City health reformer, used similar arguments from design. If urbanites correctly used the natural resources that God had granted them, there would be no unnecessary sickness or premature death. But man, "by his own wilfullness and intermeddling, and sad to say, by his own ignorance . . . creates the poison which he presents to his own lips."[18] These standard expositions always castigated Americans for their declension from a more natural order.

The purity reformers, like other contemporary analysts, moved quickly from physiology and disease to morality. They assumed that there was an interrelationship between the human body and its physical and moral environment. Since Americans lived in an undifferentiated physiological-social universe, immoderation was often blamed for imbalances of mind and body. Any indulgent acts, whether sexual or dietary, were disruptive and depraved. The romantics created arguments from design which skillfully and selectively used traditional religious notions and modern scientific theories to demonstrate the superiority of physiological vegetarianism. The premise behind this doctrine, according to Graham, was that "MAN IS NATURALLY A FRUGIVOROUS AND GRANIVOROUS OR A FRUIT AND VEGETABLE-EATING ANIMAL."[19] The purity advocates defended this statement by constructing a history of civilization that resembled a combination of Rousseau, Emerson, and Claude Lévi-Strauss.

According to Graham, there was no inherent dichotomy between man and nature. The individual was "the soul of the world—the intellectual and moral sensorium of nature." The mountains, valleys, streams, and the ocean's foamy beach were talismanic keys which awakened the appropriate tones within the human breast. Yet the history of civilization chronicled the story of man's fall from health and longevity to a state of disease and infirmity. Although most contemporary Americans impaired their natural physiological functions, mankind was not always in this deplorable condition. Changes in food consumption explained the unfortunate decline.

Graham and his followers did not write a dialectical history of eating and cooking. For them, the history of food was one of progressive complication. The food of early man (fresh fruit, dairy products, fresh water) was unrefined and simple, but it gave strength and health. Graham used the Old Testament to prove that the ancient Hebrews were so healthy that they lived almost a thousand years![20] This was the time when food practices were in a state of balance. But the paradisal conditions of early man were destroyed by a chain reaction: satiety made men eager to try new experiences. As people gradually transcended the state of nature their artificial desires increased and became so overwhelming that societies began neglecting proper health and dietary habits to devote their attention to the arts and sciences of civic life. Graham's periodization of food history was based on predominantly moral criteria without consideration for the social structure or important political and economic events. Dietary habits dictated population growth and urban expansion, influenced economic, social, and political theory, widened the horizons of commerce, inspired wars, and helped promote religion, science, technology, and medicine. For the health reformers food was the *deus ex machina* of world history.[21]

The history of diet was thus characterized by a moral antithesis between a simple, natural way of eating and the unrestrained proliferation of spurious foods. The material advances of civilization were counterbalanced by declining health, for disease and suffering increased as the human environment became more artificial. The romantics believed there was a simple and direct solution: antebellum Americans could restore their natural physiological states by adopting a natural vegetarian food diet and primitive health habits.

Graham tried to prove that physiological vegetarianism was synonymous with natural laws by using the vitalism of Bichat to make an important distinction between animal and organic life. Animal life, Bichat believed, was "susceptible of extension and perfection" while organic life was "unchangeably fixed to the limits Nature has assigned it." The inventions and refinements of civilization were the products of animal life while organic life represented man's lower nature and was the center of man's primitive and uncontrolled drives. When the organic element dominated, people were passionate and impulsive; the animal element encouraged "sensation, perception, and intelligence." A harmonious man had the two elements in equilibrium.[22]

Graham appropriated Bichat's distinction between animal and organic life but he reversed the French doctor's appraisal of the two systems. Graham was not impressed by man's supposed superiority over the lower forms of animals; since they had few mental powers (animal life), they could not violate their instincts (organic life). Thus Graham admired traits shared by both man and the animal kingdom.

Using Bichat, Graham tried to prove that organic life developed earlier than animal life and could continue to survive without the aid of the animal system. The brain was not the source of nervous energy, which maintained the body's vital processes; the stomach, which supplied the body's nutritional needs, was the key to human survival: "whatever is unfriendly to the vital properties, or impairs the nervous power and muscular contractility of the stomach . . . always leads to disease of the organ itself, and tends to induce morbid irritability."[23]

Graham reduced human existence to the performance of the body's internal functions. Animal life, which was responsible for the benefits of material civilization, actually helped destroy human health. The major purpose of the five senses and the brain was to protect the organic system, which alone maintained life.

Since he believed that the stomach was the major organ of the body, hunger, which irritated the stomach, was compared to lust, which inflamed the sexual organs. In a revealing analogy, Graham claimed that hunger produced a kind of erection in the stomach:

> This condition consists in a concentration of vital energy in the
> tissues of the organ . . . the nerves of organic life receive an increase of
> vital stimulus: the vessels become somewhat more injected with blood
> . . . preparatory to the secretion of the gastric juice: the temperature of
> the stomach is slightly elevated . . . and the whole organ becomes more
> red, and has something of an excited appearance.[24]

Hunger was controlled by the amount and the kind of food consumed.
A married woman provoked less desire than a mistress, and similarly a
vegetarian diet reduced the need for meat. Graham again used a sexual
analogy when he argued that vegetarians had "nothing of that despotic,
vehement and impatient character which marks the craving desire of the
flesh eater."[25] He thus concluded that antebellum dietary habits encouraged the abuse of the organic system by irritating the stomach.

Graham illustrated his principles with the dramatic story of Casper
Hauser. He allegedly was confined in a narrow, dark dungeon from early
childhood until the age of seventeen. During his imprisonment, which
ended in 1828, he was kept in a sitting posture, wore only a shirt, and
subsisted on coarse brown bread and water. Although he lacked exercise
and light, his body had developed with a "remarkable symmetry and
beauty" and he had acute powers of sight, smell, taste, and touch which
exceeded any of his Munich contemporaries. Hauser was able to identify
colors in almost total darkness, was capable of distinguishing different
people in a crowd by their distinctive footsteps, and could smell plant
leaves at extraordinary distances.

Most importantly, Hauser's acute powers alerted him to the dangers of
civilization. According to Graham, after Hauser was discovered and released, his sensitivity to urban-based stimuli caused him discomfort because he was constantly exposed to the "artificial state of things peculiar
to civic life." All alcohol, meat, and spices disgusted him while "all
farinaceous preparations and proper fruits very readily became agreeable
to him." Naturally, Graham believed that Hauser's remarkable abilities
and tastes were the product of his diet. After he began eating meat, his
powers diminished and later disappeared. Hauser had validated the Bible
and Graham's physiological vegetarianism; urban food had destroyed the
health of mankind.[26]

Graham doted over Hauser's story to prove that it was necessary for
the animal system—the brain and senses—to respond sensitively and accurately to every hostile impulse from the environment. For example, a
person with perfectly healthy olfactory nerves automatically would develop a headache, perspiration, fever, or chills upon breathing air laden
with geraniums or roses.[27]

But some will say that such an exquisitely delicate power of smell is far from being desirable;—that they would not wish to possess such keen olfactory sensibility as to feel oppressed and pained by the rich fragrance of a garden flower. . . . [But remember that] while we have high and healthy enjoyment in the proper exercise of all our faculties and powers, we cannot make the gratification of any of our senses a source of enjoyment beyond the fulfillment of the constitutional purposes for which these senses were instituted.[28]

Thus the major purpose of man's animal system was the defense of the organic system, which alone was responsible for the proper functioning of the body. A healthy individual did not have any consciousness of his internal organs.[29] Graham defined existence in a totally internalized manner; except for a necessary sensitivity to harmful outside stimuli, a person did not have to think or emote. Traditional dietary reforms tried to place the individual in a more harmonious relationship to his environment. Graham's vegetarianism was designed to remove man from a hostile environment and promote a passivity which maintained the vital processes of the organic system. Any other activities were superfluous and unhealthy.

Graham's vitalism was not an isolated and idiosyncratic scientific system that was confined to Broussais, Bichat, and some Philadelphia physicians. The Paris school of medicine, through Graham, pervaded the entire health-reform movement. Robert M. Hartley, a patrician New York City health reformer, asked his fellow citizens, "Is so large a number of His rational offspring born with such feeble power of vitality that life necessarily becomes extinct on the threshold of existence?"[30] And Russell T. Trall, the most prominent nineteenth-century water-cure advocate, argued that stimulating foods "are in reality the evidences of the resistance which the vital powers make to the injurious or impure substance. . . . The energies of the system are roused into unnatural intensity of action to defend the vital machinery."[31] Graham and the French physicians convinced many health reformers that all stimulation and excitement were pathological conditions that contributed to debilitating diseases. A meat diet was dangerous because it excited the body "by the violence and unnatural heat of an overstimulated and precipitate circulation."[32]

In addition to biblical proofs, moral arguments, and vitalistic scientific theories, the reformers closely followed contemporary physiological research to find proof that vegetarianism was superior to a meat diet. In their desire to appear scientifically respectable, they published two types of experiments. Studies which proved the high nutritional value of vegetarianism were accepted and promoted. And research that questioned vegetarian verities was attacked and always considered invalid. Their reactions to the studies of François Magendie, Justus von Leibig, and William Beaumont were indicative of the health reformers' attempts to make science conform to their philosophical system.

Magendie, an early–nineteenth-century French scientist, performed some important experiments with food concerning the nutritional value of meat and vegetables. He was puzzled by the origins of nitrogen in animal tissues and wondered how herbivores could supply their bodies with such seemingly large amounts of nitrogen (protein). In 1816, Magendie fed dogs on nitrogen-free rations and discovered that all the animals sickened and died. He concluded that the needed nitrogen was extracted from food, although some critics pointed out that albumen and gelatin, which were high in nitrogen, also failed to sustain life.[33] Vegetarians such as Alcott and Joel Shew supported Magendie's interpretation, for it seemed to prove that the bulkiness of a vegetarian diet was nutritionally superior to meat.[34]

The purity advocates received unexpected support for this argument from the distinguished German scientist Justus von Leibig. He argued in his influential *Animal Chemistry* (1842) that the nitrogenized food of herbivorous animals was identical with the composition of blood, animal fibrine, and albumen. Needed proteins were already present in plants so that even carnivores obtained their protein from vegetable sources.[35] The physiological vegetarians were exultant because von Leibig apparently demonstrated that vegetables contained more protein than meat, which originally was formed by plant proteins.[36]

The reformers' uses of Magendie and von Leibig illustrated their willingness to seek scientific support for their vegetarianism. But the controversy over Beaumont's dramatic research indicates that vegetarianism was basically a moral and cultural position with science used at best as an ancillary support. Beaumont, the United States Army surgeon, in a famous series of experiments on Alexis St. Martin, a French Canadian trapper afflicted with a gastric fistula, concluded that vegetables required more time and effort to digest than meat.[37]

The purity advocates denied the validity of Beaumont's experiments because he argued that meat was less stimulating and less wearing on the digestive organs than vegetables. The American Physiological Society, an organization devoted to promoting Grahamism, invited St. Martin to visit Boston so further experiments could be performed.[38] When this effort failed, Graham published a lengthy review both attacking and complimenting Beaumont. On the critical side, Graham claimed that Beaumont was not a *"truly scientific physiologist"* and therefore "not qualified to make the best of his peculiar advantages."[39] Beaumont, according to

Graham, mistakenly reduced physiology to chemistry rather than analyzing it under vitalistic laws. The digestibility of food was measured not by time, but by the expenditure of vital force. Because the body was weakened more by meat than vegetables, a vegetable diet was less stimulating. Not surprisingly, Graham believed that meat eaters always felt "more stupid and dull during gastric digestion" and experienced a "much greater degree of exhaustion than vegetarians."[40] These could be the sole proper conclusions of any "profound physiologist of enlarged views and of acute powers of observation."[41] Evidently only Graham and his supporters could understand the true import of the observations on St. Martin.

But Graham was also adept at salvaging critical works and turning them into supporting arguments for physiological vegetarianism. In the same review, he claimed that Beaumont's experiments proved that fatty meats, butter and oily substances, condiments, and alcohol impaired the digestive system and injured the stomach. The distinguished United States Army surgeon also reinforced romantic conceptions of hygiene. Anger, fear, and grief disturbed the digestive process while gentle exercise and sound sleep promoted digestion and general health.[42] The controversy over the Beaumont case showed that the health reformers would always use vitalism to defend their beliefs, which meant that the conclusions were drawn before the experiments had been performed. But they grudgingly admitted that even orthodox physicians could illuminate the subject of diet in rare instances.

Graham and his followers were obviously confident that their cause would triumph, for religion, morality, and some scientific experiments appeared to support their contentions. Alcott concluded that "if man is as well off on vegetable food as without it, we have moral reasons of so much weight" to reject meat.[43] Health reformers believed that God had designed humans to be herbivorous because the ingestion of vegetables was healthier and less stimulating than meat. Because they associated physiological vegetarianism with sound personal health, the purity advocates rapidly transformed their doctrines into a form of sectarian medicine:

> Nature's Dietetic laws lay hid by night,
> Let Vegetarians be to give us light.
> Or in other words,
> Mankind in the dark ages were mostly Carnivorous,
> But now the light shines, let us all be Frugivorous.[44]

Sectarian medicine developed during the early nineteenth century as an alternative to the orthodox medical profession. Suspicion of the regular doctor because of his heroic therapy deepened in the years before the Civil War as democratic sentiment, anti-intellectualism, romantic individualism, and opposition to the pretentions and exorbitant fees of orthodox physicians increased. Many states deregulated the medical profession and adopted a laissez-faire attitude toward all healers. As Lemuel Shattuck, a pioneering Massachusetts sanitary reformer lamented, "any one, male or female, learned or ignorant, an honest man or a knave, can assume the name of physician, and 'practice' upon any one, to cure or to kill, as either may happen, without accountability. It's a free country!"[45] In this atmosphere the principal sectarian rivals to established doctors were botanical medicine, homeopathy, and patent medicines. Physiological vegetarianism absorbed many followers from the botanical and homeopathic movements because they emphasized natural cures and unstimulating foods. Although the purity advocates never established any medical schools on a large scale, their books, lectures, and water-cure establishments helped change the nineteenth-century American diet.

Active therapy was the hallmark of the orthodox medical profession. Patients were dosed, bled, blistered, and purged by physicians who believed that the best treatment produced the most rapid and desirable changes in a patient. Actual medical practice was based on two major principles. First, the pathological state of the organism could be understood exclusively by relying on external symptoms. And second, anything which produced desired changes in the pathological symptoms of the patient was useful therapy. The most vigorous therapies were purgatives, emetics, and bloodletting. The most drastic and immediate form of medicine was calomel, a cathartic made from chloride of mercury. First, purging and salivation occurred. Later the gums, tongue, and salivary glands became inflamed and painful; sometimes the teeth and jaw bones disintegrated. Although most physicians recognized calomel's drastic effects, they continued to administer it liberally. Heroic medicine became institutionalized in antebellum America, and physicians who did not conform were considered amateurs or quacks.[46] J. Marion Sims, a pioneer gynecologist, wrote that when he began practicing, "I knew nothing about medicine, but I had sense enough to see that doctors were killing their patients . . . and that it would be better to trust entirely to Nature."[47]

Many physicians and patients agreed with Sims and rebelled against heroic therapy. Perhaps the principal beneficiary of these forces was Samuel Thomson, who popularized botanical medicine in antebellum America. He believed that all diseases were caused by cold and cured by heat. Following the ancient Greeks, he argued that all animal bodies were formed of four elements—earth, fire, air, and water. An imbalance in

these elements diminished body heat and led to illness. Heat could be
restored to its natural state directly through steambaths and botanicals
such as red pepper, or indirectly through emetics, purgatives, enemas,
and sweat-producing herbs. These medicines would clear the body of all
obstructions, allow the stomach to function naturally, and restore the
natural heat balance among the four elements. Although Thomson's
therapy was rigorous and heroic, it did not include bloodletting or the use
of mineral medicines.

Thomsonian medicine became successful for four basic reasons. First,
Thomson had considerable entrepreneurial skill; aggressive agents
throughout America sold the rights to use his system. For twenty dollars
a family could buy a book of directions and the privilege of preparing and
using the botanical remedies. Purchasers in a local area belonged to
Friendly Botanic Societies and could share their experiences, but Thomson's secrets could not be revealed to nonmembers. His attempt to create
a monopoly failed, however, for Thomsonian journals, botanical colleges, and human gregariousness spread his ideas throughout America.
Second, there was nothing exotic about Thomson's approach; botanical
medicine had been practiced throughout the colonial period and was
considered beneficial. Third, Thomson's crusade against conventional
physicians struck a sympathetic chord among those who were disap-
pointed with standard heroic therapy. And last, Thomson exploited the
public's concern over exorbitant medical expenses. Botanical medicine
has the virtue of simplicity: patients could become less dependent upon
doctors by purchasing his book and curing themselves. Like Graham,
Thomson tried to lead an increasingly specialized and urban society back
to rural virtue where everyone could be his own physician.[48]

Botanical medicine was practiced by self-taught laymen in rural areas
among the poor. Homeopathy, a popular nineteenth-century medical
doctrine, was practiced by regular physicians among wealthy urbanites.
This controversial form of medicine was created by a German physician,
Samuel Hahnemann, who criticized contemporary heroic therapies and
the overuse of pharmacological products. By experimenting with cin-
chona bark on himself, he concluded that what caused illness in a healthy
person would cure the same illness in a sick person. Hahnemann also
believed that large doses disguised the true effects of any drug and so he
recommended smaller doses to reduce superfluous symptoms. Bloodletting, blisters, and large doses of drugs were condemned by Hahnemann,
and his medical regimen consisted of small, mild doses of medicine combined with fresh air, exercise, proper diet, and personal hygiene.

Homeopathy became respectable partly because it was created by a
famous physician and was practiced by highly educated and cultured

doctors. The social position of homeopathy's physicians and clientele helped make the movement successful. Conventional doctors were often bitterly hostile to homeopaths because they threatened heroic medicine's prestige and income. Heroic physicians tried to expel homeopaths from the regular medical societies, prosecuted them in the courts, and tried to separate homeopathy from regular medicine. In these desperate actions, conventional physicians were not completely successful.[49]

Perhaps the single most popular antebellum alternative to heroic therapy was patent medicine. This industry grew rapidly because of low postal rates, the growth of inexpensive newspapers, and a popular distrust of orthodox medicine. Patent-medicine producers advertised that they had no mercury or calomel in their preparations and they promised mild treatment. Although most of their medicines had no curative powers, their harmlessness and therapeutic philosophy were a welcome alternative to vigorous cures.[50]

Thomsonianism and homeopathy were expansive doctrines that could not be restrained within conventional boundaries. For many botanicals, the condemnation of unhealthy food, alcohol, tobacco, and conventional heroic medicine led to an appreciation of diet and personal hygiene. Botanical journals increasingly stressed natural foods and physiology. Alva Curtis, a leader in the botanic movement, symbolized this shifting emphasis when he converted to Grahamism. Curtis, a former teacher in a girl's school, had joined the Thomsonians in the mid-1830s when he purchased their patent to practice medicine. By 1840 he had moved his botanical college and journal to Cincinnati and adopted a new medical system, which was signified by renaming the school the Physio-Medical College.[51] In the pages of his journal Curtis defended Graham and assorted health reforms. For example, one of his local followers claimed that "twenty years have now elapsed since we openly proclaimed against the use of alcohol, tobacco, tea, coffee, etc. We have nine children . . . and I do not recollect that I ever saw one of them drink a cup of tea or coffee."[52]

The remnants of the botanical movement were held together solely by the presence of Samuel Thomson. When he died in 1843, the botanical sectarians became restive. One group of Thomsonians followed his son John while another splinter organization dubbed themselves the Independent Thomsonians. The sect disintegrated and by the Civil War the movement was extinct. Dedicated healers such as Alva Curtis gravitated toward Graham's physiology because of its nature cures and hostility toward orthodox physicians.

Homeopathy was also related closely to physiology, for many homeopaths believed in temperance, dietary reform, and personal hygiene. Orthodox physicians recognized the affinity between homeopathy and other medical reforms. For example, one hostile regular doctor complained that the homeopaths "were equally full of transcendentalism, the year before of homeopathy, the year before of animal magnetism, Grahamism, phrenology."[53] Health reformers absorbed followers from both groups and became part of a diverse public-health movement because the physiological vegetarians combined religious perfectionism, a democratic ideology, and a belief in natural foods and health cures with a stinging attack on the established medical profession. Graham was the Ivan Illich of the antebellum era[54]; he believed that conventional physicians and heroic therapies were the problem not the solution. These doctors were incapable of curing diseases because they had erroneous concepts of health. He completely rejected the conventional medical wisdom when he stated that "ALL MEDICINE AS SUCH, IS IN ITSELF AN EVIL."[55] Either an acknowledged quack or a conventional physician could overdose a diseased patient. The skilled physician, by contrast, was one

> who assists our nature to throw off disease and recover health, with the least use of medicine. . . . [He] is the best friend to our constitution and evinces the most true science and skill, and deserves our highest respect and warmest gratitude.[56]

Graham's criticism of contemporary medicine was more radical than that of the Thomsonians, homeopaths, and defenders of patent medicine. He did not want to replace heroic therapy with milder medicines; Graham wanted to eliminate the entire medical profession because they did not acknowledge his constitutional laws of nature. Graham vehemently argued that "DISEASE IS NEVER THE LEGITIMATE RESULT OF THE NORMAL OPERATION OF ANY OF OUR ORGANS."[57] Since health was defined as the correct condition and proper functioning of the human body, all irritations and excitements such as hunger or sexual desire exhausted the body, reduced its ability to resist "foreign, morbific and pestilential causes,"[58] and increased the chance of disease and death. Graham's solution to health problems was simpler than Thomson's; Grahamite diet, personal hygiene, and sexual moderation would counterbalance man's animal nature, the enervating effects of urban civilization, and restore the reign of the organic system.

Other physiological vegetarians had similar perspectives. Alcott, who studied orthodox medicine at Yale, admitted that after he was licensed it was not apparent "how well qualified I was supposed to be."[59] As he became more involved in the health-reform movement, his criticisms of regular physicians mounted. Alcott believed that orthodox medicine of-

ten failed because too many doctors relied heavily on nosology: "to name
the disease is to cure it."[60] Since the physician's primary role was to
maintain health, he suggested that practitioners negotiate an annual contract with families to provide that a nominal cost for each day's sickness
be deducted from their yearly stipend. Alcott hoped that a sound knowledge of physiology would prevent almost all diseases and make physicians unnecessary.[61] Trall also condemned orthodox physicians because
they refused to admit that drug medication was not curative and often
poisoned the patient. He always differentiated between the "drug and
hygienic systems of medication."[62] And Dr. Isaac Jennings, a good friend
of Alcott, based his rejection of drug therapy on the concept that disease
was a natural vital action aimed at removing a noxious substance.[63] Thus,
the purity advocates cleverly inverted the standard criticisms applied to
them and accused orthodox physicians of being quacks because their
concepts of medicine were erroneous and dangerous. The physiological
vegetarians concluded that their ideology represented the salvation of
mankind:

> Physiology gives us the most full and complete instruction. It points
> out, also, the relation which subsists between the various kinds of
> food, drink and medicine in common and daily use among mankind,
> and this extensive digestive appartus; and enables us to determine, in
> no measured degree, what quantity, quality, etc. of food and drink are
> best adapted to sustain health, and prolong life; and which of them . . .
> tend directly or indirectly, to produce disease.[64]

Aside from sexual excesses, the reformers believed that the dietary
concepts and habits of antebellum Americans represented the greatest
threat to contemporary health. Indeed, the two fears were related because
overstimulating food caused masturbation and frequent sexual intercourse. Irritations of the stomach abused the organic system by taxing the
body's mental and physical functions, and thus the health reformers developed a searching critique of mid–nineteenth-century American food.

Throughout the antebellum period, all foods were thought to have
much the same value; they supposedly contained one essential element
that kept the body warm and repaired the tissues. The basis of the American diet was indigenous corn that was made into bread. In New England,
cod, corn, and whole wheat were common while in the South and West,
sweet potatoes, corn, and salted pork were popular. The major fault with
both the urban and the rural diet was the lack of milk, fresh fruits, and
leafy vegetables.

Modern standards of diet, however, are not applicable to antebellum
rural Americans. Although the infant mortality rate was high, adults lived

longer than their European counterparts. Farmers benefited from a vigorous life and fresh air. Bread was made from whole meal rather than refined flour. Spruce beer, a popular drink, was an anti-scorbutic and twig chewing supplied vitamins. Since grain was plentiful, meat was abundant and was commonly found even in poor houses. The liberal use of meat was one of the chief reasons that European travelers admired the diets of Americans. Hungry laborers could buy a pound of blood pudding for three or four cents and make a meal out of it with butter crackers.

Until the 1840s, rural Americans probably had better diets than urbanites. Citydwellers suffered from the lack of fresh milk, fruits, and vegetables partly because of the difficulty in supplying perishables to urban markets. Refined-bread consumption was higher in the cities than in rural areas. Salads and fruits were considered unhealthy and were cooked rather than eaten raw. Milk often was obtained from cows fed on distillery mash, and unscrupulous dealers sometimes added chalk, plaster of Paris, and molasses to give it a more pleasing appearance. Contemporaries agreed that urbanites, who were more sedentary than their rural kinfolk, subsisted principally on refined bread, meat, and potatoes, consumed unhealthy or poisonous milk, and ate their food in too concentrated a form.[65]

Graham associated urbanism with the animal system and the Pyrrhic triumphs of a mechanical, artificial civilization. Since he believed that biblical history, morality, and scientific laws indicated that man was a natural vegetarian, Graham condemned the use of meat, potatoes, milk, and bread in their urban forms. He admitted people could subsist on a mixed diet of meat and vegetables and sometimes attain good health and longevity. But Graham distinguished between an intensive and extensive life; meat always produced more vital intensiveness than a vegetarian diet, and thus led to debility and disease. When discussing food or sex, Graham always portrayed the body as a closed energy system. Therefore any irritations to the organic system were dangerous because they overburdened the nervous system and vital organs. Moderation in diet and moderation in sex were synonymous, for they both allowed the body to function properly by minimizing contact with the outside world. Nonreproductive sex and a meat diet were perceived as irritating and unnecessary parts of the social and cultural system.

Graham used butchers to illustrate the dangers of an urban diet. Although they consumed choice cuts of meat and appeared healthy, their diseases were violent and were apt to terminate fatally. Butchers rarely lived long; their healthy and robust appearances were attributable more to their regular habits and open-air employment than to their consumption of meat. Health was deceptive: Graham believed longevity was the surest measure of a worthy diet. He recommended, in a rare burst of tolerance, that if meat was eaten, it should be consumed raw soon after it was killed![66] Those who followed Graham's advice probably became confirmed vegetarians after their gastronomic experience.

Milk was also criticized by Graham, for it symbolized the poisonous and destructive nature of urban life. He claimed that milk in urban areas "always becomes highly charged with the odor and taste of filth: and when besides all this, the cows are fed on the vile dregs of distilleries and other improper substances, their milk is anything but wholesome."[67]

Graham's charges of adulteration and poisoning were not new. Throughout Europe and America, if a product was scarce or expensive, wholesalers and retailers increased the quantity and reduced the price by putting cheap additives into the genuine produce. Perhaps the most sensational early–nineteenth-century revelations were supplied by Frederick Accum. He discovered that London pickles owed their appetizing green color to copper, that the rainbow hues of candy were produced by poisonous copper and lead salts, that most commercial bread was laced with alum, and that the orange rind of Gloucester cheese often acquired its color from red lead. Enraged manufacturers forced the German chemist to flee England.[68] Other health reformers supported Graham's and Accum's charges. John Mullaby believed that unhealthy milk was often responsible for rotted teeth and a high infant mortality rate in urban areas.[69] And Augustus K. Gardner, a prominent purity advocate, agreed that "cows not in a natural condition . . . could not give milk of a natural character."[70] In the case of milk, Graham recommended that it be procured from healthy grazing cows raised in open fields who were fed hay during the winter and housed in clean, well-ventilated stables. But Graham did not believe that changes in the quality of milk alone would improve urban health. His solution to the problems of urban diet was bread, which had changed dramatically during his lifetime.

During the antebellum period, flour was transformed by advances in mechanization; this process completely altered the structure and content of bread. In the colonial period, most people baked bread in their fireplaces. Before baking, the flour was aged for a few months, lost its natural creamy color, and became pure white. The bread was baked thoroughly, was neither soft nor spongy, and the tough crust formed a natural protection against spoilage and dehydration.

By the 1830s, the production and consistency of bread began to change. Most urbanites did not have ovens. Since fireplace fuel was more expensive than purchasing bread, increasing numbers of citydwellers became consumers rather than producers of bread, which was being created mechanically. This process had been developed by Oliver Evans on the banks of the Red Clay creek near Philadelphia. By the 1790s, he had mechanized the craft of the miller by utilizing a continuous-line production from the unloading of grain to the processing of flour. Antebellum bakers copied Evans's mechanical techniques.

The mechanization of the milling process produced an artificial product. The oleaginous germ that made the flour somewhat greasy, and which contained the most nutritional elements, was excluded. Traditional milling techniques crushed the grain very finely and were responsible for the loss of more than 60 percent of the pure flour. This process also destroyed the aleuron cells under the pericarp which contained a very high percentage of protein, minerals, niacin, and other B_{12} vitamins. Thin-crusted bread, made of finely milled flour, was produced because it baked more quickly than the traditional kinds of bread. Characteristics that were once considered admirable became defects, such as toughness, thickness, and cracks. Antebellum bakery-produced bread was becoming soft, almost crustless, and aesthetically pleasing rather than nutritional. Interest centered around the production of finer and whiter flour.[71]

Graham wanted to restore urban man's contact with organic life through nutritional bread and personal hygiene. He did not know precisely what vital elements were contained in the germ or the husk of the grain, but Graham recognized an important principle: food should not be robbed of its nutritional values in the course of preparation. For this reason he attacked the growing urban practice of buying bakery bread. Since superfine flour, harmful additives, and mechanical baking techniques had destroyed its nutritional quality, Graham gave detailed directions on the selection, preservation, grinding of wheat, and the fermentation of homemade bread that later bore his name. When some physicians objected that Graham's coarse wheat bread was indigestible, he angrily countered that the stomach muscles, like the arms or legs, needed exercise to remain healthy.[72]

Although Graham's "scientific" principles appear primitive today, they were quite bold and perceptive during his lifetime. Not until 1846 did Justus von Liebig describe living tissues and foods as being composed of carbohydrates, fats, and proteins. During the later part of the century, minerals and different types of proteins also were isolated. Finally, in the early twentieth century, Dutch and German biochemists identified those vitamins which are fat-soluble. By the 1920s, the general pattern of contemporary food values had been established. Considering his times, Graham's dietary pronouncements were an intelligent evaluation of the bulky and increasingly mechanized nature of antebellum urban food. The philosophy and practices of present-day health-food advocates are quite similar to physiological vegetarianism.

Graham's dietary and hygienic regimen was inexpensive, both moral and scientific, and apparently appealed to insecure urbanites and recent migrants from the countryside. His principles meshed with the popular reforms of the period and so physiological vegetarianism attracted the greatest support throughout the Northeast, where commercialism and urbanism had made the greatest inroads on a rural economy and way of life.

Individuals who were cured by the physiological regimen readily testified to its effectiveness. Their activities paralleled the steps of a repentant sinner. They felt intense personal anxiety until undergoing a conversion experience which gave them a joyous sense of freedom. For example, F. W. Bird of East Walpole, Massachusetts, suffered from insomnia and the "complete prostration" of his nervous system because he used meat, alcohol, and tobacco. After he stopped consuming those harmful products and switched to a diet centered around unsifted wheat bread, his health miraculously improved. The only suffering that Bird now felt was the "constant violation of the laws of health and happiness by others, and the consciousness of it in myself." He concluded that "if such be the nature and the fruits of the Grahamic delusion, may I be under it as long as I live!"[73] Case histories such as these indicate that sympathetic Americans believed physiology promised salvation from disease through the application of the natural laws discovered by its founder. Whether discussing sexuality or diet, the health reformers always echoed Alcott's pithy advice: "Keep cool, keep cool!"[74]

Of course, the reformers' opponents rejected this treatment, for they denied that there was any connection between diet and morality and believed that meat was much healthier than vegetables. One reviewer suggested that the vegetarians were "charlatans and dupes" who believed that the "human race is to be regenerated solely through the medium of the palate."[75] Another wag concluded that "emasculation is the first fruit of Grahamism."[76] And more serious critics wondered whether a vegetarian diet was sufficiently nutritious since it was a low-protein regimen. In practice, however, most orthodox vegetarians advocated a mixed diet of vegetables and approved the consumption of dairy products and fish; Graham and Trall even created dietetic rules for boardinghouses and water-cure establishments which permitted small amounts of meat.[77] And at the 1852 annual meeting of the American Vegetarian Society, the banquet included over thirty varieties of food which was intended to prove that a vegetarian diet would not lead to poor health or starvation.[78] Thus intelligent physiological vegetarians had balanced, healthy diets low in starches and saturated animal fats and high in unsaturated fats and vegetable proteins.

Although the strict physiological vegetarianism of the romantics was never emulated by large numbers of Americans, the health reformers did help modify nineteenth-century dietary habits. Between 1790 and 1830, Americans consumed enormous amounts of alcohol because they believed it was healthful, nutritious, stimulating, and relaxing. The preference for strong drink also might have been linked with a rising abundance of cheap whiskey due to the planting of Midwestern grain and a desire to wash down poorly cooked, greasy, salty, or rancid food. After the 1830s, alcoholic consumption rapidly declined as temperance crusaders such as the romantics persuaded many Americans to drink moderately or abstain. This movement also was aided by improved transportation, which opened new markets for surplus corn, by rising economic prosperity, which encouraged people to accumulate capital rather than spend money on liquor, and by the adoption of an industrial ethic which was antithetical to heavy drinking. The result was that per capita consumption of alcohol among Americans age fifteen and over declined from 5.8 U.S. gallons in 1790 to 1.9 in 1880.[79]

Because land was cheap and food was abundant, pork, a form of condensed corn, was the most popular American table food. From 1830 to 1839, per capita meat consumption was 178 pounds annually, the highest in American history. Average meat consumption, however, declined after the 1830s as the use of wheat, flour, fruits, and vegetables increased.[80]

Perishable-food supplies became more popular in urban areas as Americans changed their dietary habits and as railroads made fruits and vegetables more available. Until the antebellum period, most Americans believed that fruits and vegetables yielded little nutriments in proportion to the labor spent in cultivation. But as fruits and vegetables became more valued, railroads were built radiating from major cities to bring perishables greater distances. Strawberries, for example, could be purchased about one month a year in Northern city markets during the 1830s. By 1865, consumers could eat strawberries from April through June. Along with improved transportation, the invention of mechanical refrigeration and canning greatly boosted the amount of cereals, fruits, and vegetables in the average American diet.[81]

Graham and his followers first popularized the idea that Americans should eat more fruits and vegetables and less meat and white flour. According to the purity reformers, the use of heavy foods such as meat and bread made from sifted flour caused indigestion and other gastrointestinal problems which encouraged people to use condiments and alcohol as digestive aids. Graham wanted food made simpler, plainer, and more natural, and so he and his supporters tried to convince Americans to use mild dishes and fewer courses in their meals. Graham's espousal of roughage and whole grains as a source of bulk gradually was recognized and accepted. Most Americans probably rejected the more extreme doctrines of physiological vegetarianism, but Graham and his followers were the first and most important group in mid–nineteenth-century America to advocate sound eating habits.

Graham's physiological vegetarianism mirrored the romantic and perfectionist spirit in antebellum America. The health reformers' criticisms of contemporary urban life were part of a growing hostility toward cities. During the eighteenth century, the American city had not become too large or so unattractive as to stir people into passionate ideological arguments about the virtues and vices of urbanism. But during the antebellum period, commerce, industry, massive migration, chaotic expansion, and a visible and growing lower class marked the city with the scars that offended antebellum thinkers. For the transcendentalists and writers such as Herman Melville, Nathaniel Hawthorne, and Edgar Allan Poe, the city represented heartless commercialism, poverty, pollution, crime, the decline of morality, and personal defeat. Since they perceived America as an agrarian Eden that was losing its innocence through urbanization and its attendant evils, they were deeply offended by the city's effects on the human spirit.[82] Graham's criticisms were novel, but they were part of an increasing distaste for urban life.

Ralph Waldo Emerson, for example, based his theory of knowledge partly on a dichotomy between urban and rural life. Understanding was empirical and analytical, while Reason was man's creative power and the key to the universe. The Understanding was an urban faculty and Reason belonged to the countryside:

> The city delights the understanding. It is made up of finites; short, sharp, mathematical lines, all calcuable. It is full of varieties, of successions, of contrivances. The country on the contrary offers an unbroken horizon, the monotony of an endless road, of vast uniform plains, of distant mountains, the melancholy of uniform infinite vegetation [;] the objects on the road are few & worthless [;] the eye is invited ever to the horizon & the clouds. It is the School of Reason.[83]

Both transcendentalism and physiology were antebellum examples of a strong sense of expectancy and millennialism which was not just confined to chiliast sects such as the Millerites, a religious sect which confidently predicted the end of the world in 1844, but characterized many reformers. This optimism had secular and religious roots. The republican ideal combined with evangelical hopes and material expansion to foster a dynamic vision of national perfection. During this period, traditional forms of social control were breaking down as rapid economic and geographical expansion modified social class, religion, and the state. Revivalism and romantic reform partly were responses to these conditions; both movements promoted the idea that divine grace or an awakened moral conscience had to replace external authority. Throughout the antebellum era, reformers such as William Lloyd Garrison, Theodore Parker, and Walt Whitman articulated a popular American belief that individuals could fulfill themselves outside of institutions. The dream of an autonomous consciousness, where the mind was the origin and judge of its own "reality," was the central doctrine of romantic reform.[84]

Graham resembled these romanticists in his career and ideology. He was a reformer who had no fixed place in the community and no institutional loyalties. He repudiated any inherited or assumed social roles; like Emerson, Graham was a former minister who had left the church to make the world his pulpit. Reformers and evangelicals looked to transcendental reason and the inner promptings of the spirit to work a moral revolution. Graham devalued reason because it was an unnecessary part of animal life and argued that the "constitutional laws of human nature," or physiology, were the surest guide to action. Graham, however, also resembled these romantic reformers because he too displaced authority from society and institutions to the individual. Ethics were reduced to hygiene. Grahamite man was a solitary figure, protected by his ability to recognize danger (sexual desire, stimulating food, an unhealthy environment) and avoid it, and was secured from within by a regimen which minimized his body's demands. The world could be confronted and bested without any external sources of strength. For Graham, essence and existence were synonymous.

The physiological vegetarianism of the reformers was not simply a nineteenth-century expression of a perennial condemnation of gluttony that substituted vegetarian arguments for a mixed diet. The ideology of the health reformers symbolized a major change in attitudes toward the human body. Graham and his followers articulated a new belief that meat-eating, like masturbation and frequent sexual intercourse, was an antisocial and debilitating expression of an unhealthy urge. The desire for food, except to satisfy hunger, was a depraved habit and an invitation to disaster. Ideally, after following Graham's strictures, a person felt neither sexual desire nor the need for stimulating food; his body was almost a self-sustaining organism whose sensitivity protected him against urban life.

Graham's insecure and problematic life was mirrored in his philosophy. He rarely discussed culture, government, friendship, voluntary organizations, or the family. Instead, he reduced the complexity of human life to the proper operation of an individual's bodily functions. Graham's strongest fear was the loss of control, of gratifying impulses without restraint. The body must be kept in check because from it emanated all the dangerous impulses, especially sexuality. To be able to survive with only the minimal amount of food or sex proved that life was possible without others. Graham's dual obsession with food and sex was complimentary; both drives represented dangers to complete self-control and independence. Graham and his followers promoted a solipsistic individualism to insulate themselves through rigid prohibitions from an environment that they perceived as hostile and undependable.

These traits, in a less extreme form, helped modernize Americans. Although the health reformers were profoundly ambivalent about mid–nineteenth-century social and cultural changes, they helped Americans adjust to their new environment. The purity advocates marched into the future with their heads turned backwards toward an idealized past where there was a sense of community and stability. While their values were nostalgic and bucolic, the behaviors they encouraged were very modern. By helping Americans transform their personalities to meet the novel demands of city life, romantic health reform became part of middle-class American culture. Graham's concepts of diet and health so permeated American society that they influenced a set of beliefs that ostensibly appeared completely opposite his doctrines of extreme moderation— Victorian free love.

NOTES

1. Sylvester Graham, *Thy Kingdom Come; A Discourse, on the Importance of Infant and Sunday Schools, delivered at the Crown St. Church, Philadelphia* (Philadelphia: W. F. Geddes, 1831), pp. 24–25.

2. Sylvester Graham, *A Lecture to Young Men* (Providence, R.I.: Weeden and Cory, 1834), p. 30.

3. Sylvester Graham, *Lectures on the Science of Human Life*, 2 vols. (Boston: Marsh, Capon, Lyon, and Webb, 1839), 2:496. After his retirement from the lecture field, Graham continued to work on this subject. His posthumous material was published in *The Philosophy of Sacred History Considered in Relation to Human Ailment and the Wines of Scripture*, ed. Henry S. Clubb (New York: Fowlers and Wells, 1855).

4. Graham, *Science of Human Life*, 2:327.

5. Ibid., 2:537 (Graham's emphasis).

6. For other studies of physiological vegetarianism, see the relevant pages in William B. Walker, "The Health Reform Movement in the United States, 1830–1870" (Ph.D. diss., Johns Hopkins University, 1955); Stephen Nissenbaum, "Careful Love: Sylvester Graham

and the Emergence of Victorian Sexual Theory in America, 1830–1840" (Ph.D. diss., University of Wisconsin, 1968); James C. Whorton, " 'Tempest in a Flesh-Pot': The Formulation of a Physiological Rationale for Vegetarianism," *Journal of the History of Medicine and Allied Sciences* 32 (1977):115–39; "Christian Physiology": William Alcott's Prescription for the Millennium," *Bulletin of the History of Medicine* 49 (1975):466–81.

7. *American Vegetarian and Health Journal* 4 (1854):74.

8. Charles W. Forward, *Fifty Years of Food Reform: A History of the Vegetarian Movement in England* (London: The Ideal Publishing Union, Ltd., 1898), pp. 13–15; Gerald Carson, *Cornflake Crusade* (New York: Holt, Rinehart and Winston, 1957), pp. 15–17; *American Vegetarian and Health Journal* 4 (1854):69–72; *Library of Health* 4 (1840):69.

9. For the history of Western vegetarianism, see Nissenbaum, "Careful Love," pp. 35–58; Frederick W. Hackwood, *Good Cheer, The Romance of Food and Feasting* (London: T. F. Unwin, 1911), pp. 324–30; Janet Barkas, *The Vegetarian Passion* (New York: Scribner, 1975), pp. 1–84, 134–42.

10. William A. Alcott, *Vegetable Diet: As Sanctioned by Medical Men, and by Experience in All Ages* (Boston: Marsh, Capon & Lyon, 1838), p. 212.

11. Luigi Cornaro, *Discourses on a Sober and Temperate Life*, ed. John Burdell (New York: Fowlers and Wells, 1842), p. 26.

12. Cornaro, *Discourses*, pp. 35, 75, 100–101; William B. Walker, "Luigi Cornaro: A Renaissance Writer on Personal Hygiene," *Bulletin of the History of Medicine* 28 (1954):525–34.

13. Lewis Cornaro, *Discourses on A Sober and Temperate Life*, ed. Sylvester Graham (New York: M. Day, 1832), pp. ix–xiv, 165–78.

14. Burdell, *Discourses*, pp. 14, 27, 33, 102, 156.

15. Graham, *Discourses*, p. xi.

16. Perry Miller, *The Life of the Mind in America: From the Revolution to the Civil War* (New York: Harcourt Brace and Jovanovich, 1965), pp. 3–95; Sacvan Bercovitch, *The American Jeremiad* (Madison, Wisc.: University of Wisconsin Press, 1978).

17. *The Harbinger* 1 (28 June 1845):33. At Ripley's Brook Farm, there was a Graham table that had an optional menu for the members of the commune.

18. John H. Griscom, *Improvements of the Public Health and the Establishment of a Sanitary Police in the City of New York* (Albany, N.Y.: Van Benthuysen, 1857), p. 3.

19. Graham, *Science of Human Life*, 2:356 (Graham's emphasis).

20. For a fascinating discussion of vegetarianism in the Old Testament, see Jean Solet, "Sémiotique de la nourriture dans la Bible," *Annales, E.S.C.* 28 (1973):943–55.

21. Graham, *Science of Human Life*, 1:22–26, 2:21–41.

22. Xavier Bichat, *Physiological Researches upon Life and Death* (Philadelphia: Smith and Maxwell, 1809), pp. 2–3, 43–47, 63–64, 108–9.

23. Graham, *Science of Human Life*, 1:351.

24. Ibid., 2:485.

25. Ibid., 2:337.

26. Ibid., 2:289–99.

27. Ibid., 1:493–94.

28. Ibid., 1:494–95.

29. Ibid., 1:121–57.

30. Issac Smithson Hartley, *Memorial of Robert Milham Hartley; Edited by His Son* (Utica, N.Y.: Curtiss & Childs, 1882), p. 331.

31. Russell T. Trall, *Fruits and Farinacea the Proper Food of Man* (New York: Fowler and Wells, 1854), p. 171.

32. *Library of Health* 4 (1840):221.

33. James M. D. Olmsted, *François Magendie: Pioneer in Experimental Physiology and Scientific Medicine in XIX Century France* (New York: Schuman's, 1944), pp. 68–69.

34. *Moral Reformer* 1 (1835):278; *American Vegetarian and Health Journal* 4 (1854):74; Joel Shew, *Hydropathy; or, the Water-Cure: Its Principles, Modes of Treatment, &c.* (New York: Wiley and Putnam, 1844), p. 291.

35. Justus von Liebig, *Animal Chemistry* (Cambridge, Mass.: J. Owen, 1842), pp. 47–48.

36. *American Vegetarian and Health Journal* 1 (1851):22–24, 2 (1852):2, 30, 163.

37. William Beaumont, *Experiments and Observations on the Gastric Juice, and the Physiology of Digestion* (Plattsburgh, N.Y.: F. P. Allen, 1833), pp. 36, 46–47, 144, 275.

38. *Graham Journal of Health and Longevity* 1 (1837):225.

39. Ibid., p. 264.

40. Graham, *Science of Human Life*, 2:112.

41. *Graham Journal of Health and Longevity* 1 (1837):264.

42. Ibid., pp. 264–70. For a similar argument, see Mary S. Gove, *Lectures to Women on Anatomy and Physiology* (New York: Harper & Brothers, 1846), pp. 9, 29, 104–5.

43. Alcott, *Vegetable Diet*, p. 165.

44. *American Vegetarian and Health Journal* 4 (1854):131.

45. Lemuel Shattuck, *Report of the Sanitary Commission of Massachusetts, 1850* (Cambridge, Mass.: Harvard University Press, 1948), p. 58.

46. Phyllis Allen, "Etiological Theory in America Prior to the Civil War," *Journal of the History of Medicine and Allied Sciences* 2 (1947):489–520; William G. Rothstein, *American Physicians in the Nineteenth Century* (Baltimore: Johns Hopkins University Press, 1972), pp. 41–62; Richard H. Shyrock, *Medicine and Society in America: 1660–1860* (Ithaca: Cornell University Press, 1960), pp. 117–66.

47. J. Marion Sims, *The Story of My Life* (New York: D. Appleton and Company, 1884), p. 150.

48. Joseph F. Kett, *The Formation of the American Medical Profession* (New Haven, Conn.: Yale University Press, 1968), pp. 97–107; James Harvey Young, *The Toadstool Millionaires* (Princeton, N.J.: Princeton University Press, 1961), pp. 44–57; Rothstein, *American Physicians*, pp. 125–51; Alex Berman, "A Striving for Scientific Respectability: Some American Botanics and the Nineteenth Century Plant Materia Medica," *Bulletin of the History of Medicine* 30 (1956):7–31; "Neo-Thomsonianism in the United States," *Journal of the History of Medicine and Allied Sciences* 9 (1956):133–55; Philip D. Jordan, "The Secret Six, An Inquiry into the Basic Materia Medica of the Thomsonian System of Botanic Medicine," *Ohio State Archeological and Historical Quarterly* 52 (1943):347–55.

49. Martin Kaufman, *Homeopathy in America: The Rise and Fall of a Medical Heresy* (Baltimore: Johns Hopkins University Press, 1971); Kett, *American Medical Profession*, pp. 132–64; Rothstein, *American Physicians*, pp. 152–74. In antebellum America, there was about one sectarian doctor for every ten orthodox physicians. Approximately 2,400 homeopaths practiced medicine between 1835 and 1860. There were about 4,000 eclectic and botanical practitioners between 1845 and 1860. See Kett, *American Medical Profession*, pp. 185–86.

50. James Harvey Young, "American Medical Quackery in the Age of Common Man," *Mississippi Valley Historical Review* 47 (1961):579–93; *Toadstool Millionaires*, pp. 16–43.

51. Jonathan Forman, "Alva Curtis," *Bulletin of the History of Medicine* 21 (1947):772–87.

52. *Botanico-Medical Recorder* (Cincinnati), 21 September 1844, pp. 356–57.

53. *Boston Medical and Surgical Journal* 38 (1848):518.

54. See Ivan Illich, *Medical Nemesis: The Expropriation of Health* (New York: Pantheon Books, 1976).

55. Graham, *Science of Human Life*, 2:234 (Graham's emphasis).

56. Ibid., p. 233.

57. Ibid. (Graham's emphasis).

58. Ibid., p. 238.

59. William A. Alcott, *Forty Years in the Wilderness of Pills and Powders* (Boston: J. P. Jewett, 1859), p. 38.

60. *Library of Health* 5 (1941):79.

61. Ibid. 1 (1837):21; William A. Alcott, *The Young Husband* (Philadelphia: n.p., 1835), p. 374.

62. Russell T. Trall, *Nervous Debility; The Nature, Causes, Consequences, and Hygienic Treatment of Invalids Suffering from Prematurely Exhausted Vitality* (New York: Davies & Kent, 1861), p. 17; *Water Cure Journal* 27 (1859):65.

63. *Graham Journal of Health and Longevity* 3 (1839):23; Isaac Jennings, *Medical Reform: A Treatise on Man's Physical Being and Disorders* (Oberlin, Ohio: Fitch & Jennings, 1847), pp. 326–27.

64. *Constitution of the American Physiological Society: With a Catalogue of its Members and Officers* (Boston: Marsh, Capon & Lyon, 1837), p. 8.

65. Richard Osborn Cummings, *The American and His Food* (Chicago: University of Chicago Press, 1941), pp. 4, 10–42; Waverly Root and Richard de Rochement, *Eating in America* (New York: William Morrow, 1976), pp. 104–46; Thomas De Voe, *The Market Assistant* (New York: Hurd and Houghton, 1867), pp. 104–5.

66. Graham, *Science of Human Life*, 2:361–84.

67. Ibid., pp. 396–97.

68. Frederick Accum, *A Treatise on Adulterations of Food, and Culinary Poisons* (London: J. Mallett, 1820).

69. John Mullaly, *The Milk Trade in New York and Vicinity* (New York: Fowlers and Wells, 1853), pp. 115–16.

70. New York City Board of Health, *Majority and Minority Reports of the Select Committee of the Board of Health, Appointed to Investigate the Character and Condition of the Sources from which Cow's Milk Is Derived, for Sale in the City of New York* (New York: n.p., 1858), p. 69.

71. Siegfried Giedion, *Mechanization Takes Command* (New York: W. W. Norton, 1969), pp. 169–200; Greville Bathe and Dorothy Bathe, *Oliver Evans* (Philadelphia: The Historical Society of Philadelphia, 1935); pp. 10–18; Charles Byron Kuhlmann, *The Development of the Flour-Milling Industry in the United States* (Boston: Houghton Mifflin Co., 1929), pp. 93–103.

72. Sylvester Graham, *Treatise on Bread, and Bread-Making* (Boston: Light and Stearns, 1837), pp. 17–126; *Science of Human Life* 2:399–479; Asenath Nicholson, *Nature's Own Book* (New York: Wilbur and Whipple, 1835), pp. 17–18.

73. *Constitution of Physiological Society*, pp. 9–21.

74. William A. Alcott, *Familiar Letters to Young Men on Various Subjects* (Buffalo, N.Y.: Geo. H. Derby and Co., 1850), p. 176.

75. *New York Review* 1 (October, 1837):336.

76. *Boston Medical and Surgical Journal* 14 (1836):169.

77. Sylvester Graham, *Lecture on Epidemic Disease Generally, and Particularly the Spasmodic Cholera* (New York: M. Day, 1833), p. 79; Russell T. Trall, *The Hydropathic Encyclopedia*, 2 vols. (New York: Fowlers and Wells, 1852), 1:420–22.

78. *American Vegetarian and Health Journal* 2 (1852):160.

79. W. J. Rorabaugh, "Estimated U.S. Alcoholic Beverage Consumption, 1790–1860," *Journal of Studies on Alcohol* 37 (1976): 357–64.

80. Cummings, *American and Food,* pp. 258–59; John T. Schlebecker, *Cattle Raising on the Plains, 1900–1961* (Lincoln, Neb.: University of Nebraska Press, 1963), p. 10; U.S. Bureau of the Census, *Historical Statistics of the United States: Colonial Times to 1970* (Washington, D.C.: Government Printing Office, 1975), pp. 329–31.

81. Cummings, *American and Food,* pp. 53–74; *Journal of Health* 4 (1833):145–46; *Moral Reformer* 1 (1835):165.

82. Morton White and Lucia White, *The Intellectual Versus the City* (Cambridge, Mass.: Harvard University Press, 1962), pp. 13–62; Harry Levin, *The Power of Blackness* (New York: Alfred A. Knopf, 1958), pp. 165–200; Leo Marx, *The Machine in the Garden* (New York: Oxford University Press, 1964), pp. 145–353.

83. Ralph Waldo Emerson, *The Journals and Miscellaneous Notebooks of Ralph Waldo Emerson,* ed. William H. Gilman et.al., 14 vols. (Cambridge, Mass.: Harvard University Press, 1960), 7:288.

84. John L. Thomas, "Romantic Reform in America, 1815–1865," *American Quarterly* 17 (1965): 656–81; Rush Welter, *The Mind of America, 1820–1860* (New York: Columbia University Press, 1975), pp. 77–104, 165–89; R. W. B. Lewis, *The American Adam* (Chicago: University of Chicago Press, 1955), pp. 1–53, 77–109; Wilson Carey McWilliams, *The Idea of Fraternity in America* (Berkeley and Los Angeles: University of California Press, 1973), pp. 229–53, 280–300.

6

The Paradox of Victorian Free Love

Sylvester Graham and the health reformers not only theorized about diet and sexuality, but they also became influential analysts of love and marriage. Although Graham focused upon young males rather than married couples, some of his supporters critically examined marriage, condemned the institution, and developed a systematic theory of what they called free love. Perhaps the two most notorious Grahamite free lovers were Thomas and Mary Nichols, who believed God had created the human passions so that they might have "freedom for development, freedom of action, freedom of enjoyment."[1] While the celibate Shakers, the pantagamous Oneida community, and the polygamous Mormons boldly experimented with alternatives to monogamous marriage, the Nicholses also were intent on radically transforming romantic relations in antebellum America.

The Nicholses' arguments seemed completely opposed to mid–nineteenth-century sexual behavior and "respectable" sexual mores. Throughout this period, we have seen that American sexual ideology and behavior became more restrictive. Beginning in the late eighteenth century, there was a precipitous decline in premarital pregnancies and illegitimacy, and contemporary medical, biological, and instructional literature increasingly became concerned with the strict control of sexual activities. For moral and health reasons premarital sexual activities were condemned and infrequent sexual relations after marriage were championed.

The lyrical and descriptive language Thomas Nichols used to describe sexual intercourse seemed completely different from the chaste circumlocutions of his contemporaries:

> The expressions of love antecedent to, and connected with its ultimation, are varied and beautiful, involving the whole being. . . . [When]

.e bolder hands of man wander over the ravishing beauties of woman
. . he clasps her waist, he presses her soft bosom, and in a tumult of
delirious ecstasy, each finds the central point of attraction and of pleasure, which increases until it is completed in the sexual orgasm—the
most exquisite enjoyment of which the human senses are capable.[2]

Yet the Nicholses were not nineteenth-century critics of Victorian sexuality who glorified sexual intercourse. Their doctrine of free love, which
implied to contemporaries uncontrolled passion, was in reality as restrictive as the sexual mores of middle-class antebellum America. Thomas
Nichols, for example, contradicted his paean to sexual intercourse with a
medical philippic. Precisely because sexual intercourse was such an intense and consuming activity, it could be experienced only under very
strict circumstances. If Nichols's readers followed his advice, they might
have found themselves entitled to only as many acts of coitus as the
number of their children![3]

The Nicholses shared similar views with such professed sex radicals as
Robert Dale Owen, John Humphrey Noyes, and Stephen Pearl Andrews.[4] Their free-love arguments bore a striking similarity to conventional Victorian morality. Like their horrified critics, they were
obsessively concerned with human sexuality and linked the progress of
civilization with its careful control. Paradoxically, through contrasting
arguments, the Nicholses and their conservative opponents arrived at
similar forms of sexual behavior. They all believed that sexual promiscuity was a profanation of the body and that chastity was morally and
physiologically sound. But the Nicholses and other Grahamite sexual
theorists broke with contemporary opinion when they defended the concept of birth control through voluntary motherhood. Like other romantic health reformers, the Nicholses were both repressive and
perfectionist. They condemned contemporary American dietary, physiological, and sexual behavior and demanded that individuals radically
change their lives in the direction of greater self-control. At the same
time, the Nicholses confidently expected that their lectures, books, and
institutions would purge American society of its imperfections and lead
to the physiological millennium. The example of the Nicholses and contemporary sexual radicals demonstrates how the sexual ideology of Sylvester Graham so permeated American culture that it became the
foundation for Victorian free-love theories and practices.

When Thomas Nichols published his major work, *Esoteric Anthropology* (1853), both he and his wife had become prominent followers of
Sylvester Graham.[5] Nichols was born in Orford, New Hampshire, in
1815 and raised by strict and sturdy Congregational farmers. He studied

medicine at Dartmouth College, but left without completing his degree. After traveling to western New York, he achieved local notoriety as a newspaper editor in Buffalo when he received a four-month jail sentence for his unflattering descriptions of local politicians. He then moved to New York City in the late 1830s, became a respected newspaper editor, and dabbled in Democratic party politics and romantic literature. After he married Mary Gove in 1848, however, Nichols abandoned journalism and decided to become a physician.[6]

Since Mary already was a highly respected Grahamite, Thomas chose to study hydropathy. He entered medical school and graduated from New York University in 1850. Soon after he became a physician, the Nicholses opened their first water-cure establishment on the west side of Manhattan above Greenwich Village. Concurrently, Thomas became a regular contributor to the *Water Cure Journal* and he also helped organize the American Vegetarian Society and the American Hygienic and Hydropathic Association of Physicians and Surgeons. Although Thomas Nichols was trained as a regular doctor, he was uninterested in a standard medical practice because it was dominated by the unconscionable techniques and values of orthodox physicians. Thomas believed that only hydropathy and the Grahamite health principles he had learned from his wife could prevent disease and educate people about the laws of health.[7]

Throughout his hydropathic career, Thomas generously attributed his reputation and success to his wife, whose sympathetic understanding guided him to health reform. Mary Gove Nichols was one of the most dramatic and influential mid–nineteenth-century female reformers. Her ideology and career vividly illustrates how Grahamism influenced Victorian culture and reform.

Mary Sargaent Neal was born in Gofftown, New Hampshire, in 1810 and later moved to Vermont. She was a quiet, introspective child who enjoyed reading and studying religion. If she had a satisfying marriage, Mary probably would have become a competent schoolteacher and minor writer. Her problems began in 1830 when she met a Quaker, Hiram Gove, who convinced her to marry him a year later. From the beginning, their relationship was marred by marital problems and tragedy. Their first child, Elma Penn, lived to adulthood but four other pregnancies ended in miscarriage and stillbirths. And Hiram was no consolation, for he tyrannized his young wife and forced her to support the family through needlework.[8]

To compensate for her unhappy life, Mary began studying physiology and discovered the inspiring principles of Sylvester Graham.[9] In Lynn, Massachusetts, Mary lectured on Grahamite anatomy and physiology at the local lyceum and by 1838 she had opened a girl's school whose students lived according to a Grahamite system.[10] At the same time, Mary became involved with the American Physiological Society and delivered very popular lectures to women in the fall of 1838. Her audiences averaged around 500 and when she gave a free talk on tight lacing, almost 2,000 women attended. For the next few months, Mary repeated her successful lectures in Boston, Lynn, and Haverhill, Massachusetts, Providence, Rhode Island, and New York City. Rapidly she blossomed into a prominent Grahamite and female lecturer. Hiram disapproved of his wife's independence and career but grudgingly allowed her to continue because he collected the fees for her activities.[11]

Mary's reform activities were not universally admired, and she was condemned for the same reasons people criticized Graham and the other purity advocates. The Quakers denounced her unseemly activities until she left the Society of Friends. And when Mary began lecturing and publishing on the "solitary vice,"[12] newspapers attacked her because they considered talks about masturbation offensive and obscene.[13] Her books, however, received excellent reviews and she continued to attract large and enthusiastic audiences wherever she lectured.[14]

Inasmuch as Mary believed that contemporary women suffered from mistreatment and illness, she advocated Grahamite physiology as a cure for female problems. Dress reform was one of her major principles: women should "loosen the death grasp of the corset, and send the now imprisoned and poisoned blood rejoicing through the veins."[15] She also defended the standard Grahamite regimen of fresh air and plentiful exercise, sound personal hygiene and daily bathing, abstinence from meat, tea, coffee, alcohol, and drugs, and a diet based on vegetables and whole-wheat bread. She felt, however, that Grahamism was becoming synonymous with mere vegetarianism and so Mary broadened her physiological principles to include a variety of reforms whose goals were the liberation of women legally and physiologically.

As Mary developed a successful, independent career, her marriage became intolerable. When she asked for a separation, Hiram threatened to take custody of Elma and destroy his wife's reputation. Mary was able to leave him in 1842 only because her father threatened to sue Hiram for a loan he had never repaid. After Mary's father died in 1845, Hiram seized Elma for three months until some of Mary's friends kidnapped the daughter back to her mother's home. Fortunately, Hiram decided to marry another woman and so he secured a divorce in 1848. Ironically, Hiram eventually became a highly respected homeopathic physician in Salem and Boston.[16]

After her separation, Mary became more deeply involved in the health-reform movement. Conversations with Bronson Alcott and Charles Lane reinforced her physiological principles, and she spent three months studying and lecturing at a hydropathic establishment in Brattleboro, Vermont. In December of 1845 she saw patients and gave talks at Joel Shew's water cure in New York City and during the spring of the next year she opened her own hydropathic center on Tenth Street in lower Manhattan. At the same time, her literary career flowered. Soon after she moved to New York, the editor of *Godey's Lady's Book* paid her fifteen dollars for a short story. Later more stories and a number of sentimental novels followed, and her water cure became a gathering place for such antebellum luminaries as Edgar Allan Poe and Albert Brisbane.[17]

After their marriage, the Nicholses opened their own water-cure establishment. The next year they created the American Hydropathic Institute, which was a medical school based on Grahamite principles. The first term began in September of 1851 with twenty-six students; three months later, twenty students, including nine women, were awarded diplomas. During the following year they moved to a new water-cure establishment in Port Chester, New York, to open a School of Integral Education where people could study hydropathy while they lived at the institution.[18] By the early 1850s the Nicholses were well-known literary and reformist figures on the New York cultural scene.

While the Nicholses were establishing their hydropathic credentials, Thomas was writing *Esoteric Anthropology*, which frankly explained their ideas about social relations and physiology:

> As the material basis of all reform, and all progress of humanity toward its true destiny, the world wants health. Individuals are sick, communities are sick, nations are sick. The very earth is diseased. All must be cured together, but the work must begin with the individual. Every man who purifies and invigorates his own life, does something for the world. Every woman who lives in the conditions of health, and avoids the causes of disease, helps the race. . . . [Both] do a noble work for the redemption of universal humanity.[19]

Although Nichols's book discussed physiological reform and the water cure, the most sensational chapters described the anatomical and physiological aspects of sexual intercourse and their views on marriage and sexuality. The book was considered scandalous, and even hydropathic reformers such as Trall denounced it,[20] but if reviewers had studied the work carefully, they would have discovered that the Nicholses used Grahamite principles to denounce conventional marriage in the name of chaste health. Free love, according to the Nicholses, was not license, for they attached so many dietary and physiological conditions to sexual intercourse that healthy couples would rarely engage in any sexual activities. Along with their next work, *Marriage* (1854), this book dramatically demonstrates how Grahamism, which appeared radical and destructive to some Americans, actually was a conservative ideology that bolstered Victorian morality and sexual behavior.

As we have seen, Graham believed that American youths and adults were suffering from an increased incidence of debility, disease, and weakness of the brain. He blamed these conditions on sexual excesses, poor diet, and improper hygiene. Graham demanded that people radically change their diets, follow the "constitutional laws of human nature," and hoped that healthy and robust adults would limit the number of times they had sexual intercourse. Frequent intercourse would impair people's constitutional powers, shorten life, and increase disease and suffering.

Graham and Thomas Nichols agreed that sexual excitement was inevitably debilitating. Both men rejected Tissot's theory; it was not the loss of semen which produced sexual exhaustion, but the drainage of nervous energy. Too much sex, Nichols argued, left the nervous system flaccid.[21]

Therefore sexual intercourse was permitted only under certain conditions. Nichols's criteria included the physical and intellectual maturity of both partners, the presence of mutual love, the financial means to support any children, a female pelvis of sufficient size, and the absence of any hereditary defects or "distressing singularities of mind." This category included "diseased amativeness," a phrenological term for nymphomania. Thus, too intense a desire for sexual intercourse was a good reason to remain chaste. Finally, even under ideal conditions, sexual intercourse was to be avoided if experienced recently, since overindulgence was as harmful as any abuse. Sexual intercourse was permissible twelve times a year if all other indications were positive.[22]

Nichols used Graham's physiological principles to demonstrate the tragic results of sexual exhaustion. Consistently, Thomas Nichols argued that too much sex led to such varied diseases as dyspepsia, epilepsy, and most women's problems. His diagnosis was always the same; the nervous exhaustion caused by sexual activities was a universal source of most American medical problems.[23]

The Nicholses cleverly inverted Graham's ideas to attack the institution of marriage. Graham could only ruefully defend the state of matrimony. While all sex was inherently harmful, marital sex was less harmful than other kinds because it was less enjoyable. Although marriage was founded on biblical and civil laws, it ultimately was based upon the "physiological principles established in the constitutional nature of man."[24] Graham's attempt to refute theorists such as Stephen Pearl Andrews and Robert Dale Owen paradoxically succeeded in destroying his own argument for marriage. If health reformers such as the Nicholses believed that marital sex was less healthy than free love because it was more frequent or intense, marriage became an immoral and debilitating social institution.

In *Esoteric Anthropology* and *Marriage*, the Nicholses boldly concluded that marriage was incompatible with a healthy and moral society. It promoted violent and degrading sexual practices. Most importantly, marriage rendered all sexual activity unnatural by denying love's instinctive regulations. Based on their observations and their medical practice, the Nicholses believed marriage was little better than sexual slavery, for the wife was supposed to submit to her husband's demands. When coitus became "morbid lust" for the husband and a "loathsome act" for the wife, debilitation and disease were the predictable results.[25]

Thomas Nichols suggested that the "whole train of what are called female diseases [were] mainly caused by the legalized and sanctified brutalities of the civilized marriage."[26] Mary supported her husband with graphic illustration. In the Medical College at Albany, she explained,

> There is an exposition of indissoluble marriage, which should be studied by all those who begin to see that a legalized union may be a most impure, unholy, and consequently, unhealthy thing: in glass vases, ranged in a large cabinet . . . are uterine tumors, weighing from half a pound to twenty-four pounds. A viscus that in its ordinary state weighs a few ounces, is brought, by the disease caused by amative excess—in other words, licentiousness and impurity—to weigh more than twenty pounds.[27]

In opposition to contemporary medical, biological, and popular opinion, the Nicholses argued that marriage had unfavorable psychological consequences. Inasmuch as the marriage bond was indissoluble, spouses often developed a callous attitude toward each other. Thus marriage led to such vices as slovenliness, the use of tobacco, liquor, and meat, and sexual infidelity. Thomas Nichols claimed that the exhaustion, monotony, and disgust that characterized many marriages was primarily responsible for the high incidence of alcoholism. Moreover, by forcing couples to engage in sexual relations under such unhealthy circumstances, marriage led to masturbation and other disgusting sexual excesses.[28]

Brutality, alcoholism, and disease; these were the unfortunate results of the allegedly sacred institution of marriage. But their critics argued that the Nicholses' free-love doctrines would promote greater excesses than marriage. The Nicholses disagreed and revealed the conservative implications of their philosophy.

In *Marriage*, the Nicholses argued that, although women had the same sexual desires as men, they did not believe in promiscuous relationships because unwanted children would be the result.[29] For Mary Nichols, free love meant that women would have total control over their bodies and decide when to have sexual relations. She attacked the double standard which counseled submissiveness for the female and condoned aggressive violations of morality and health in the male. Thomas agreed, arguing that free love would destroy lust because sexual freedom would naturally moderate sexual activity better than marriage. Inasmuch as sexual desire attained "a morbid activity in the constraints and repressions of civilization,"[30] the Nicholses' brand of free love would relieve this morbid activity. If the artificial constraints of civilization were responsible for poor health and sexual excesses, a return to natural regulations would cure these problems and usher in the physiological millennium.

In March of 1856 the Nicholses announced their intention of establishing a utopian water-cure community in Yellow Springs, Ohio.[31] They were excited by the prospect of operating a hydropathic establishment in a rural village and organizing a society based on their free-love principles. Attracted by the anarchist concepts of Stephen Pearl Andrews and Josiah Warren, they once had considered moving to Andrews's Modern Times commune in 1853. There they were promised one hundred free acres to establish a School for Life, which would develop the spiritual and physiological harmony promised by Graham and the water cure. But the needed funds did not appear, and instead, the Nicholses began studying spiritualism and decided to move west and establish a community that would satisfy the needs of the individual in a collective setting.[32]

The village of Yellow Springs appeared to be an ideal place for the realization of the Nicholses' dreams. Besides its bucolic atmosphere, the community had a reputation for supporting reformist institutions. A small group of Owenite utopians had briefly settled there in the late 1820s and the town was the home of an integrated and coeducational school, Antioch College, whose president was Horace Mann. In this community the Nicholses planned to open Memnonia, which was named after the legendary statue on the Nile in ancient Egypt that sang when enveloped by the morning rays of the sun.[35]

But their writings and reform activities made them suspect in the area. Mann feared that his experiment in liberal education was threatened by the Nicholses and their free-love disciples. Some Antioch students had purchased the Nicholses' books and one withdrew from school rather than stop selling their works.[34] The academic community and the leading citizens of Yellow Springs fought the Nicholses with protest rallies, intimidation, and violence. The Grahamites replied with similar tactics, including an abortive attempt to take control of their water-cure establishment before their lease began. Finally, they occupied their buildings in July of 1856 and the commune officially opened in September.[35]

Even after Memnonia opened, Mann continued to oppose the Nicholses. He condemned their free-love doctrines as the "superfoetation of diabolism upon polygamy"[36] and feared that many female students would leave the college because of its proximity to the depraved Grahamites. Eventually Yellow Springs accepted the Nicholses because their spiritualist doctrines were sympathetically received by the townspeople. Mann still condemned the health reformers, and even expelled a male student who lived at Memnonia and sold the Nicholses' books.[37]

If Mann and his followers had dispassionately examined the Nicholses' free-love doctrines, they would have realized that their fears about sexual excesses were unjustified. The Nicholses' regimen, which was organized around the slogan "FREEDOM, FRATERNITY, CHASTITY,"[38] far exceeded the strictest rules of the contemporary sexual ideology and behavior they supposedly were combatting. Persons wishing to join the community were asked to adopt the Canons of Consecration printed in the *Nichols' Monthly*. Members pledged to be pure in spirit, drink only water, take daily baths, eat only vegetables and dairy products, and ingest only bread and fruit on Fridays and Sundays. Couples were expected to be monogamous and follow the Nicholses' strict rules regarding sexual intercourse. Daily confessions were required and disobedient residents were assigned penances.[39] The regimen appealed to about twenty individuals who were Englishmen and Easterners who "had met with disappointments and grief in the life of the affections—the unrequited and the divorced."[40]

Mary provided the doctrinal justification for the Memnonia regulations. She condemned the institution of marriage because it enslaved women and deprived them of control over sexual intercourse. But Mary also believed that frequent sexual intercourse depleted the body's vital energy. Her Law of Progression in Harmony, which stated that sexual intercourse was a debilitating act, brought accusations of asceticism and Shaker celibacy upon this health reformer. Other critics such as Mann, who did not understand the conservative implications of her doctrines, considered Mary depraved and promiscuous.[41] Soon after the commune opened, the Nicholses decided that its members were not yet spiritually prepared for the doctrines of free love, for baleful institutions such as marriage had corrupted them. The "temporary" solution was total and unqualified celibacy for the entire membership.[42] Memnonia was not an anarchistic utopia such as Modern Times, but was a closely regulated Grahamite community whose members developed wisdom and health through rigorous discipline and austerity.

Within a few months, personality conflicts and financial losses made the commune a shaky venture. Also, the Nicholses were abandoning orthodox Grahamism and gravitating toward spiritualism and Roman Catholicism. Spiritual seances were held every morning and on Friday and Sunday evenings. In the fall of 1856 Roman Catholic apparitions began appearing who informed the Nicholses that their goals were similar to the Jesuits. After Mary began receiving personal messages from Ignatius Loyola, the Nicholses converted to Roman Catholicism and abandoned the colony.[43]

A contemporary account of the Memnonia experiment was written by Moncure Conway, a reformer who was then pastor of the First Congregational Church in Cincinnati. In a book review of one of Thomas Nichols's novels, he described the colony and unwittingly explained the paradoxical and the conservative implications of antebellum free love:

> Memnona [sic], when in its most flourishing condition, numbered about twenty inmates. . . . It was represented to the country chiefly through the terrible denunciations of Horace Mann. . . . This community, however, had reason to know that Mr. Mann was mistaken; and so far from Memnona [sic] being a seat of sexual license, it inaugurated in its actual life the asceticism and celibacy which afterwards carried its leading characters into the Church of Rome.[44]

The Nicholses seemed chastened by the failure of their community, for they stopped writing about free love and lectured for several years in Catholic institutions throughout the Mississippi Valley. Thomas gave talks on religion while his wife taught hygiene. Their anonymous followers cannot be traced. Early in 1861 they returned to New York City, but quickly sailed for England because they had no sympathy for the Lincoln government. There they wrote, lectured, and operated a water-cure establishment and Graham food store in the health resort of Malvern. Mary died in 1884 and Thomas continued to run his business until he retired to the Continent, where he died in 1902.[45] Their careers after Memnonia were devoid of the free-love doctrines that had made them famous antebellum reformers.

Although critics accused the sexual radicals of destroying traditional monogamy by abetting the breakup of families and providing social alternatives to marriage, the impact of Victorian sexual radicals on antebellum mores was far more ambiguous than their outraged detractors recognized. Most Victorian sexual radicals such as the Nicholses fruitfully questioned but could not escape the dominant beliefs of their age about the human body. Their ambiguity about sexual relations appeared in its most striking form in John Humphrey Noyes's Oneida community. He believed that "the Shakers and Grahamites [were] right" in arguing that sexual intercourse was "wasteful of life and cannot be natural."[46] But in contrast to prevailing sexual norms, Noyes thought sexual intercourse could be practiced regularly without procreation and that sex should be enjoyed by women as well as by men. Noyes told his followers that "sexual communion differs only by its superior intensity and beauty from other acts of love"[47] and he believed that sexual expression was "love in its most natural and beautiful form."[48] Thus sexual intercourse was encouraged among consenting men and women. But Noyes qualified his doctrines by establishing the principle of male continence. During intercourse, the male partner was not permitted to have an orgasm. Instead, upon entering the woman, he remained stationary until his erection had subsided naturally or until the woman had an orgasm. Noyes defended this practice by dividing sexual intercourse into two distinct physiological acts. The "amative" was sexual, beautiful, and healthy. The "procreative" was merely sensual, ugly, and unhealthy.[49]

Noyes's sexual doctrines probably were based on his own unfortunate experiences. In *Male Continence*, he poignantly explained why he and his wife decided to practice birth control in the 1840s:

> The [decision] was occasioned and even forced upon me by very sorrowful experiences. In the course of six years my wife went through the agonies of five births. Four of them were premature. Only one child lived. . . . After our last disappointment, I pledged my word to my wife that I would never again expose her to such fruitless suffering.[50]

Noyes never completely accepted the doctrines of physiology because they appeared to deny the importance of the spiritual life. But he admired Graham and believed that dietary temperance was an important adjunct to sexual control because the "stomach and the bowels are intimately connected with the brain, and thus are specially subject to the action of the mind." Noyes confessed that once he was "sorely tempted to give up my bowels to runaway merriment" but his willpower prevailed.[51] He also condemned the use of alcohol, coffee, tea, tobacco, and meat; dietary restraint was a "sacrifice to God" which helped guarantee a physical and spiritual unity to man.[52] "We sanctify that which we take into ourselves."[53] Although Noyes's sexual practices violated Grahamite prohibitions about the frequency of sexual intercourse, both the purity advocates and the Oneidans believed they were restoring health and purifying the race. Perhaps the distance between the two groups was not so great. When the Oneida community was about to dissolve in 1881, Noyes suggested that the communitarians abandon complex marriage and become celibate.[54]

The sexual mores of Noyes and his followers helps explain the Nicholses' free-love doctrines. Like other contemporary sexual radicals, the Nicholses attacked the double standard and the male sexual license it condoned. Men were depicted as aggressive destroyers of female innocence and happiness and thus women's safety lay in a militant effort to control men's sexual values and autonomy. The Nicholses' rhetoric betrayed an unmistakable and deeply felt resentment toward a male-dominated society.

Their solution to the problem of male domination was the idea of voluntary motherhood. Romantic health reformers were the first important group to defend this concept, which in the late nineteenth century was appropriated by some suffragists, members of the social-purity crusade, and small numbers of secular free lovers. The Nicholses believed that, since marriage enslaved and degraded women, they should develop the institutions and courage to control their own sexuality. If society and especially the institution of marriage had destroyed people's natural self-regulating mechanisms, voluntary motherhood would restore the innate, moderate sexual instincts. Voluntary motherhood, according to the Nicholses and other Grahamites, was directed against the social and legal practice of female submission to her husband's sexual demands.[55]

Interestingly, the Grahamites' analysis both supported and rejected the dominant opinions of nineteenth-century physicians, who saw women as uniquely conditioned by their reproductive systems. Purity advocates such as the Nicholses agreed with respectable medical opinion that women were the products and prisoners of their sexual organs. But they gave this contemporary diagnosis a feminist twist. Because women had delicate reproductive systems, they had to have liberty and autonomy. Women needed control over their own bodies; without this, they were the slaves not only to the sexual desires of their husbands but also to endless childbearing and childrearing. Trall, a close friend of the Nicholses until the publication of *Esoteric Anthropology*, concisely summed up the radical argument when he claimed that a "woman's equality in all the relations of life implies her absolute supremacy in the sexual relation. . . . It is her absolute and indefeasible right to determine when she will and when she will not be exposed to pregnancy."[56]

The Nicholses, however, dissented from these same conservative physicians by arguing that the exclusive aim of sexual intercourse was not the procreation of children. Sexual intercourse was an act of love and tenderness between individuals. Sex was justifiable as an essential and irreplaceable form of human affection; no man could demand this act unless it was freely given. By selectively using Grahamite principles, the Nicholses tried to destroy the link between male sexual prerogatives and procreation. "Mothers who loved in loving union, and obeyed the health-laws which I [Mary] taught them, obtained immunity from suffering"[57] and delivered healthy babies. Thomas agreed that "Heaven conferred" upon women the "right to choose the father of her babe. Every child should be a love-child," for this was the "only legitimacy that nature knows."[58] The Nicholses' support of female sexual autonomy and their condemnation of the double standard in the name of purity and virtue was the essence of their sexual radicalism.

Mid–nineteenth-century health reformers such as the Nicholses rejected all forms of contraception because they feared it would encourage promiscuity. They wanted women to avoid pregnancy, but they did not believe that it was essential for women to engage freely in sexual intercourse. For birth control they recommended abstinence. Self-regulation was directed against the attitude that male sexual desire was an uncontrollable urge. The Nicholses' doctrines of free love were designed to bring about a natural sexual moderation that bound sexual intercourse within Grahamite notions of proper health and physiology.

This attitude was common throughout the nineteenth century. Ezra Heywood, for example, who courageously defended free-love doctrines, condemned contraception as "unnatural, injurious, or offensive."[59] And Tennessee Claflin, one of the century's most notorious free lovers, argued that the

> washes, teas, tonics and various sorts of appliances known to the initiated [are a] standing reproach upon, and a permanent indictment against, American women. . . . No woman should ever hold sexual relations with any man from the possible consequences of which she might desire to escape.[60]

The arguments against contraception reflected a romantic yearning for the "natural" as opposed to the artificial. The Nicholses' sexual doctrines were based firmly on the individualistic and laissez-faire ethics of the period. The entire physiological foundations of the Grahamites' concepts of sexuality were predicated on a return to a more simple and natural form of regulation that allegedly existed before the creation of an artificial, urban civilization.

Nineteenth-century free-love doctrines[61] and behavior, which were founded on the physiological theories of Sylvester Graham, posed no threat to the established order or Victorian sexual morality. Although the free lovers attacked marriage and all forms of compulsion between men and women, they expected individuals to regress to a natural regulatory system that was characterized by severe dietary and sexual self-restraint. They also hoped that women would use their new freedom to reject frequent sexual intercourse, which led to promiscuity and overburdened families. Like the other sexual radicals, the Nicholses were obsessed with the rationalization and sublimation of sexuality through careful prudence. On this issue, there was little disagreement among nineteenth-century middle-class Americans.

NOTES

1. Thomas Low Nichols, *Esoteric Anthropology* (New York: Thomas L. Nichols, 1853), p. 256..

2. Ibid., p. 153.

3. Ibid., pp. 152–53, 234–48, 437–38.

4. Stephen Pearl Andrews, like Thomas Nichols, argued that sexual freedom would "moderate the passions instead of inflaming them, and so . . . contribute, in the highest degree, to a general Purity of Life." Owen expressed a similar opinion. See Stephen Pearl Andrews, *Love, Marriage, and Divorce, and the Sovereignty of the Individual* (New York: Stringer and Townsend, 1853), p. 20; Robert Dale Owen, *Moral Physiology; Or, A Brief and Plain Treatise on the Population Question* (London: J. Watson, 1841), pp. 12–13, 21–22; John Humphrey Noyes, *Male Continence* (Oneida, N.Y.: Office of Oneida Circular, 1872), pp. 5, 15–20, and *Essay on Scientific Propagation* (Oneida, N.Y.: Oneida Community, 1872), p. 24.

5. For other studies of the Nicholses, see Bertha-Monica Stearns, "Two Forgotten New England Reformers," *New England Quarterly* 6 (1933):59–84; Irving T. Richards, "Mary Gove Nichols and John Neal," *New England Quarterly* 7 (1934):335–55; John B. Blake, "Mary Gove Nichols: Prophetess of Health," *Proceedings of the American Philosophical Society* 106 (1962):219–34; Stephen Nissenbaum, "Careful Love: Sylvester Graham and the Emergence of Victorian Sexual Theory in America, 1830–1840," (Ph.D. diss., University of Wisconsin, 1968), pp. 243–57. Blake's article is the most detailed study of Mary Nichols. The influence of Graham, however, is not emphasized. Nissenbaum's chapter perceptively analyzes the Nicholses' thought but neglects their reform activities, especially the Memnonia experiment.

6. Thomas Low Nichols, *Forty Years of American Life* (London: J. Maxwell and Company, 1864), pp. 15–253.

7. *Water-Cure Journal* 9 (1850):153–54.

8. Mary Gove, *Mary Lyndon, or Revelations of a Life* (New York: Stringer and Townsend, 1855), pp. 5–147. This autobiographical novel is a frank discussion of Mary Nichols's life.

9. Mary Gove Nichols, *Experience in Water-Cure* (New York: Fowlers and Wells, 1850), p. 23.

10. *Graham Journal of Health and Longevity* 2 (1838):128.

11. Ibid., pp. 325–30, 337–42, 357–59, 373–75, 3 (1839):20, 37, 69; Gove, *Mary Lyndon*, pp. 155, 159.

12. Mary Gove Nichols, *Solitary Vice. An Address to Parents and those Who have the Care of Children* (Portland, Maine: Journal Office, 1839).

13. *Graham Journal of Health and Longevity* 3 (1839):181.

14. *Library of Health* 6 (1842):6; *Boston Medical and Surgical Journal* 25 (1841):374, 36 (1842):97–98.

15. Mary Gove, *Lecture to Women on Anatomy and Physiology* (New York: Harper & Brothers, 1846), p. 97.

16. Gove, *Mary Lyndon*, pp. 148–60, 227–72; William Henry Gove, *The Gove Book* (Salem, Mass.: S. Perley, 1922), pp. 204–5.

17. Nichols, *Experience in Water-Cure*, pp. 29–30; Gove, *Mary Lyndon*, pp. 273–344; Franklin B. Sanborn, *Bronson Alcott at Alcott House, England, and Fruitlands, New England (1842–1844)* (Cedar Rapids, Iowa: The Torch Press, 1908), pp. 13–18, 22–24.

18. *Water-Cure Journal* 11 (1851):91, 129–30, 12 (1851):10–11, 65–66, 73–75, 97–100, 114, 13 (1852):8, 19–20, 40–41, 64–65, 78, 14 (1852):13–14, 67–68, 75, 80.

19. Nichols, *Esoteric Anthropology*, pp. iv–v.

20. Thomas Low Nichols and Mary Gove Nichols, *Nichols' Medical Miscellanies; a Familiar Guide to the Preservation of Health, and the Hydropathic Home Treatment of the Most Formidable Diseases* (Cincinnati, Ohio: T. L. Nichols, 1856), p. 5; *Nichols' Journal of Health, Water-Cure, and Human Progress* 1 (1853):5, 44–47.

21. Nichols, *Esoteric Anthropology*, pp. 268–69, 398–400.

22. Ibid., pp. 230–38, 400–38.

23. Ibid., pp. 248–49, 357–61.

24. Sylvester Graham, *A Lecture to Young Men* (Providence, R.I.: Weeden and Cory, 1834), pp. 33–37.

25. Thomas Low Nichols and Mary Gove Nichols, *Marriage: Its History, Character and Results* (Cincinnati, Ohio: V. Nicholson & Co., 1854), pp. 185–90.

26. Ibid., p. 93.

27. Ibid., p. 207.

28. Ibid., p. 359; Nichols, *Esoteric Anthropology*, p. 212.

29. Nichols and Nichols, *Marriage*, p. 204.

30. Ibid., p. 345.

31. For other studies of Memnonia, see Bertha-Monica Stearns, "Memnonia: The Launching of a Utopia," *New England Quarterly* 15 (1942):280–95; Philip Gleason, "From Free Love to Catholicism: Dr. and Mrs. Thomas L. Nichols at Yellow Springs," *Ohio Historical Quarterly* 120 (1961):283–307.

32. *Nichols' Journal of Health, Water-Cure and Human Progress* 1 (1853):21, 29, 31, 38, 49–50; *Nichols' Monthly* 1 (1855):53–60.

33. *Nichols' Monthly* 2 (1856):170.

34. Ibid., 3 (1856):234.

35. Ibid., 233–37, 313–14.

36. Moncure D. Conway, *Autobiography, Memories and Experiences* 2 vols.(Boston and New York: Houghton, Mifflin and Company, 1904), 1:263.

37. *Nichols' Monthly* 3 (1856):117, 180–81, 233–34.

38. Ibid., 2 (1856):219.

39. Ibid., 3 (1856):151.

40. Conway, *Autobiography*, 1:263.

41. *Nichols' Monthly* 2 (1856):306–9, 321, 375, 378, 431.

42. Ibid., pp. 141, 306–9, 375–79, 3 (1856):337.

43. Ibid., 2 (1856):115–16, 179; Conway, *Autobiography*, 1:263.

44. *Dial* (Cincinnati), May 1860.

45. Nichols, *Forty Years*, pp. 170–77; Blake, "Mary Gove Nichols," p. 233.

46. Noyes, *Male Continence*, p. 13.

47. *John Humphrey Noyes: The Putney Community*, ed. George Wallingford Noyes (Oneida, N.Y.: n.p., 1931), p. 114.

48. *Bible Communism: A Compilation from the Annual Reports and Other Publications of the Oneida Association and Its Branches* (Brooklyn, N.Y.: Oneida Community, 1853), p. 31.

49. Noyes, *Male Continence*, pp. 2–8; Havelock Ellis, *Sex in Relation to Society* (Philadelphia: F. A. David Company, 1911), p. 553. Ellis's information was based upon correspondence with a former member of Oneida, George Noyes Miller.

50. Noyes, *Male Continence*, pp. 10–11.

51. *The Oneida Circular* 1 (1856):64.

52. *The Witness* 2 (1842), 101, 148–49; *The Oneida Circular* 1 (1856):92.

53. *The Oneida Circular* 1 (1852):188.

54. Constance Noyes Robertson, *Oneida Community: The Breakup, 1876–1881* (Syracuse: Syracuse University Press, 1972), pp. 144–66.

55. Hal D. Sears, *The Sex Radicals: Free Love in High Victorian America* (Lawrence, Kansas: Regents Press of Kansas, 1977), pp. 3–27; Linda Gordon, *Woman's Body, Woman's Right: A Social History of Birth Control in America* (New York: Viking Press, 1976), pp. 95–115. These otherwise excellent accounts err in dating the concept of voluntary motherhood from the 1870s and in assuming that the pioneer free lovers defended female sexual impulses. For a good anthology of nineteenth-century free love, see *Free Love in America: A Documentary History*, ed. Taylor Stoehr (New York: AMS Press, 1979). The book is unfortunately marred by the editor's flippant and contemptuous attitude toward free lovers.

56. Russell T. Trall, *Sexual Physiology: A Scientific and Popular Exposition of the Fundamental Problems in Sociology* (New York: Miller, Wood, 1866), pp. xi, 202.

57. Nichols, *Experience in Water-Cure*, pp. 17–18.

58. Nichols and Nichols, *Marriage*, p. 205; Nichols, *Esoteric Anthropology*, pp. 142, 172.

59. Ezra Heywood, *Cupid's Yokes: or, The Binding Forces of Conjugal Life* (Princeton, Mass.: Co-operative Publishing Co., 1876), p. 20.

60. Tennessee Claflin, *The Ethics of Sexual Equality* (New York: Woodhull & Claflin, 1873), pp. 9–10.

61. The only antebellum free lovers who defended and practiced an unregulated form of serial monogamy were the Townerites of Berlin Heights, Ohio, and they had to abandon their scheme to join the Oneida community. See *Berlin Heights: Free Love and the New Faith in Ohio, 1857–1871*, ed. William F. Vartorella (New York: AMS Press, 1979).

7

Grahamite Health Reform

Graham's *Lectures on the Science of Human Life* was designed to educate the public about correct physiology, diet, and morality. But the book was long, turgid, and repetitive; consequently book reviews were unfavorable and sales low. A one-volume edition was published simultaneously in London and a posthumous condensation appeared twenty years later in America. The failure of Graham's last book contrasted sharply with the popularity of his *Lecture to Young Men* and the bestselling works of Alcott and the other health reformers. Graham felt rejected and ominously believed that his influence was waning. He immediately embarked on a strenuous lecture tour throughout upstate New York in 1837 to improve his finances and reputation. His speeches were not enthusiastically received and in a few months he returned home to Northampton, Massachusetts, after suffering a nervous breakdown.[1] From 1838 until his death, Graham remained a semi-invalid, wrote only a few articles and delivered rare lectures, and fitfully worked on a book examining biblical attitudes toward flesh and wine. His direct influence over the health-reform movement declined, and he was forced to issue pathetic appeals for charity in order to survive.[2]

Northampton was a congenial setting for the last decade of Graham's life. Situated in the Berkshire mountains, the area was a center for the water-cure treatment, and several institutions promoted a simple vegetarian diet, natural hygiene, and outdoor exercise. In a house on Pleasant Street, Graham cultivated his vegetable garden, pondered the depravity of America, and became increasingly misanthropic. The town considered their famous resident a curiosity because every day they observed him mumbling incoherently as he walked through the main street in a bathrobe to go swimming. Graham also poured out his grief in a series of pathetic poems with such titles as "Thoughts on Madness" and "Thoughts on Clearing the Dead and Decaying Vegetable Matter from

Garden, Wednesday, Oct. 30th 1850."[3] He had foreseen his demise as
ly as 1835 when he lamented that "while the People of our country are
⌣⌣ entirely given up . . . to the untiring pursuit of wealth it is perhaps
wholly in vain for a single individual to raise his voice in a subject of this
kind."[4]

As Graham languished in bitter retirement, he considered himself a
failure. His *cri de coeur* represented the conviction that mechanical civilization was causing the death of organic man. After August of 1850,
Graham became very ill and an eclectic doctor began treating him with
the medicines and foods he detested. Graham died on September 11,
1851, after taking Congress water and a tepid bath. His wife and two
children, Henry Earl (1833–1873) and Sarah (1828–?), survived him.[5]

Graham's prediction about the demise of his ideas was premature.
Until the late nineteenth century, Graham's ideas permeated and influenced the health-reform movement, American dietary habits, and sexual behavior, and romantic reformers helped modernize the hygienic
practices of many Americans. Ironically, Graham's early retirement gave
the more moderate purity advocates the opportunity to create institutions
which developed their leader's concepts. College dining halls, boardinghouses, and sectarian physiological societies were not successful in dis-
seminating Grahamism because the public considered them too spartan
and extreme. But phrenology and water-cure establishments became
popular and influential in mid–nineteenth-century America. By modifying and disguising Graham's extremism, they were able to inspire and
reinforce important dietary, hygienic, and sexual changes in America life.
The followers of Graham were not merely abstract ideologues; like all
successful sects, they succeeded in institutionalizing their philosophy and
helped establish the foundation for a diverse and influential health-reform
movement.

As a biological phenomenon, the causes of disease always have been
sought in the realm of nature. But in man, disease has another dimension—it is mediated and modified by social activity and the cultural environment. Medical practice inevitably has been linked with social and
economic conditions, but these relations traditionally were considered
unclear. During the nineteenth century, however, medicine developed as
a social science and the principles of public health and social medicine
were clarified. These concepts center around three basic themes. First,
the health of people is a matter of direct social concern. Second, social
and economic conditions have an important effect on health and disease,
and these factors must be subject to scientific investigation. And third,
steps must be taken to promote health and combat disease, for every

member of the community is entitled to health protection, just as people are entitled to protection of liberty and property.[6]

Previous studies of nineteenth-century health reform indicate that the crusade was composed of three major groups. Physicians and zealous public servants emphasized the importance of increased medical sophistication and government interference in promoting improved public health. This was in great contrast to the colonial period, when the government assumed little responsibility for the promotion of individual or community health. Except for the quarantining of incoming ships in the face of disastrous epidemics, the local community or private philanthropy was responsible for public health.

The humanistic aspect of public health was initiated early in the nineteenth century as rapid industrial and urban development convinced local communities that they had a direct responsibility for the promotion of individual and familial health. This new perspective developed as health reformers pondered child labor in textile mills, malnutrition among factory workers, the terrible housing conditions of the urban poor, and the cholera epidemics of 1832, 1849, and 1866. By the late 1800s, medical science had become immersed in the study of the etiological factors in disease production, and health reformers began stressing the epidemiological approach in the control of disease. Armed with new knowledge and confidence, government boards of health and the science of bacteriology revolutionized American concepts of health and disease which in turn led to a group responsibility for health promotion.[7]

Christian perfectionism was another important factor in the triumph of health reform and perhaps it even overshadowed the rationalistic approach to public health. Much of the same spirit of enthusiasm that sparked the Second and Third Great Awakenings and fueled camp meetings motivated the leaders of health reform. In the more liberal theological and meliorative atmosphere of antebellum America, public-health advocates rejected the idea that disease had been sent by a wrathful God in just punishment for man's sins. Instead, disease was perceived as the failure to live in accordance with the natural laws established by a benevolent God. Health reformers such as John H. Griscom and Robert M. Hartley assumed there was an intimate relationship between the environment, health, and morality. A pious moralism and a dedicated environmentalism were the most characteristic aspects of both social welfare and health reform by the Gilded Age.[8]

Finally, romantic health reformers promoted improved public health. Inspired by such charismatic individuals as Graham, Thomson, and Alcott, the movement emphasized preventive hygiene and natural cures—hydropathy, homeopathy, animal magnetism, physical culture, and herbal medicines. The irregular healers, who often helped individuals not reached by orthodox medicine, were part of a more democratic medical tradition. Although their hygienic recommendations were rejected by the regular medical profession, the popular-health physicians belatedly were recognized for their valuable medical advice.[9]

Clearly, a concern with hygiene was an integral part of nineteenth-century reform. Indeed, the health crusade converged with many better-known reforms such as college education, abolitionism, and women's rights. A cursory glance at the men and women who promoted health reform also indicates that, like other reformers, they came from the middle-class population of the Northeast. While physicians, public servants, and Christian perfectionists promoted improved individual and community hygiene, it should now be apparent that social medicine and health reform were first inspired by the purity advocates, who began in the 1830s to advocate massive changes in contemporary hygienic practices. Their advice ironically promoted many of the economic and social habits they condemned. Graham and his followers were unintended modernizers; before the orthodox medical profession belatedly accepted the importance of health reform, the purity advocates were defending values and habits that encouraged survival and success in a competitive and commercial society. They were the first group in nineteenth-century America to develop a comprehensive solution to urban America's health problems.

American health reform was associated with a rising mid–nineteenth-century interest in personal hygiene. This impulse was stimulated by sectarian medicine, which flourished around New England from the antebellum period to the 1870s. The medical dissenters encouraged such social phenomena as the daily bath, moderation in diet and sexual behavior, exercise, athletics, and the vogue for the outdoor life. Although most of the sectarians were Grahamites, they were involved in a variety of health reforms, for as one hostile regular physician contemptuously stated, "One sort of *ism* generally begets another."[10] A good example both of the vocational diversity and the thematic unity of the movement was the New York Hygeio-Theraputic College, which opened in 1854 and three years later obtained a charter from the New York State legislature to offer a medical degree.[11] Russell T. Trall, the founder of the school, taught materia medica, female diseases, and medical jurisprudence. Dr. Lydia Fowler, a phrenologist and feminist, taught obstetrics, and her husband, Lorenzo, a phrenologist, taught mental science and phrenology. Dr. James Caleb Jackson, a hydropath and an expert on diet, was one of the curators. Although these individuals had different backgrounds and interests, they had one common characteristic—a belief in Grahamite physiology.

Perhaps the earliest health-reform institutions were the Oberlin College program, the Graham boardinghouses, and the physiology clubs. A Graham Club had been formed by eight students at Wesleyan College in Middletown, Connecticut, to promote simple vegetarian meals. In 1839, a Physiological Society was founded by thirty students at Wesleyan to discuss hygiene and purchase health books for the library.[12] At Williams College, an association of students formed a Grahamite club based "upon the principle of abstinence from tea and coffee and the use only of food the simplest in every respect." And some Lane Seminary students in Cincinnati agreed to dispense with tea and coffee and tried to survive on the principles of "Christian simplicity and economy."[13] But these physiological activities were ephemeral compared to the dietary experiment at Oberlin College.

Oberlin College had been founded in 1833 as a unique coeducational experiment[14] to develop, in the words of the prominent evangelist Charles G. Finney, "men and women for God and God's cause."[15] Women comprised almost half the student body; they mixed freely in classes, at meals, and during social occasions, but were separated during religious services. Most of the women graduated from the "Ladies Department," which had a different course of study from the male Liberal Arts program. Although the Oberlin faculty educated antebellum women traditionally, Finney and his colleagues believed that society had an obligation to train women, whose presence would be beneficial to the male students' manners and morals. But coeducation also caused problems because it promoted frequent contacts between the sexes. Finney believed that, unless the male student strictly controlled his body, it would become "so fierce and overpowering a source of temptation to the mind as inevitably to lead it to sin." According to him, diet was especially important because the wrong food led to the most "vile affections."[16] Improper diet caused a high level of excitement which induced "inflammation of the brain, and consequent insanity."[17] Oberlin attempted to solve these problems by developing a health program based on Graham's principles.

In 1839, David Cambell, a Garrisonian abolitionist who had been one of the early members of the American Anti-Slavery Society and was an editor of the *Graham Journal of Health and Longevity*, announced that Finney had asked him to become the steward of Oberlin College. When the college was founded in 1833, tea, coffee, highly seasoned meats, and rich pastries had been prohibited. Two years later, boarding fees were changed so that a meat diet was more expensive than the vegetarian fare, which cost 75 cents a week.[18] Oberlin's president, Asa Mahan, who had addressed the American Physiological Society in 1839, believed reformers should become concerned with "intemperance, licentiousness, war, [and] violations of physical law in respect to food, drink, [and] dress."[19] He had been in contact with New England health reformers and perhaps convinced Cambell to accept the new position.

After Cambell became steward, the elective meat table was discontinued and only vegetarian dishes were served in the dining hall. Around the same time, a Physiological Society was established with Mahan and Finney as the faculty sponsors, and the "Female Society for the Promotion of Health" promised not to expose their feet in cold weather or wear corsets and tight clothes. Graham, who praised Oberlin's activities to his friends, was invited to lecture there, but declined because he was physically incapacitated. When Alcott spent ten days lecturing and visiting at Oberlin in 1840, he was so excited by the regimen that he seriously considered relocating there to found one of his many journals.

The Oberlin faculty and students appeared to support the major tenets of Graham. In addition to the vegetarian fare, regular exercise outdoors was encouraged through a manual-labor program, orthodox medicine was used only in extreme cases, and clothing was not supposed to be too warm or too tight. Students slept seven hours per day on hard mattresses and they bathed regularly even though water had to be carried from the outdoor pump to the stove-heated rooms. Violators sometimes were punished severely; a faculty member was allegedly dismissed partly because he used a pepper shaker in the dining hall![20] Other members of the college community were more positive about their experiment. One student claimed that after adopting the Grahamite regimen, "my mind immediately . . . resumed its pristine vigor [and] . . . my youth . . . returned again."[21]

Eventually the dismissed professor and a group of hungry, lanky students raised a protest over the college's health program. Parents complained that their children were unhealthy and rumors of death through starvation circulated throughout Oberlin. Finally in April of 1841, Cambell was forced by administrative pressure and public opinion to resign as steward, although he remained at Oberlin on friendly terms with the college. The Graham diet became elective once again and in 1845 Finney publicly repented his former adherence to Grahamism although he continued to believe that dietary reform would minimize sexual excitement.[22] A local sectarian physician articulated the health reformers' crestfallen attitudes when he lamented that the students and faculty had "rushed with precipitous and confused haste back to their flesh pots" and "with the riotous eating of swine's flesh . . . they succeeded in arresting a necessary renovating work."[23]

Oberlin was a unique example of antebellum health reform, for it was the only college to adopt Graham's physiology. After Cambell's fall, Oberlin rechanneled its constant millenial zeal into other areas of reform such as pacifism, abolitionism, and evangelical religion. But the legacy of Graham continued; physiology remained a required but popular course, outdoor manual labor continued as an integral part of the curriculum, and students could substitute a mild vegetarian diet for the traditional meat dishes. Oberlin persisted as a novel experiment in student health and romantic reform, but Cambell's orthodox Grahamism was considered too extreme by many students and the surrounding community.

At the same time, the romantics attempted to extend their influence by establishing two Graham boardinghouses in the Northeast. For three years Cambell managed one in Boston, but the more famous New York City house was founded in 1833. A private home was renovated into a hostel, and the daily routine revolved around a strict schedule of meals, exercise, and sleep. During the summer, guests awakened at 4:00 A.M. to bathe and exercise before breakfast. The curfew was 10:00 P.M., when the lights went out and all the boarders were supposed to be indoors. Tea, coffee, chocolate, liquor, and tobacco were prohibited, and everyone was encouraged to drink large amounts of filtered rainwater. Breakfast consisted mostly of organic, unsifted bread which had been cooked at least twelve hours before the meal. At dinner, the boarders could eat some meat but they were expected to consume moderate quantities of bread and vegetables. Meat, fish, and fruit were prohibited at supper; guests chose plain bread, milk, oatmeal, or barley gruel for their last meal of the day. When the boarders were not eating or working, they were encouraged to exercise outdoors, preferably by walking or horseback riding, and wash regularly with cold water.[24] This health regimen, according to Graham, increased the "buoyancy and elasticity" of the spirits and thus produced a "saluatory acceleration of the vital functions."[25]

Initially the Graham boardinghouse was patronized by temperance advocates and other reformers. Although the guests appeared to enjoy the regimen, one wit described the boarders as "lean-visaged cadaverous disciples" who sat around the dining table with "their looks lit up with a certain cannibal spirit," hoping to eat some healthy, invigorating food.[26] The boardinghouse's vegetarian diet and exercise program were not unusual because physiological reformers initiated similar regimens throughout the nineteenth century. The guest list, however, provides some important insights into antebellum reform. According to William S. Tyler, a visitor,

The Boarders in this establishment are not only Grahamites, but

Garrisonites—not only reformers in diet, but radicalists in Politics. Such a knot of Abolitionists I never before fell in with. Slavery, Colonization, &c. constitute the unvarying monotonous theme of their conversations except that they give place to an occasional comment upon their peculiar style of living. Arthur Tappen, [William] Goddell, & [C. W.] Dennison are the most prominent characters. . . . Garrison & [Joshua] Leavitt are sometimes at the Graham house.[27]

As Ronald Walters has cogently argued, the abolitionists, like most antebellum reformers, believed that the loss of moral and physical control and the consequent growth of licentiousness were major threats to American civilization. Slavery appeared the worst offender. The abolitionists often described the South in erotic terms because slavery marked the outer limits of disorder, debauchery, and social anarchy.[28] Abolitionists were attracted to Grahamism because it represented the fusion of bodily and social control. Henry B. Stanton and Lewis Tappen attended the Grahamite American Health Convention in 1839, and the Welds, Sarah Grimké, William Goodell, LaRoy Sunderland, Amasa Walker, William Lloyd Garrison, and Thomas Wentworth Higginson fervently believed in the physiological principles of moderation in diet and sexual behavior, gymnastic exercise, and outdoor culture.[29]

The abolitionists were attracted to Grahamism not just because they wanted to improve the quality of life, but also because they wanted to control man's sexual appetite. Theodore Weld wrote his fiancée Angelina Grimké in 1838 that "it will be a relief to you to know that I have acquired *perfect self control,* so far as any *expression* or *appearance* of deep feeling is visable to others."[30] Higginson preached that "a vigorous life of the senses [exercise] not only does not tend to sensuality in the objectionable sense, but it helps to avert it."[31] And William Goodell lectured at the American Health Convention that no abolitionist efforts would "ever raise human beings, of any complexion to the true dignity of freeman, so long as they permit themselves to be the slaves of their own appetites, the panders of their own lusts, the forgers of their own fetters."[32] Dietary reform, like the antislavery crusade, focused on man's erotic nature in order to overcome it. Not surprisingly, after the Civil War and Reconstruction, former abolitionists were attracted to the social-purity alliance. They wanted to abolish prostitution, eradicate the brothel, and suppress the white-slave traffic.[33] This alliance had been forged during the antebellum period; the Oberlin College program and the Graham boardinghouse in New York City illustrate the deeper currents of antebellum reform that health reform tapped.

While the reformers were promoting better health in their college organizations and boardinghouses, they also were founding societies to reach a broader public. Before Cambell moved to Oberlin College he had been an officer of the first physiological organization in the world, the American Physiological Society. When Graham lectured in Boston during the winter of 1835 and 1836 one of his most enthusiastic followers was John Benson, a wealthy merchant who had been enslaved to tea, coffee, rum, chewing tobacco, and large quantities of meat. Since he also suffered from rheumatism, gout, dyspepsia, and vertigo, he adopted the Graham regimen with impressive results. On December 23, 1836, he chaired a meeting of Graham supporters at which five complimentary resolutions were passed. An organizational meeting was held on February 11, 1837, and Alcott presented a preamble and constitution of the American Physiological Society, which was signed by 124 men and 39 women. He was elected president and Cambell was made the corresponding secretary.[34]

During its three-year existence, the society conducted a variety of health-reform activities. The organization's members were encouraged to subscribe to Cambell's new publication, *The Graham Journal of Health and Longevity,* which never attained a large circulation, or Alcott's more popular *Journal of Health.* Lectures were delivered on Graham's philosophy at the monthly and annual meetings, and case studies were published demonstrating the wonders of a vegetarian diet. To promote a better knowledge of physiology the organization raised fifty dollars to purchase a health library which could lend books to subscribers for a week. And in 1838 the society attempted to broaden its support by sponsoring a series of lectures at Amory Hall in Boston where physicians discussed Grahamite physiology and where Graham delivered two sets of well-attended lectures on diet and the Biblical attitude toward wine and flesh. In addition, in May of 1838 the society issued a call for a physiological conference which later developed into the American Health Convention. It met in Boston and New York in 1838 and 1839 to pass resolutions and hear testimonials about Graham's diet.[35]

The third annual meeting of the American Physiological Society was the final one. After many members had written testimonials and passed repetitious resolutions, there was nothing to do. Also, the nation was still recovering from the depression of 1837 and many benevolent enterprises had difficulty raising funds. This coincided with ferment in the antislavery crusade, and some reformers might have moved in that direction. As a result of all these factors, the society's lectures drew progressively smaller audiences, and eventually members forgot to pay their dues or renew their subscriptions to the *Graham Journal of Health and Longevity.* When Graham retired to Northampton and drastically cut down his lecture schedule, the organization lost its *raison d'être* and expired.[36]

Considering the backgrounds of the American Physiological Society's members, the organization should not have disintegrated. According to Alcott,

> Most of these individuals were more or less feeble, and a very large proportion of them were actually suffering from chronic disease when they became members. . . . Not a few joined it, indeed, as a last resort, after having tried everything else. . . .
> Nearly all . . . of the members of this society, as well as most of their families, abstain from animal food, and have done so ever since they joined the society. Some of them even adopted the vegetable system more than two years ago.[37]

The fate of the Graham experiments at antebellum colleges, boarding-houses, and the American Physiological Society illustrates the limits of an undiluted Grahamite physiology. Although these institutions were part of a diverse public-health movement, they had a limited impact and few people made long-term commitments to them. Evidently a pure Graham-ite regimen was too spartan for most Americans.

There were a number of reasons for the failure of orthodox Graham-ism. One was Graham's personality and activities. Many supporters con-sidered him conceited, boring, and insufferably verbose. They supported his philosophy while they condemned his personality, platform style, and literary work. For example, Graham's success in New England was marred by continual and probably unnecessary clashes with the regular medical profession. The first major dispute was precipitated when Dr. Luther V. Bell was awarded the prestigious Boylston Prize in 1835 for his study of diet. Although he conceded that most people ingested too much meat, Bell believed "a diet of both animal and vegetable food is adapted to the condition of the New England laborer" and consequently "no radical change" in diet was needed.[38] Graham disagreed, of course, and argued that a vegetarian diet would enable someone to work "ten or twenty years longer" than a "flesh eater." But then Graham attacked Bell's character and accused him of propagating "errors whose only authority is . . . ignorance and depravity." If Bell had presented the facts "instead of sneer and sarcasm," concluded Graham, his book would have been "as good as can reasonably be expected from a young physician."[39] Finally, after interminable charges and countercharges, the editor of the *Boston Medi-cal and Surgical Journal* refused to accept any more contributions on the subject and regretted that so little of the arguments had been devoted to the efficacy of certain diets.[40] Graham often was intemperate or abusive in his discussions, and this repelled some people from the health crusade.

Second, when Graham had an opportunity to advance his philosophy, he always reduced his regimen to a proper diet. After the early 1830s, Graham ceased writing and lecturing on sexuality, and became known as the philosopher of bran bread. Of course, he considered this change to be an evolutionary development arising from his earlier discoveries; a proper diet supposedly moderated sexual desire and sexual activity. But Graham never made the relationship between diet and sexuality clear in his later lectures and books. Perhaps he stopped discussing sexuality because of adverse public criticism. One newspaper asserted that people had walked out of Graham's lectures, and added that "a greater humbug or a more disgusting writer never lived."[41] When he tried to repeat a course of lectures at Amory Hall, there was "great excitement . . . but so great was the tumult made by persons adverse to Graham . . . that the object was defeated." Sometimes he was threatened for attempting to advocate his theories, and a newspaper summarized hostile opinion by rhetorically asking Graham whether his lectures could "be *not* indecent."[42] Once the Grahamites were even attacked. In the winter of 1837 a violent mob of bakers surrounded Amory Hall in Boston where Graham was lecturing on vegetarianism. When the owner of the Marlborough Hotel offered Graham his dining room to lecture soon after the Amory Hall incident, loyal supporters barricaded the lower story and a shovel brigade manned the roof with slacked lime. When another mob of bakers refused to disperse, they were pelted and the lecture continued without interruption.[43] These hostile comments and activities made Graham more aloof, suspicious, and hypersensitive, and forced him and his supporters to discuss sexuality in Aesopian language. Grahamism became associated with the unattractive, monomaniac personality of its founder, and it lost adherents who once were sympathetic to its doctrines. Alcott, antebellum America's most prominent advice writer and a believer in Graham, was an excellent example of Graham's inability to keep his supporters committed and loyal.

Alcott, unlike Graham, became concerned about public health and personal hygiene early in his life. After becoming a Connecticut schoolteacher, he gained a regional reputation for such innovations as more comfortable school benches, improved ventilation and heating, changes in the curriculum, and educational reforms such as the introduction of dancing as a school exercise. Alcott had suffered from poor health since childhood, and so he decided to leave the teaching profession and study medicine. He spent two years with a local physician while he taught school, and after one year of residence, Alcott obtained a diploma from Yale College in 1826.

After graduation, Alcott attempted to operate a model school, but a recurrence of pulmonary disease forced him to make medicine his major vocation. He alienated his Connecticut patients by calling attention to the unsanitary conditions in their homes and by insisting on frequent bathing, exercise, and fresh air. Paradoxically, Alcott's experience and academic studies convinced him that popular education could correct most social abuses; he now was reay to codify his health principles and present them to a broader public.[44]

In May of 1830, Alcott "abandoned all drinks but water," abstained "from animal food, and from all fermented, narcotic, and alcoholic drinks,"[45] and began to write a continuous stream of articles, best-selling books, tracts, and letters about personal health, anatomy, physiology, and diet. By the mid-1830s, Alcott was famous and well established in his career. He firmly believed that with an adequate preparation in anatomy and physiology, correct living would follow automatically. To accomplish this goal, Alcott recommended a complete vegetarian diet with unleavened, coarse-milled whole grain as the main food source and promoted strict personal hygiene while he condemned liquor, spices, butter, and any condiments.[46]

When Graham lectured in Boston during the winter of 1835, he discovered that Alcott already was championing his doctrines. Although he believed that Graham's ideas were not wholly original and were only a partial answer to the problem of proper physiology, he supported his fellow health reformer because their philosophies were similar.[47] Alcott admitted that he owed many of his concepts to a " 'Lecture to Young Men' lately published in Providence" and elaborated dietetic ideas that clearly were patterned after Grahamite physiology.[48]

Alcott's preoccupation with Graham's vegetarianism provoked harsh criticism. One newspaper condemned him by arguing that total abstinence from meat was "more than any man of sound mind will contend."[49] Another correspondent wondered "why was not the Yankee race extinct?"[50] if meat was so unhealthy. What evidence could Alcott offer except

> his own case, and . . . the cases of half-a-dozen gaunt, wry-faced, ghostly looking invalids, who . . . are so many walking proofs—(those that are able to walk)—of his system . . . Dr. Alcott . . . has been no more successful than the advocates of other absurd opinions.[51]

Alcott's reply indicated that he was uneasy over his relationship with Graham. He condemned the attempt "to throw dust in everybody's eyes by the perpetual cry of 'bran bread' " and denied that he "joined Mr. Graham in applauding the virtues of abstinence and starvation."[52] Significantly, Bostonians began to criticize Alcott when he became an open supporter of Graham. But Alcott also was chagrined at the treatment he was receiving from Graham's supporters, for he admitted that "my great sin in this region is that I will not join Mr. G."[53] Alcott concluded that vegetarianism was just one aspect of a broad hygienic program. While he continued to support Graham's ideas of diet and sexual behavior, Alcott expanded his philosophy to include personal cleanliness, outdoor exercise, sound sleep, a positive mental attitude, and preventive medicine. These concepts were an extension of his earlier interest in school architecture and student health and could be defended without referring to Graham.[54]

Horace Mann, an avid phrenologist and an admirer of Graham who once stated that a dyspeptic stomach was "an abomination in the sight of God,"[55] was so impressed with Alcott's ideas that he appended special supplements to his first, sixth, and eleventh annual reports to the Massachusetts Board of Education on the need for hygienic instruction among teachers and students and the necessity for a proper physical environment in the classroom. After 1850, the Massachusetts General Court responded to Mann's reports by requiring the teaching of physiology and hygiene in all public schools.[56] While Mann was responsible for these hygienic recommendations, he openly acknowledged his debt to Alcott for his physiological principles. Alcott successfully promoted health reforms because he broadened and deepened Graham's principles and made them acceptable to a wider audience.

When Graham retired in 1838 amid bitter controversy, his supporters and opponents realized that his personality and reputation were restricting the scope of the public-health movement. Even his disciples admitted that "reform is too often . . . a mere discontinuing the use of flesh meat and adopting . . . bran bread and water."[57] Graham's excessive reliance on bran bread was compounded by a similar obsession with the "solitary vice." By attempting to create a monistic health movement based principally on diet and a masturbation phobia, Graham endangered the more comprehensive ideal of promoting health reform through personal hygiene. This is why the Graham college experiments, boardinghouses, and the American Physiological Society failed—they were considered too simplistic and extreme. Alcott had discovered the solution that would be imitated by successful health reformers; he accepted Graham's basic principles but subsumed them into a less controversial and broader program.

Romantic health reform allied itself with phrenology, which became popular in America because it combined European scientific principles with a concern for health and morality. Phrenology had been created in the early nineteenth century by two Austrian physicians, Franz Joseph Gall and Johan Casper Spurzheim, and it became popular in America through Spurzheim's lectures and the efforts of Scotland's George Combe. Phrenologists believed mental phenomena had natural causes that could be determined by studying the anatomical and physiological characteristics of the skull, which was divided into thirty-seven personality traits in localized areas of the brain. According to their principles, the brain was related intimately to the body, and therefore physical health was essential to happiness and proper morality.[58] There was a curious mixture of hereditarianism and perfectionism in phrenology which made it attractive to romantic health reformers. Phrenologists believed that characteristics were inherited, including the moral ones rooted in the "organs" of the brain. But they also argued that these characteristics, which were reflected in the shape of the skull, could be improved by modifying one's environment, thinking, or behavior. When the phrenologists discussed education and health reform, they usually meant physical education and physiology. For example, at one of George Combe's American lectures, he stated that

> again, phrenology shows us that, to improve the human mind, we must begin by improving the condition of the brain; and . . . to attain success in this object . . . teaching must be conducted in harmony with the laws of physiology.[59]

To dramatize his principles, the windows were opened in the middle of the lecture, and the skeptics were converted when they found the supposed noxious night air refreshing. Spurzheim, Combe, and other phrenologists believed that many Americans were suffering from a general debility due to incorrect personal hygiene and dietary habits.

Although the phrenological analysis of physiological processes was different from Graham's explanations, many phrenologists believed that the two systems were compatible and thus they combined them enthusiastically. Graham devoted about seventy pages of his *Lectures on the Science of Human Life* to a discussion of phrenology, and concluded that he was "strongly disposed" to favor the principles of Gall despite his neglect of the human nervous system. Graham used Spurzheim to prove that as the alimentary desires of the body increased, the selfish and evil passions of man predominated.[60]

While Combe and other European phrenologists appealed for more physical exercise, the Americans Orson and Lorenzo Fowler popularized this branch of phrenology by melding it with Grahamite dietary and sexual principles. After the Fowlers arrived in New York City from Amherst in 1835, they established an office in lower Manhattan that rapidly became a combination lecture-booking bureau, publishing house, and phrenological museum. They published hundreds of inexpensive books and manuals on temperance, tobacco, vegetarianism, physiology, anatomy, agriculture, horticulture, architecture, and works by Walt Whitman, Andrew Jackson Davis, Robert Dale Owen, and Ralph Waldo Emerson. The Fowlers were the first practical phrenologists who parlayed their promotional schemes into a successful and influential enterprise. Their *American Phrenological Journal,* which was founded in 1837, attained a circulation of 50,000 by 1847, which was one of the largest monthly distributions in the country.[61]

The Fowlers believed that Americans should "look well to the welfare of your *bodies* if you would promote the welfare of your minds."[62] Orson, who had encountered Grahamism as a student at Amherst, was convinced that phrenology and Graham's principles reinforced each other and so he devoted an entire section of the *Journal* to physiology and lectured on the subject many times. Graham spoke at the Fowlers' and Wells's auditorium in New York City, and the *Journal* strongly recommended Graham's unsifted bread, which Orson lived on "almost exclusively"[63] as well as Graham's vegetarian plan, personal hygiene, and concepts of proper clothing.[64] The Fowlers' defense of Graham extended beyond the *Journal* and physiology lectures; most of their practical books on health and diet were phrenological glosses of Graham's *Lectures on the Science of Human Life.* For example, in Orson's *Physiology, Animal and Mental* (1847), he used Graham's vitalism and concepts of the nervous system to discuss anatomy, physiology, temperance, the correct preparation of Graham bread, and the benefits of a vegetarian diet. Fowler based his dietary principles on the concept that meat and other stimulants inflamed the lower area of the brain which controlled physical drives and emotions.[65] Graham had argued exactly the same point ten years before Fowler:

> It is one of the most important doctrines of phrenology, that the greater the proportionate width of the head between the head and the back of the ears . . . the more the animal propensities will predominate . . . and that flesh meat is decidedly more stimulating and heating than proper vegetable food, and increases . . . the animal instincts and propensities.[66]

The Fowlers also analyzed sexuality from a Grahamite perspective. Lorenzo's *The Principles of Phrenology and Physiology* (1842) quoted approvingly the banner of a women's group in Rochester, New York: "*Total abstinence from all licentiousness and all that intoxicates, or no husbands.*"[67] According to Lorenzo, America was populated by invalids; this deplorable condition was caused by an improper diet and other violations of physical laws which in turn ruined courtship and marriage.

Amativeness, which was responsible for the attraction between the sexes, was excited and perverted by the "indulgence of the appetite in the too free use of stimulating food and drink."[68] He recommended a strict vegetarian diet as the cure for all social and sexual problems, for this regimen would destroy the passionate and animalistic propensities in people and encourage natural sexual moderation.

Orson was even more explicit in his debt to Graham's sexual concepts. In *Amativeness* (1846), he based his sexual principles on Graham's *Lecture to Young Men*.[69] Throughout his book, Orson discussed the prevalence of sensuality throughout America, the effects of masturbation, promiscuous indulgence, and marital excesses, and bolstered his opinions by quoting Samuel Woodward, Mary Gove Nichols, and Alcott. Predictably, Fowler recommended total abstinence from tea, coffee, tobacco, condiments, meat, and all rich food, for they caused "an irritated, craving state of the nervous system, which aggravates desire . . . by inflaming the nervous system, and of course the base of the brain." Oatmeal, milk with unsweetened fruit, and "coarse or Graham bread" would obviate any inflamations and allow the body to heal naturally.[70] This was a typical phrenological and Grahamite analysis: alimentiveness and amativeness, or food and sex, were located in the primitive part of the brain and could be excited and perverted by too intensive food. A vegetarian diet would restore natural health and allow a person's hunger and sexuality to operate normally, or seldom. The popular books from the Fowlers and Wells publishing company dominated the field of physiology and promoted Graham's system until the late 1800s.

Through public lectures, the activities of the local phrenological societies, books, and journals, the new science achieved wide public notice in mid–nineteenth-century America. Phrenology was extrapolated rapidly from the cautious and limited anatomical deductions of Spurzheim and Gall to an encyclopedic system of social philosophy that had recommendations for every facet of human life. In Europe, phrenology was considered a mental science which had little relationship to physiology or personal hygiene. Significantly, the phrenologists in America superimposed Graham's principles onto their science, and American phrenology became oriented toward the physiological. Graham recognized the affinities between his principles and phrenology, for both philosophies claimed to be scientific, based on experiment and direct observation, and made broad deductions from their discoveries. The health reformers and American phrenologists reversed European phrenology's hierarchy of the importance of the mental faculties and, instead, argued that the physiological condition of the body determined the effectiveness of the mental operations. Both Graham and American phrenology mutually reinforced each other, and after Graham's orthodox principles were discredited in the late 1830s, the phrenologists appropriated them in the cause of mental science.

Phrenology played a similar role to physiology. Both movements tried to order life and make intelligible and predictable relations between strangers. Allan S. Horlick has discovered that phrenology was especially attractive to businessmen and community leaders because it provided an allegedly objective, scientific system for evaluating job applicants and individuals migrating from rural areas to cities who lacked job credentials or recommendations.[71] Phrenology and health reform both wanted to create stable relationships in a seemingly chaotic commercial environment, and so not surprisingly the two reforms combined and developed together.

The Fowlers also became involved in hydropathy, or the water-cure movement, which most clearly grafted European physiological concepts with Graham's philosophy. The hydropathic system developed as a rival to the homeopathic method and emphasized the free administration of two powerful therapeutic agents, cold water taken internally and externally, and skin perspiration. Although water always has been used as a medical agent, the nineteenth-century interest in hydropathy was the creation of a Silesian peasant, Vincenz Priessnitz.[72] Americans were sympathetic to his principles, for unlike many Europeans, Americans always had taken water with their meals and recognized the curative powers of mineral and natural springs. By the 1830s, sympathetic articles on hydropathy began appearing in American medical journals and from 1843 to 1900, 213 separate water-cure institutions were established through America, especially in New York, Pennsylvania, and Massachusetts.[73] Although there were different forms of treatment, the wet sheet became the most common technique. A sheet of cotton or linen dipped in cold water was spread on several thick woolen blankets. A patient would be encased in this cocoon from twenty-five minutes to several hours, and then he was unswathed and took a cold bath. The most popular kind of bath was the sitz bath, which used water just deep enough to cover the abdomen.

There were clear parallels between hydropathy and physiology. First, hydropathy was a health cure that avoided heroic medicine and emphasized the superior healing art of nature. Joel Shew, an influential hydropathic doctor and a devoted follower of Graham, explained that hydropathy,

when taken with all its adjuncts, is an *artificial* primitive condition to which the sick man *temporarily* submits himself for a temporary purpose, viz., that of giving nature, assisted by art, a fair opportunity of healing his diseases.[75]

Second, according to the Priessnitzian method, a strict dietary regimen was an integral part of the cure. The Austrian peasant believed that the intake of stimulating food at high temperatures was injurious, and so only cold foods and water were permitted. The major part of a patient's diet was fresh cold water, and believers consumed from five to forty glasses in twenty-four hours. Water was supposed to cleanse and regularize the system and help shed any excess weight.[75]

And third, hydropathic patients were expected to exercise vigorously. Walking in the open air was the most common exercise, but many establishments encouraged gymnastics, chopping wood, dancing, and bowling, especially after drinking water and cold baths. Since most of the water cures were located in attractive rural areas or in the mountains, they became popular centers for the sickly or for people who wanted an energetic vacation.[77]

Like phrenology, as hydropathy became accepted in antebellum America, it was combined with an established Grahamite regimen. Both the Priessnitzian water cure method and health reform were romantic, anti-urban, oriented toward natural cures and natural food, and emphasized strict personal hygiene. The American water-cure establishments became the lineal descendants of the defunct Graham boardinghouses and dining halls; the personnel and the health practices often were exactly the same. In the spring of 1845, David Cambell became the steward and manager of Joel Shew's water cure at New Lebanon Springs, New York.[78] Elsewhere, abolitionists abandoned the Graham boardinghouses and became involved with hydropathy. David Ruggles, an infirm runaway slave who had become an abolitionist lecturer, helped operate the Round Hill Water-Cure in Northampton.[79] And the country's most famous water cure, at Dansville, New York, was owned and managed by James Caleb Jackson, the former secretary of the American Anti-Slavery Society and a former coeditor with Nathaniel P. Rogers of the *National Anti-Slavery Standard.*[80]

The activities of the water cures indicated their affinity with earlier Grahamite institutions. Trall's establishment in lower Manhattan contained sleeping, dining, bath facilities, and a gymnasium for its boarders, who were expected to obey a strict diet and health regimen. Vegetarian meals were served at prescribed hours and the house was closed at 10:00 P.M. nightly. Alcohol, tobacco, drug medicines, and "similar trash" were prohibited and guests were cautioned not to lounge on the sofas or sit in "uncouth or ridiculous attitudes." By the early 1860s, Trall was manufacturing "all kinds of farinaceous preparations" and was selling Graham flour to the public.[81]

Graham's principles provided the theoretical underpinning for the water-cure establishments. Although the hydropaths discussed Priessnitz and his methods in reverential terms, they turned to Graham when they analyzed diet and sexuality. Trall believed that the two phrenological propensities which people most abused were alimentiveness and amativeness. The misuse of alimentiveness produced indigestion and dyspepsia while perverted amativeness, which often was caused by youthful masturbation, induced nervous debility. Since he believed that "vitality *always* results from *nutrition,* and *never* from *stimulation,*" he recommended vegetarianism with a heavy dose of Graham bread as the way to modify an overstimulating diet and too intensive sexual desires and activities[82]:

> I regard dietetic errors as among the chief predisposing causes [of nervous debility]. The early use of flesh-food, salted provisions, condiments, and stimulating . . . beverages, as tea or coffee, certainly conduces to an inflammatory state of the whole system, and a precocious and preternatural excitement of the genital organs.[83]

Shew and Jackson also relied on Graham for their theoretical formulations. Shew appended a nineteen-page appendix to his major work on the water cure asserting that Graham's "teachings take in the whole range of the great and important subject of Human Life," and quoted him profusely to prove that vegetarianism was necessary to good health.[84] Jackson, like Trall, echoed Graham when he discussed food and sex:

> Of all the organs in our physical structure, no two sustain . . . a more vital purpose than the stomach and genitals. . . . No man, whose stomach is impaired, can have health, and no man, whose stomach is enfeebled, can possibly propagate and reproduce his kind, and have healthy offspring. . . . [G]enerally speaking, genital debility induces dyspepsia, [and] dyspepsia sometimes induces genital debility.[85]

Although most of the water-cure establishments were weakened or destroyed by the depression of 1857, the Civil War, and more restrictive medical standards, education, and licensing, the sectarians transmitted their philosophy to other health advocates who combined romantic health attitudes with the latest effective medical discoveries. Jackson's water cure in Dansville, which contained a large four-story main house and a variety of recreational and educational facilities, attracted about one hundred patients at one time after it opened in 1859. Like Trall, Jackson manufactured and marketed a variety of Grahamite health foods including a new product called Granula, which was a mixture of water and unsifted flour baked into thin sheets, ground into small pieces, and baked again. Unfortunately for Jackson, this pioneering cold breakfast cereal was unacceptable to the American palate.[86]

Granula and Jackson's water cure may have lapsed into obscurity except for the Seventh-Day Adventists, who believed that health reform was an important adjunct to their message setting forth the pressing need for the restoration of biblical truths and God's commandments. They had adopted this philosophy after June 6, 1863, when the leader of the Adventists, Ellen G. White, had a vision that converted her followers to health reform:

> I saw that it was a sacred duty to attend to our health and arouse others to their duty . . . to come out against intemperance of every kind—intemperance in working, in eating, in drinking, in drugging—and then point them to God's great medicine: water.[87]

In 1865 the Adventists visited Jackson's water cure to study his philosophy and methods and then they established a health-reform institute in Battle Creek, Michigan. Around 1878 the Battle Creek Sanitarium began manufacturing Granula under the supervision of a young hydropathic and sectarian physician named John Harvey Kellogg, who had studied with Trall.

Trall had trained two Adventists for the Western Health Reform Institute in Battle Creek. In May of 1868 he was invited there and gave several lectures. Attendance was high, interest was keen, and much to Trall's surprise, hundreds of women appeared in their bloomer outfits. He made such an impression that Trall was asked to become a regular contributor to the Adventists' new journal, the *Health Reformer*.[88] Kellogg also was first trained at Trall's Hygeio-Therapeutic College during the winter of 1872.[89] After completing his medical training at Bellvue Hospital, he returned to Battle Creek and turned the sanitarium into a world-famous health institution while he wrote voluminously about sex, diet, and health and experimented with different vegetarian recipes.

Kellogg's concepts of health came from Trall and Graham. Like his mentors, Kellogg believed that the use of the sexual organs produced a nervous shock to the entire system. Even those who engaged in sexual intercourse for reproductive purposes had to limit their activities or else insanity would result.[90] Kellogg constructed a physiological regimen to avoid sexual reveries and activities that combined Graham's vegetarianism with hydropathy. Healthy individuals were advised to drink about eight glasses of natural water a day, take cold enemas and hot sitz baths, wear a wet girdle to bed, and avoid stimulating foods such as alcohol, tobacco, tea, coffee, and spices.[91] Kellogg's advocacy of extreme self-denial was related to his vision of the city, the center of luxury, corruption, and sexual indulgence. His books and sanitarium were designed to counteract urban civilization by re-creating rural life and habits, which were synonymous with natural health and sexual restraint.

Kellogg's influence spread far beyond Battle Creek. In 1885 the Woman's Christian Temperance Union established a department of social purity which was headed by Kellogg and his wife. The WCTU, the most effective organization in the post–Civil War purity reform movement, used the Kelloggs to attack prostitution, sexual abuse, and public indecency. And on April 14, 1896, the United States government granted Kellogg a patent for the manufacture of a flaked cereal food, and the cornflakes boom commenced a few years later. By 1915, Kellogg had expanded his health activities and coauthored school textbooks on physiology which emphasized asceticism and chastity. Along with his sanitarium, a more modern and epic version of a Graham boardinghouse, Kellogg institutionalized and popularized the dietary and sexual principles which Graham first articulated in the 1830s.[92]

Perhaps even more important than health reform's influence on Kellogg and the Adventists was their work with women, who were one of the primary constituencies of the hydropaths and the female physiologists. The sectarians believed the American woman's new domestic situation required a knowledge of health and hygiene, and so male and female health reformers took a strong interest in marriage, childbearing and childrearing, family diet, and health. At its second annual meeting, The American Physiological Society recognized women's central role in health reform when they

> *Resolved*, that woman, in the character of wife and mother, is only second to the Deity in the influence which she exerts on the physical, the intellectual and moral interests of the human race, and that her education should be adapted to qualify her in the highest degree to cherish those interests in the wisest and best manner.[93]

Other reformers voiced similar sentiments. Mary Gove Nichols wanted "to teach mothers how to cure their own diseases, and those of their children; and to increase health, purity, and happiness in the family and the home."[94] Alcott believed that the improvement of female health could lead to social regeneration: "If all wives loved and delighted in their homes as Solomon would have them, few husbands would go down to a premature grave through the avenues of intemperance and lust."[95] And

Jackson summarized the sectarians' great hopes for women when he said that "God punishes as well as rewards mankind *through woman*."[96]

Women's changing roles in antebellum America led them to participate actively in health-reform organizations. Until the early nineteenth century, most women experienced the family, home, and work as an organic, stable structure. But as new concepts of childhood and childrearing developed and as the home ceased to be a productive economic unit, masculine and feminine spheres became more separated. Middle-class urban women became primarily wives and mothers, and the prototype of the modern family—small, nuclear, emotionally intense, a haven from a hostile environment, and supervised by a woman—appeared as the distinguishing characteristic of the middle-class family. Although women often were described as weak, sickly, unintellectual, and dependent, they also were exalted and invested with power and responsibility within their sphere.[97] The health reformers rejected the first characterization and supported the second, and thus they helped women to adjust to a more industrial and urban world by giving them information, responsibility, and a sense of self-worth.

As Regina Markell Morantz has perceptively suggested, the health reformers concentrated on good female health, personal hygiene, and sexual mores.[98] Since women had important roles to play in their families and society, only a healthy woman could bear such responsibility. Impractical clothing immobilized women and ruined their anatomies and health. Reformers considered dress reform a moral imperative,[99] and one female health reformer thundered that

> woman was neither made a toy nor a slave . . . and as such devolves upon her very many important duties and obligations which cannot be met so long as she is the puny, sickly, aching, dying creature that we find her to be. . . . [S]he must throw off the shackles that have hitherto bound both body and mind.[100]

Because procreation was an important familial function, health reformers concerned themselves with conception, gestation, and parturition. They viewed childbirth as a natural process and severely criticized the regular medical profession for hiding the medical facts about procreation from women and for treating them as invalids. Since most of the purity advocates believed in the inheritance of acquired characteristics, they wanted pregnant women to get exercise, fresh air, and a proper diet so that their children would be healthy.[101]

While the health reformers exalted marriage and parenthood, they believed couples should limit their offspring; romantics were the first group in America publicly to advocate birth control (in the form of abstinence).

Because excessive childbearing endangered female health while it made women less able to care adequately for their children, the health reformers linked sexual restraint to family limitation.[102] This attitude was typified by Henry Clarke Wright, who believed that since the object of sexual intercourse was the *"perpetuation and perfection of the race,"*[103] couples should have intercourse rarely unless they were willing to have children.

Graham articulated the relationship between the movement he inspired and women by relating the two groups to food:

> I say again, there must be a judgment, an experience, a skill, a care, a vigilance, which can only spring from the sincere affections of a devoted wife and mother, who accurately perceived and duly appreciates the importance of these things [food].[104]

Ironically, Graham idealized a mother he never possessed. A similar irony characterized the health reform movement, for while they tried to adjust female roles to coincide with traditional values, they unwittingly helped erode the veracity of the ancient pieties by giving women more active control over their lives, their bodies, and their society. The romantic reformers rejected the traditional attitude that disease was primarily a spiritual dilemma which involved introspection and fatalism. They argued that poor health violated religious and natural laws and that people had a moral obligation to be healthy. The purity advocates promoted the assumption that both women and men had responsibility for their own health, the health of their families, and the health of American society.

The emergence of romantic health reform as a vigorous crusade was part of the modernization process. Health reformers insisted upon the efficacy of individual action and zealously believed that people could improve themselves by manipulating the environment and by controlling their personal health, diets, and sexual behavior. As Mary Gove Nichols stated, "Many seem to have no idea that there are established laws with respect to life and death, and that the transgression of these laws is followed by disease."[105]

Health reform promoted autonomy. Mastery of diet, health, and sexual behavior meant mastery over one's self and one's destiny. Like evangelical Protestantism and most nineteenth-century reforms, a Graham regimen instilled discipline and a willingness to forego gratification, which helped lead to success in an increasingly commercial and urban environment.

On the surface it appears that Grahamism and romantic health reform ought to have combined with the public-health movement so well studied by recent historians. That was not the case. The public-health crusade took little notice of the purity advocates and so these different health reformers functioned without reciprocal influence. This bifurcation had a major impact on the nature of modern American public-health activities.

During the last half of the nineteenth century, American physicians had different definitions of disease, divergent therapeutic procedures, and various kinds of training. Challenges to the status of orthodox physicians, the largest group of doctors, were intensified by the successful practices of sectarian physicians, the public recognition of varied medical theories and techniques, and the growing availability and acceptance of hospitals, which were beginning to attract middle-class patients who formerly shunned them because hospitals had been associated with charity cases. Both doctors and the public were concerned about the lack of unanimity among American physicians.

Faced with an obligation to justify and promote orthodox medicine, regular physicians in the public-health movement used their growing authority and power to exclude "amateurs" and defined public health in a narrow, orthodox fashion that minimized the importance of environment in favor of the identification and treatment of major diseases. No longer a loose association of humanitarian individuals who wanted to alleviate all conditions which promoted poor health, the late–nineteenth-century public-health movement was distinguished by its professional outlook. Trained specialists in the American Public Health Association and the local boards of health redefined disease in a privitized, bioscientific manner. Orthodox physicians defended the concept, which was shared by many of their patients, that regulations based on considerations of general welfare might vitiate accepted ideas of responsibility and lower their professional status.[106]

By the early 1900s, discussions of the social and environmental influences on disease were becoming a dim memory. For example, Charles V. Chapin, a pioneer health officer for the Providence (Rhode Island) Board of Health and later a prominent spokesman for public-health experts within the American Medical Association, believed that physicians should conform to acceptable scientific methods and theories and sharply distinguish medicine from humanitarianism or benevolence. Health departments should not assume responsibility for the control of the environment, nor "should [they] work for free transfers, cheaper commutation tickets, lower prices for coal, less shoddy in clothing, or more rubber in rubbers—all good things in their way and tending toward comfort and health."[107] Public health had been defined in such a way as to place major health problems beyond the responsibility of orthodox medicine. The regular medical profession's concept of public health ironically led to the notion that good health was a private, individual responsibility best handled by physicians and their patients. Graham and the health reformers, in contrast, lived in an undifferentiated universe where the mind, body, and society all interacted and influenced each other. This romantic conception, which was private and individualistic in theory, evinced a greater concern for public health because of its emphasis on the environment.

Romantic health-reform principles, nevertheless, achieved a wide hearing through Graham-inspired journals and books, advice manuals, lectures, and the phrenology and hydropathy movements. Graham's *Lecture to Young Men* went through fifteen editions in ten years, Alcott's *Young Man's Guide* reached its twenty-first edition by 1858, Trall's *Sexual Physiology* also had twenty-one reprints by 1881, the *Water-Cure Journal* attained a monthly circulation of 10,000 by 1849, and the *Health Reformer* claimed 11,000 subscribers in 1868.[108] Throughout the mid-nineteenth century, the health reformers reached a massive audience through their popular books and journals. In the early 1850s, Orville A. Roorbach's *Bibliotheca Americana* (1855), the only full list of books in print, listed eighteen books by health reformers.[109] And in the same decade, S. Austin Alliborne's important collection of booksellers' sales figures stated that many of "Dr. Alcott's works have been very popular" and that Mary G. Nichols had "become widely known by her advocacy and application of the Water-Cure System."[110] Lectures were another important part of the health crusade. Graham spoke to thousands of people during the 1832 New York cholera epidemic and continued to draw large crowds throughout the Northeast until his retirement. Other health reformers such as Alcott and Nichols also created regional reputations through their popular talks, and phrenologists and hydropaths were in great demand in Northeastern and Midwestern lyceums. Last, health reform was further popularized by the water-cure establishments that were within easy traveling distance of major metropolitan centers such as Boston, New York, and Philadelphia. The purity advocates skillfully used the latest techniques created by the antebellum transportation and communications revolutions to spread their message throughout the North.

Unlike the government and orthodox health reformers, the purity advocates did not attempt to change state and national laws, but tried to modify the public's behavior and fundamental point of view. They helped improve American health because the influence of the health-reform movement coincided with important dietary, hygienic, and sexual changes in American life. During the mid-nineteenth century, average alcohol and meat consumption declined, the use of fruits and vegetables increased, personal hygiene improved, and Americans became more conscious of the interrelationship between environment and health.

Romantic health reformers also helped popularize the value of personal hygiene, exercise, and the outdoor life. Baths and personal hygiene formed the basis of many of their hygienic techniques. At first, the reformers considered exercise as just one method for restoring health. But Alcott's concepts of physical education helped stimulate interest in physical training for its own sake.[111] And Trall promoted swimming as a recreational activity and as a form of life-saving rather than just another water cure technique.[112] As a result, the hydropathic emphasis on healthy, outdoor activities helped lead to a renewed interest in sports, games, and fresh air exercise.

Of course, the romantics cannot be solely credited with the unprecedented improvements in the health of Americans during the last half of the nineteenth century. Male life expectancy rose at birth from forty-one in the 1850s to over fifty by the early 1900s. The crude death rate fell from approximately 22 deaths per 1,000 living people during the 1850s to about 15 deaths in 1915. And there were important changes in the types of mortal diseases. At mid-century the most dangerous diseases were infectious ones; heart diseases and ailments of old age were relatively unimportant. By the early twentieth century, the pattern had been reversed. The major decline in mortality came from reductions in infectious diseases.[113]

It is highly unlikely that improved medical practice had anything to do with this remarkable improvement in national health. For over a century, the pattern of disease trends indicates that the environment is the most important determinant of a population's general health. Tuberculosis, cholera, dysentery, scarlet fever, diptheria, whooping cough, and measles declined dramatically before the advent of bacteriological medicine, the introduction of antibiotics, and widespread immunization. The substantial reduction in mortality from these and especially from intestinal infections resulted from the introduction of sound personal health habits, improved food hygiene, and better nutrition.[114] In contrast to environmental improvements, neither the proportion of physicians in a population nor their clinical tools is significantly related to a decline in the overall disease burden or to a rise in life expectancy.[115] The health of Americans improved during the nineteenth century before intervention by orthodox physicians and their public-health movement. Most likely, a rising standard of living and better personal hygienic measures made America a healthier place to live.

The romantic health reformers were the first and most important nineteenth-century group to promote improved personal and public health. Although the purity advocates developed their physiological system to limit sexual activities, most Americans rejected the health reformers' more controversial and extreme theories and, instead, appropriated their very sensible suggestions about developing better health. Their criticisms of alcohol and meat and their espousal of exercise, improved personal hygiene, and a balanced diet inspired and reinforced mid–nineteenth-century American dietary and hygienic concepts. The medical historians, who date the triumph of the urban sanitation and public-health movements in the 1880s, have been unable to account for its rapid acceptance once city and state governments began mobilizing expertise and money to combat community health problems. Perhaps the middle-class public's belief in romantic concepts of personal hygiene prepared the groundwork for a government and orthodox medicine inspired health movement. By helping individuals deal with the traumas of modernization, sectarian health reform became part of the new environment, and by the end of the nineteenth century, romantic concepts of personal and family hygiene were accepted as a major component of middle-class urban culture.

Proper hygiene became an important way to differentiate "respectable" Americans from the new immigrants of the late 1800s, who often had very traditional values and habits about sanitation and disease. The reformers had always argued that there was a close relationship between ignorance, bad habits, and poor health. Now middle-class urbanites could use these concepts to separate themselves from their alleged inferiors, a form of behavior that had been recommended by Jackson as early as 1858:

> What with the decline of the Puritan and Cavalier stock on the one hand, and the great influx of foreign born on the other, it is not difficult to predict *our future*. In less than fifty years the New England type of manhood will have ceased to govern this Republic, and when once it ceases to govern it will cease to exist. . . . *Nothing but a bold and faithful advocacy of the laws of health can stop this ebbtide of human life.*[116]

Thus the romantics' insistence that good health and respectability were synonymous was ironically proven by the late nineteenth century as immigrants transformed the American city. The purity advocates did not spawn a second generation of reformers to promote their proposals, but by that time health reform had disappeared as a distinctive movement and became part of mainstream American values and institutions. Their demise signified the triumph of health reform.

NOTES

1. *Health Journal and Advocate of Physiological Reform* 1 (1840–1841):87.

2. *Health Journal and Advocate of Physiological Reform* 1 (1840–1841):102–3.

3. *The Northampton Book* (Northampton, Mass.: Tercentenary Committee, 1954), pp. 102–8; *Boston Post*, 2 March 1848; *Hampshire Gazette*, 12 November 1830, 19 November 1850.

4. Asenath Nicholson, *Nature's Own Book* (New York: Wilbur & Whipple, 1835), pp. 35–36.

5. *Boston Medical and Surgical Journal* 11 (1851):188; *Water-Cure Journal* 13 (1851):110–111; Helen Graham Carpenter, *The Reverend John Graham of Woodbury, Connecticut and His Descendants* (Chicago: The Monastery Hill Press, 1942), p. 190.

6. George Rosen, "What Is Social Medicine? A Genetic Analysis of the Concept," *Bulletin of the History of Medicine* 21 (1947):674–733; "Approaches to a Concept of Social Medicine, A Historical Survey," *Millbank Memorial Fund Quarterly* 26 (1948):7–21.

7. See Frederic P. Gorham, "The History of Bacteriology and Its Contribution to Public Health," *A Half Century of Public Health*, ed. Mazÿck P. Ravenel (New York: American Public Health Association, 1921), pp. 69–73; Richard H. Shyrock, "Origins and Significance of Public Health," *Annals of Medical History* 1 (1929):644–55; Howard D. Kramer, "The Beginning of the Public Health Movement in the United States," *Bulletin of the History of Medicine* 21 (1947): 352–76; "The Germ Theory and the Early Public Health Program in the United States," *Bulletin of the History of Medicine* 22 (1948):233–47; John B. Blake, "The Origins of Public Health in the United States," *American Journal of Public Health and the Nation's Health* 38 (1948):1539–50; Wilson G. Smillie, *Public Health: Its Promise for the Future* (New York: Macmillan Co., 1955); George Rosen, *A History of Public Health* (New York: MD Publications, 1958); John Duffy, *A History of Public Health in New York City, 1625–1866* (New York: Russell Sage Foundation, 1968); Barbara Gutmann Rosenkrantz, *Public Health and the State: Changing Views in Massachusetts, 1842–1936* (Cambridge, Mass.: Harvard University Press, 1972).

8. See Carroll Smith Rosenberg, "Protestants and Five Pointers: The Five Points House of Industry, 1850–1870," *New York Historical Society Quarterly* 48 (1964):327–47; Charles E. Rosenberg and Carroll Smith Rosenberg, "Pietism and the Origins of the Public Health Movement: A Note on John H. Griscom and Robert M. Hartley," *Journal of the History of Medicine and Allied Sciences* 23 (1968):16–35; Carroll Smith Rosenberg, *Religion and the Rise of the American City: The New York City Mission Movement, 1812–1870* (Ithaca, N.Y.: Cornell University Press, 1971), pp. 225–73; John B. Blake, "Health Reform," *The Rise of Adventism: Religion and Society in Mid–Nineteenth-Century America*, ed. Edwin A. Gausted (New York: Harper and Row, 1974), pp. 30–49; James C. Whorton, "Christian Physiology: William Alcott's Prescription for the Millennium," *Bulletin of the History of Medicine* 49 (1975): 466–81.

9. See Richard H. Shyrock, "Sylvester Graham and the Popular Health Movement, 1830–1870," *Mississippi Valley Historical Review* 18 (1931):172–93; William B. Walker, "The Health Reform Movement in the United States, 1830–1870," (Ph.D. diss., Johns Hopkins University, 1955); Stephen W. Nissenbaum, *Sex, Diet, and Debility in Jacksonian America: Sylvester Graham and Health Reform* (Westport, Conn.: Greenwood Press, 1980); Linda Gordon, *Woman's Body, Woman's Right: Birth Control in America* (New York: Viking Press, 1974), pp. 162–170; Ronald Numbers, *Prophetess of Health: A Study of Ellen G. White* (New York: Harper and Row, 1976), pp. 48–76.

10. *New Jersey Medical Reporter* 6 (1853):105–6.

11. *Boston Medical and Surgical Journal* 19 (1855):85; *Water-Cure Journal* 23 (1857):111.

12. *Graham Journal of Health and Longevity* 3 (1839):221–22.

13. Delavan Levant Leonard, *The Story of Oberlin; the Institution, the Community, the Idea, the Movement* (Boston: The Pilgrim Press, 1898), pp. 222–23.

14. See Roland H. Hogeland, "Coeducation of the Sexes at Oberlin College: A Study of Social Ideas in Mid–Nineteenth Century America," *Journal of Social History* 6 (1974):160–77.

15. *Oberlin Evangelist*, 10 September 1851.

16. *Oberlin Evangelist*, 22 April 1840; Charles G. Finney, *Lectures on Revivals of Religion*, 1835, ed. William G. McLoughlin (Cambridge, Mass.: Harvard University Press, 1960), pp. 416–17.

17. Charles Grandison Finney, *Views of Sanctification* (Oberlin, Ohio: Steele, 1840), p. 18.

18. *Moral Reformer and Teacher on the Human Constitution* 2 (1836):97.

19. *Advocate of Moral Reform*, 15 June 1839.

20. Robert Samuel Fletcher, "Bread and Doctrine at Oberlin," *Ohio State Archaelogical and Historical Quarterly* 49 (1940):59–65; *A History of Oberlin College, from its Foundation through the Civil War*, 2 vols. (Oberlin, Ohio: Oberlin College, 1943), 1:319–25.

21. *Graham Journal of Health and Longevity* 3 (1839):396–97.

22. Fletcher, "Bread and Doctrine," pp. 63–67; *History of Oberlin*, 1:325–28.

23. Isaac Jennings, *The Philosophy of Human Life* (Cleveland, Ohio: O. Jewett, Proctor & Worthington, 1852), pp. 241–42.

24. Sylvester Graham, *A Lecture on Epidemic Diseases Generally, and particularly the Spasmodic Cholera* (New York: M. Day, 1833), pp. 78–80; *Graham Journal of Health and Longevity* 1 (1837):21, 47.

25. Graham, *Lecture on Epidemic Diseases*, p. 80.

26. *New York Review*, 14 October 1837.

27. William S. Tyler to Edward Tyler, 10 October 1833, in Thomas H. Leduc, "Grahamites and Garrisonians," *New York History* 20 (1939):190–91.

28. Ronald Walters, "The Erotic South: Civilization and Sexuality in American Abolitionism," *American Quarterly* 25 (1973): 177–201; *The Antislavery Appeal: American Abolitionism after 1830* (Baltimore: Johns Hopkins University Press, 1976), pp. 70–87.

29. *Graham Journal of Health and Longevity* 1 (1837):5, 2 (1838): 209, 3 (1839):185; Henry Villard, *Memoirs of Henry Villard, Journalist and Financier: 1835–1900*, 2 vols. (Boston and New York: Houghton, Mifflin and Company, 1904), 2:52; Thomas Wentworth Higginson, *Out-Door Papers* (Boston: Lee and Shepard, 1863), p. 142.

30. Theodore Dwight Weld to Angelina Grimké, 12 March 1838, *Letters of Theodore Dwight Weld, Angelina Grimké Weld, and Sarah Grimké, 1822–1844*, ed. Gilbert H. Barnes and Dwight C. Dumond, 2 vols. (New York: D. Appleton-Century Company, 1934), 2:602. Angelina Grimké approved of Weld's conduct. In an earlier letter she had "been tempted to think marriage was *sinful*. . . . Instead of the higher, nobler, sentiments being first aroused, and leading to the lower passions *captive* to their will, the *latter* seemed to be *lords* over the former." See Angelina Grimké to Theodore Weld, 4 March 1838 in Barnes and Dumond, *Letters*, 2:587.

31. Higginson, *Out-Door Papers*, p. 139.

32. *Graham Journal of Health and Longevity* 2 (1838):214.

33. David J. Pivar, *Purity Crusade: Sexual Morality and Social Control, 1868–1900* (Westport, Conn.: Greenwood Press, 1973).

34. *Constitution of the American Physiological Society: with a Catalogue of its Members and Officers* (Boston: March, Capon & Lyon, 1837); *First Annual Report of the American Physiological Society* (Boston: George W. Light, 1837), pp. 2–8. For the history of the

American Physiological Society, see Hebbel E. Hoff and John F. Fulton, "The Centenary of the First American Physiological Society Founded at Boston by William A. Alcott and Sylvester Graham," *Bulletin of the Institute of the History of Medicine* 5 (1937):687–734.

35. *First Annual Report*, pp. 9–86; *Second Annual Report of the American Physiological Society* (Boston: George W. Light, 1838), pp. 7, 13; *Third Annual Report of the American Physiological Society* (Boston: George W. Light, 1839), pp. 6–7, 10.

36. *Graham Journal of Health and Longevity* 3 (1839):355; *Boston Medical and Surgical Journal* 14 (1836):31.

37. *Boston Medical and Surgical Journal* 19 (1839):316–20.

38. Ibid., 13 (1835):223, 303.

39. Ibid., pp. 329, 351–52.

40. Ibid., 14 (1836):270.

41. *Boston Courier*, 21 March 1838.

42. Ibid., 6 March 1837; *American Vegetarian and Health Journal* 3 (1852):166.

43. *Harper's New Monthly Magazine* 60 (1880):190; *American Vegetarian and Health Journal* 3 (1852):166.

44. *American Journal of Education* 4 (1857):629–54; H. Thoms, "William Andrus Alcott: Physician, educator, writer," *Bulletin of the Society of Medical History* 4 (1928):123–30; Louis B. Salomon, "The Least-Remembered Alcott," *New England Quarterly* 34 (1961):87–93.

45. William A. Alcott, *Forty Years in the Wilderness of Pills and Powders* (Boston: J. P. Jewett, 1859), p. 86; *Boston Medical and Surgical Journal* 14 (1836):200.

46. William A. Alcott, *The Young Man's Guide* (Boston: Lilly, Wait, Coleman, & Holden, 1833), pp. 319–52; *The Young Mother* (Boston: Light and Stearns, 1836), pp. 22–186; *The House I Live In* (Boston: G. W. Light, 1839), pp. 13–136, 245–51; *Boston Medical and Surgical Journal* 19 (1839):186–89, 220–23, 252–55, 267–69, 281–84, 316–20, 21 (1840):334–38, 28 (1843):19–20, 32 (1845):78–80, 363.

47. *Boston Medical and Surgical Journal* 13 (1836):396–98, 14 (1836):199–201.

48. Alcott, *Young Man's Guide*, pp. 340–41; *Vegetable Diet: as Sanctioned by Medical Men, and by Experience in All Ages* (Boston: Marsh, Capon & Lyon, 1838), pp. 277–93; *The Young Housekeeper* (Boston: G. W. Light, 1838), p. 256; *Tea and Coffee* (Boston: G. W. Light, 1839), pp. 50–117; *Moral Reformer and Teacher on the Human Constitution* 2 (1836):340.

49. *Boston Recorder*, 29 June 1838.

50. *Boston Medical and Surgical Journal* 19 (1838):220.

51. Ibid., pp. 221, 269.

52. Ibid., pp. 317–18.

53. Ibid., p. 318.

54. *Moral Reformer* 1 (1835):21, 2 (1836):345–46; *Library of Health* 1 (1837):180–82, 5 (1841):41–42, 79–80, 176–77, 201–3; William A. Alcott, *The Young Husband* (Philadelphia: n.p., 1835), p. 374.

55. *American Phrenological Journal* 25 (1857):33.

56. Mary Mann, ed., *The Life and Works of Horace Mann*, 5 vols. (Boston: Walker, Fuller and Company, 1865–1868), 2:4, 33–456, 3:131–225, 5:658–62; Walker, "Health Reform Movement," pp. 97–98.

57. *Second Annual Report*, p. 13.

58. John D. Davies, *Phrenology Fad and Science: A Nineteenth Century American Crusade* (New Haven, Conn.: Yale University Press, 1955), pp. 3–11, 106–17; Robert E. Reigel, "Early Phrenology in the United States," *Medical Life* 37 (1930):361–76.

59. George Combe, *Notes on the United States of North America during a Phrenological Visit in 1838–9–40*, 3 vols. (Edinburgh: Maclachlan, Stewart, 1841), 3:428–29.

60. Sylvester Graham, *Lectures on the Science of Human Life*, 2 vols. (Boston: March, Capon, Lyon, and Webb, 1839), 1:359–416, 2:338–46.

61. Davies, *Phrenology*, pp. 46–64; Carl Carmer, "That Was New York: The Fowlers, Practical Phrenologists," *New Yorker* 12 (February 13, 1937), 22–27; *American Phrenological Journal* 7 (1845):344.

62. *American Phrenological Journal* 25 (1857):33.

63. Ibid., 18 (1853):137.

64. Madeleine B. Stern, *Heads & Headlines: The Phrenological Fowlers* (Norman, Okla.: University of Oklahoma Press, 1971), pp. 49, 67–68, 124, 138.

65. Orson S. Fowler, *Physiology, Animal and Mental: Applied to the Preservation and Restoration of Health of Body, and Power of Mind* (New York: Fowler and Wells, 1847), p. 67.

66. Graham, *Science of Human Life*, 2:338, 346.

67. Lorenzo N. Fowler, *The Principles of Phrenology and Physiology Applied to Man's Social Relations; together with an Analysis of the Domestic Feelings* (New York: Fowler and Wells, 1842), p. 79.

68. Fowler, *Principles of Phrenology and Physiology*, p. 15.

69. Orson S. Fowler, *Amativeness: or Evils and Remedies of Excessive and Perverted Sexuality* (New York: Fowler and Wells, 1846), p. 53.

70. Fowler, *Amativeness*, p. 55.

71. Allan S. Horlick, "Phrenology and the Social Education of Young Men," *History of Education Quarterly* 11 (1971):23–39.

72. Joel Shew, *Hydropathy; or, The Water-Cure: Its Principles, Modes of Treatment &c.* (New York: Wiley and Putnam, 1844), pp. 2–9; *Boston Medical and Surgical Journal* 27 (1842):283, 29 (1843):164, 31 (1844):182–83; *Water-Cure Journal* 1 (1846):49.

73. Harry E. Sigerist, "American Spas in Historical Perspective," *Bulletin of the History of Medicine* 2 (1942):133–47; Carl Bridenbaugh, "Baths and Watering Places of Colonial America," *William and Mary Quarterly* 3 (1946):151–81; Harry B. Weiss and Howard R. Kemble, *The Great American Water-Cure Craze: A History of Hydropathy in the United States* (Trenton, N.J.: The Past Times Press, 1967), pp. 1–22, 41; Marshall Scott Legan, "Hydropathy in America: A Nineteenth Century Panacea," *Bulletin of the History of Medicine* 45 (1971):267–80; *Water-Cure Journal* 18 (1854):79, 34 (1862):62.

74. *Boston Medical and Surgical Journal* 27 (1842):134–35, 35(1846):325–27, 37 (1847):495.

75. Shew, *Hydropathy*, p. 272.

76. *Boston Medical and Surgical Journal* 29 (1843):308.

77. John F. Hageman, *History of Burlington and Mercer Counties, New Jersey* (Philadelphia: Everts & Pack, 1883), p. 330; John Duffy, "Medical Practice in the Antebellum South," *Journal of Southern History* 25 (1959):67–69; *History of Medicine in Louisiana*, ed. John Duffy, 2 vols. (Baton Rouge, La.: Louisiana State University Press, 1962), 2:39; *Water-Cure Journal* 30 (1860):14, 62.

78. *Water-Cure Journal* 1 (1846):15.

79. Ibid. 3 (1847):126–27.

80. *Dansville Advertiser*, 18 July 1895; *Water-Cure Journal* 26 (1858):77.

81. *Water-Cure Journal* 18 (1854):31–32, 20 (1855):66.

82. Russell T. Trall, *The Hydropathic Encyclopedia*, 2 vols. (New York: Fowlers and Wells, 1852), 1:307, 442–43; *Pathology of the Reproductive Organs; Embracing All Forms*

of *Sexual Disorders* (Boston: B. Emerson, 1863), pp. 13–23, 126–31; *Nervous Debility; The Nature, Causes, Consequences, and Hygienic Treatment of Invalids Suffering from Prematurely Exhausted Vitality* (New York: Davies and Kent, 1861), pp. v–vii, 9–19. For an excellent discussion of Trall's philosophy and career, see Walker, "Health Reform Movement," pp. 179–92, 221–35, 246–69.

83. Trall, *Nervous Debility*, p. 10.

84. Shew, *Hydropathy*, pp. 275–96.

85. James Caleb Jackson, *The Sexual Organism, and Its Healthful Management* (Boston: Leverett, 1869), p. 184.

86. *Water-Cure Journal* 26 (1858):17; *Dansville Advertiser*, 12 April 1883; Gerald Carson, *Cornflake Crusade* (New York: Holt, Rinehart and Winston, 1957), pp. 61–68.

87. Quoted in Dores E. Robinson, *The Story of Our Health Message: The Origin, Character, and Development of Health Education in the Seventh-Day Adventist Church* (Nashville, Tenn.: Southern Publishing Association, 1955), p. 37. For White's indebtedness to contemporary health reformers and the development of her health concepts after 1863, see Ronald L. Number's excellent book, *Prophetess of Health*.

88. *Health Reformer* 3 (1868):14.

89. *Good Health* 18 (1882):92.

90. John Harvey Kellogg, *Plain Facts for Old and Young* (Burlington, Iowa: I. F. Segner, 1882).

91. John Harvey Kellogg, *Man, the Masterpiece, or Plain Truths Plainly Told, About Boyhood, Youth, and Manhood* (Battle Creek, Mich.: Modern Medicine Publication Co., 1894).

92. Carson, *Cornflake Crusade*, pp. 71–243; Richard W. Schwartz, *John Harvey Kellogg* (Nashville, Tenn.: Southern Publishing Association, 1970), pp. 17–127.

93. *Second Annual Report*, p. 20.

94. *Water-Cure Journal* 26 (1858):96.

95. Alcott, *Young Mother*, pp. 88–89.

96. *Water-Cure Journal* 26 (1858):3.

97. Gerda Lerner, "The Lady and the Mill Girl: Changes in the Status of Women in the Age of Jackson," *American Studies* 10 (1969):5–15; Glenda Riley, "The Subtle Subversion: Change in the Traditionalist Image of American Woman," *The Historian* 32 (1970):210–27; Linda Kerber, "Daughers of Columbia: Educating Woman for the Republic, 1787–1805," *The Hofstader Aegis,* ed. Stanley Elkins and Eric McKitrick (New York: Columbia University Press, 1974), pp. 39–59; Jill Conway, "Perspectives on the History of Women's Education in the United States," *History of Education Quarterly* 14 (1974):1–12; Nancy F. Cott, *The Bonds of Womanhood: "Woman's Sphere" in New England, 1780–1835* (New Haven, Conn.: Yale University Press, 1977); Keith Melder, *Beginnings of Sisterhood: The American Woman's Rights Movement, 1800–1850* (New York: Schocken Books, 1977).

98. Regina M. Morantz, "Making Women Modern: Middle Class Women and Health Reform in 19th Century America," *Journal of Social History* 10 (1977):490–507; "Nineteenth Century Reform and Women: A Program of Self-Help," *Medicine without Doctors: Home Care in American History,* ed. Guenter B. Risse, Ronald L. Numbers, and Judith W. Leavitt (New York: Science History Publications, 1977), pp. 73–93.

99. Alcott, *Essay*, p. 10; *The House*, pp. 248–49; *Young Mother*, p. 53; Trall, *Hydropathic Encyclopedia*, 1:298; Graham, *Science of Human Life*, 2:646–51; *Water-Cure Journal* 12 (1851):33, 58, 13 (1852):111, 15 (1853):7, 10, 32, 34–35, 131, 34 (1862):1–2.

100. *Water-Cure Journal* 15 (1853):131.

101. *Water-Cure Journal* 9 (1850):121, 11 (1851):57–59; Thomas Low Nichols, *The Curse Removed; A Statement of Facts Respecting the Efficacy of Water-Cure in the Treat-*

ment of Uterine Disease and the Removal of the Pains and Perils of Pregnancy and Child-birth (New York: The Water-Cure Journal, 1850): Jackson, *Sexual Organism*, pp. 261–79; Lorenzo Fowler, *Principles of Phrenology and Physiology*, pp. 67–135; Russell T. Trall, *Sexual Physiology: A Scientific and Popular Exposition of the Fundamental Problems in Sociology* (New York: Miller, Wood, 1866), pp. 247–82.

102. Jackson, *Sexual Organism*, pp. 256–61; Orson Fowler, *Love and Parentage* (New York: Fowlers and Wells, 1847), pp. 272–74; Sylvester Graham, *A Lecture to Young Men* (Providence, R.I.: Weeden and Cory, 1834), pp. 33–35; Trall, *Sexual Physiology*, pp. 201–14, 229–48.

103. Henry Clarke Wright, *Marriage and Parentage* (Boston: B. Marsh, 1855), p. 257.

104. Sylvester Graham, *Treatise on Bread, and Bread-Making* (Boston: Light and Stearns, 1837), p. 126.

105. Mary S. Gove, *Lectures to Women on Anatomy and Physiology* (New York: Harper & Brothers, 1846), p. 20.

106. James G. Burrow, *AMA: Voice of American Medicine* (Baltimore: Johns Hopkins University Press, 1963), pp. 1–53; Rosemary Stevens, *American Medicine and the Public Interest* (New Haven, Conn.: Yale University Press, 1971), pp. 34–66; William G. Rothstein, *American Physicians in the Nineteenth Century* (Baltimore: Johns Hopkins University Press, 1972), pp. 298–322; Barbara Gutmann Rosenkrantz, "Cart Before Horse: Theory, Practice and Professional Image in American Public Health, 1870–1920," *Journal of the History of Medicine and Allied Sciences* 29 (1974):55–73.

107. Charles V. Chapin, *The Sources and Modes of Infection* (New York: J. Wiley and Sons, 1910), p. 28.

108. Carl Bode, *Antebellum Culture* (Berkeley and Los Angeles: University of California Press, 1959), p. 125; *Water-Cure Journal* 8 (1849):18; *Health Reformer* 10 (1875):256.

109. Orville A. Roorbach, *Supplement to the Bibliotheca Americana, A Catalogue of American Publications* (New York: O. A. Roorbach, 1855), pp. 5, 72, 141, 178, 197, 217.

110. Samuel Austin Alliborne, *A Critical Dictionary of English Literature and British American Authors*, 3 vols. (Philadelphia: Childs & Peterson, 1859), 1:45, 2:1, 426.

111. William A. Alcott, *Essay on the Construction of Schoolhouses* (Boston: Hilliard, Gray, Little and Wilkins, 1832), p. 15; *Young Mother*, p. 232.

112. Trall, *Hydropathic Encyclopedia*, 2:44–47.

113. Edward Meeker, "The Improving Health of the United States, 1850–1915," *Explorations in Economic History* 9 (1972):353–75; Paul H. Jacobson, "Cohort Survival for Generations Since 1840," *Millbank Memorial Fund Quarterly* 42 (1964):36–53.

114. Rick J. Carlson, *The End of Medicine* (New York: Wiley, 1975); René Dubos, *The Mirage of Health: Utopian Progress and Biological Change* (New York: Harper and Row, 1959); Ivan Illich, *Medical Nemesis: The Expropriation of Health* (New York: Pantheon Books, 1976); Thomas McKeown, *The Modern Rise of Population* (London: Arnold, 1976).

115. Charles T. Stewart, Jr., "Allocation of Resources to Health," *Journal of Human Resources* 6 (1971):103–21.

116. *Water-Cure Journal* 26 (1858):4.

Conclusion:
Victorian Sexuality and the Eclipse of Community

American sexual ideology and behavior underwent a major transformation during the late nineteenth and early twentieth centuries. As a result, Victorian sexual ethics were attacked and seriously weakened by World War I. Critics of nineteenth-century sexuality denied that sexual experience was a threat to society and the individual or a drain on vital bodily energies. Instead, they pictured sexual activity as a worthwhile experience which was essential to individual and social health. Like the European romantics of the early nineteenth century, the sexual moderns affirmed the essential worth of erotic encounters, criticized the repressive values of traditional Christianity, and encouraged a more experimental attitude toward sexuality. The modernists triumphed and thus the conceptual and behavioral foundations of Victorian sexuality have been seriously eroded in the twentieth century.[1]

According to the systematic and quantitative studies of premarital sex in America, there were also important changes in premarital sexual relations around the turn of the century. Although most of the research was done with urban, middle-class, and college-educated individuals, the studies indicate that sexual ideology and behavior were changing simultaneously throughout America. Lewis M. Terman interviewed 792 married couples in California during the 1930s and discovered that 60 percent of the men and 37 percent of the women reported premarital sexual relations.[2] In the 1940s Alfred Kinsey studied 6,000 females and 5,000 males. About 50 percent of the women said they had premarital sexual intercourse while the male rate was over 90 percent.[3] More important for our discussion in the Terman and Kinsey surveys are changes in premarital rates of sexual intercourse for women by decade of birth. Both studies claim that women born before 1900 had rates of premarital sexual inter-

176

course of about 22 percent. But the percentage of women born after 1900 having premarital sexual intercourse jumped to about 50 percent.[4] Thus on the basis of available evidence, it appears the greatest changes in the rates of premarital sexual relations before the 1960s occurred in the early twentieth century, when Victorian sexual values and behavior were heavily battered.

At the same time, the health-reform movement also changed. The crusading spirit of the purity advocates sustained romantic health reform, but it also contained a darker side. Precariously balanced between the goals of repression and perfection, Graham and his followers simultaneously were, in Orestes Brownson's characterization, "the party of the Hopeful and that of the Fearful."[5] Moralists such as the health reformers responded to new urban conditions and the modernization process in two ways: they tried voluntarily to prohibit or encourage specific forms of behavior and they also attempted to design an environment that would lead to the type of society they admired. The purity advocates hoped to achieve these goals by insisting on proper individual physiology and by encouraging Americans to improve their surroundings. Excessive zeal, however, frequently degenerates into a smug and nagging moralism. After the Civil War, the eclipse of romanticism and the intense challenge of industrialization, urbanization, and the new immigration led to a different kind of health crusade. Anthony Comstock, Godfrey Lowell Cabot and the Boston Watch and Ward Society, the American Purity Alliance, and the numerous other censorship and vigilance societies were motivated more by fear than hope. While they wanted to reconstitute society upon a new cultural foundation, the Gilded Age purity reformers reduced their message to vapid exhortations on behalf of individual morality and the fear of punishment. They seemed more interested in controlling people than in improving them. The millennial hopes of the antebellum romantics were replaced by pietism and punitive legislation. Late–nineteenth-century purity crusaders refused to acknowledge that genuine moral problems were also social problems that could not be adequately dealt with merely from the standpoint of personal betterment.[6]

The Victorian sexuality that Comstock and the social purity advocates so hysterically defended was first articulated, as we have seen, by Sylvester Graham and other romantic health reformers. They advocated a repressive sexual morality to help Americans function in a fluid and disorderly society. The purity reformers developed a plausible theory to explain contemporary America: the disintegration of generational ties, commercialization, and the decline of the patriarchal agricultural family led to chaos and a sense of rootlessness. Because traditional institutions were unable to handle the seeming disorder of antebellum society, the romantics wanted to restore order and morality by relocating the source of authority within the individual. Proper physiology, which was synonymous with extreme self-restraint, could compensate for the destructive temptations and habits of mid–nineteenth-century America.

The health reformers' ideology, careers, and impact calls into question traditional theories of modernization and suggests that we must reevaluate our interpretations of mid–nineteenth-century America. The overarching concept of modernization marching relentlessly through the centuries is an example of the problems inherent in any unilinear theory of history which ignores the intensity of social and intellectual changes, the lack of uniformity in trends, and the failure of various changes to fit into the paradigm. Modernization theorists are correct in identifying the progressive erosion of five traditional values. The first of these values is the sense of community *(Gemeinschaft)*, which decayed as an impersonal, meritocratic, competitively individualistic urban society developed. The second value is the sense of authority and deference, which was weakened by the development of a democratic society. Social stability, the third value, was undermined by increasing geographical, social, and occupational mobility. The secularization of society undermined the fourth traditional value, the concept of the sacred. And the last value, a physical and psychological sense of rootedness, was destroyed by the growth of autonomy and independence, which led to alienation and anomie. Although this concept of modernization reduces the rich diversity of nineteenth-century American experience to a uniformity it never possessed, the theory does provide a general explanation for the changes that first occurred in the Northeastern United States.

But the traditional theories of modernization do not explain the sexual ideology and behavior of nineteenth-century Northeastern urbanites. The sexual-sublimation model fits the demographic and cultural evidence but the metahistorical theories of the Freudian left and the changing intensity of the Protestant ethic cannot explain American sexual behavior. There was cultural disintegration, but it did not lead to a more liberal sexuality or to an influential subculture of gratification. And the decline-in-religiosity model can only work among individuals who were heavily influenced by religion. Besides, the data are too contradictory to arrive at any definite conclusions about religious beliefs and sexual behavior. These models cannot accommodate Victorian American sexuality because they picture modernization as an irreversible process leading to affective individualism, which supposedly erodes the strict sexuality of traditional societies. But eighteenth-century American sexuality was more permissive than the sexuality of the next century. And although nineteenth-century Americans were more individualistic than their predecessors, affections were increasingly confined to the small, intimate circle of the family and self.

The causes of this wave of repressive sexuality were related to a sense of social and cultural crisis, a fear that the social structure and traditional morality were in danger. Victorian sexual ideologues erected stern and unforgiving natural laws whose vengeance fell inexorably on all sinners. As traditional secular and religious institutions lost authority and power, the purity reformers substituted a rigid personal code allegedly based on physiological laws to control themselves and their middle-class allies.

The incredible emphasis on sexual repression also was congruent with bourgeois values of status and success. The most valued of nineteenth-century middle-class attributes was respectability, which took the form of severe self-restraint buttressed by evangelical piety and reinforced by the internalization of strict moral laws. These values were developed by aggressive reformers and their followers through vigorous propaganda and health institutions. Their prohibitions were acceptable because they appeared to be scientific and did encourage social mobility and financial success.

And last, the middle-class Victorian family, which the romantics rarely discussed, helped develop a more prudish sexuality. Within the family, wives and children were sexually repressed and society developed a strong emotional and religious concern for their welfare. The subordination of women and the sublimation of children's sexual drives occurred in an atmosphere where the emotional life of the family members were almost entirely focused within the tight boundaries of the nuclear family. The modern family—emotionally intense, isolated, fearful of the outside world, where children were socialized by women—developed partly as a response to the need for protection from a society that appeared untrustworthy and destructive. Thus Grahamism helped create and reinforce the doubts mid–nineteenth-century Americans had about their environment; prudery, sexual repression, and the isolated nuclear family were partial responses to that situation. Graham and his supporters affirmed the relationship between extreme moderation, social order, and health. Although their physiological theories were sometimes inaccurate, their diagnosis and therapeutics had an emotional and symbolic truth which helped adjust Americans to a new society while the Grahamites helped erode a sense of community.

Most literature in the social sciences describes a great change that destroyed the notion of community and gave birth to modern society. But as Thomas Bender has wisely argued,[7] the concept of community is not just a base line for historical change; it is also a fundamental and enduring form of social interaction. This is an important concept because the community-breakdown model provides the structure for many studies treating different periods of American history from the colonial era to the present. Although these books are quite persuasive, they collectively portray a cultural impossibility—the collapse of community during the lives of successive generations of Americans.

The modernization process in early–nineteenth-century America did not destroy the viability of the community but, instead, brought a new configuration to local life. While most antebellum Americans continued to act out their lives within the context of the town, the experience of community took on a new quality during this era. In Kingston, New York, and in the Berkshires of western Massachusetts, for example, the creation of a nationally integrated economy and society revitalized towns and secondary urban centers and thus created a countercurrent of parochial, community-oriented action and identity.[8] The bonds of geography and mutuality, however, that defined community became more complicated than they were a century earlier. Locality remained an important focus for community, but the growth in the size and complexity of local life and the loss of some community autonomy encouraged people to create new social networks that were independent of geography. Institutions identified with the nation gained in scope while local ones became less important. What had once been a seamless web of community life broke into fragments. Thus Bender and other historians have correctly warned us about the dangers of discarding the concept of community during the Jacksonian era. If community is a traditional pattern of social relations, the task of the historian is not to date the moment when one of the worlds of social interaction is replaced by another; it is to probe their interaction and assess their importance to peoples' lives. Graham and the health reformers certainly did not destroy any geographical communities, but they did challenge some of the traditional bonds of community and helped devalue public life.

While Bender and other social scientists have alerted us to the endurance of communities, they have sometimes neglected the psychic changes taking place in mid–nineteenth-century America that might have sundered many of the community's foundations. The romantic reformers' extreme individualism and lack of faith in the integrating power of community were indicative of broader cultural changes taking place in antebellum America. These cultural transformations, set in motion by the modernization process, helped weaken the concept of community in the ways described in the recent provocative social theorizing of Quentin Anderson, Christopher Lasch, and Richard Sennett.[9] These writers have helped reorient our evaluation of the American character by modifying some of Alexis de Tocqueville's speculations, which were concerned with the values and habits of people obsessed with themselves.

In the first volume of *Democracy in America* (1835) Tocqueville argued that democracy, which he equated with equality, was dangerous because the majority could suppress deviants and minority groups. The second volume (1840) shifted from politics in an egalitarian society to the social conditions of everyday life. Tocqueville believed that intimate life would become more important in a society consumed by a passion for equality because public affairs would be handled by the state while important issues became more psychological in character. In other words, citizens would abandon public life because it was outside the intimate realm. When this occurred, people would harbor no great passions since their eruption would threaten the stability of intimate life. Emotional relationships, according to Tocqueville, could only become meaningful when they were part of a broader system of social relations and so this situation would ironically constrict emotional gratification. Tocqueville ascribed these changes to a shift away from a deferential society where "the father is not only the civil head of the family but the organ of its traditions. . . . He is listened to with deference, he is addressed with respect."[10] He found the change particularly noticeable in England and America and he believed that the spirit of independence was fostered by the ideology of individualism.

Anderson, Lasch, and Sennett have modified this cautious analysis by arguing that the individualistic tendencies Tocqueville discerned have now become a form of narcissism. Having lost our sense of communion with the past, we feel no responsibility for the future. The final product of bourgeois individualism is psychological man, who is rootless, alienated, lives entirely in the present, and yet exists in a state of restless, unsatisfied desire. The new narcissism means a sense of inner emptiness, boundless repressed rage, an intense fear of old age and death, the decline of the play spirit, and strained relations between the sexes. Lasch associates this narcissism with specific twentieth-century developments, but Anderson and Sennett locate its origins in mid–nineteenth-century America and western Europe respectively. Their analysis applies to the health reformers, who exhibited an intense individualism that was coupled with an unwillingness to promote community-oriented values.

Individualism, in its most positive nineteenth century form, was the willingness of Americans to engage their energies, inventiveness, and adaptability in commercial and industrial enterprises. But individualism also negated the social bonds which bound Americans together. The Grahamites incarnated this flight from community to romantic individualism, for they spurned society and judged it irrelevant to human purposes. The purity reformers desperately took the only step available to save what they thought was essential: the self became the repository of society. To preserve what they embodied, one had to act alone. The individual consciousness became a secular incarnation and a means of becoming one's own redeemer. The Grahamites rejected the social world as a place of affirmation and instead pictured it as a snare and a danger to the fragile individual. They were complete and consistent in their negation: the health reformers denied the source of religious authority, the importance of society, and any meaning to history. Repression and internalization replaced any dialectical relationship with others. Many of Graham's followers probably understood and welcomed the tie between themselves and the world of the self because it answered the same emotional need in them that it fulfilled in Graham: the fantasy that transcendence could be achieved through self-absorption. They wanted the freedom to imagine themselves as having the power to dispose of the whole world. The abolition of pain, terror, anxiety, and death were the exorbitant demands made on reality by the Grahamites. As Emerson preached:

> The height of culture, the highest behavior, consists in the identification of the ego with the universe; so that when a man says, I hope, I find, I think, he might properly say, the human race finds or thinks or hopes. And meantime he shall be able continually to keep sight of his biographical Ego—I have a desk, I have an office, I am hungry, I had an ague,—as rhetoric or offset to his grand spiritual Ego, with impertinence, or ever confounding them.[11]

This study of romantic health reform and the works of Anderson, Lasch, and Sennett reverses the famous argument David Riesman made in *The Lonely Crowd* (1950). He contrasted an inner-directed society, in which people make commitments based on goals and sentiments they feel within themselves, to an other-directed society, in which feelings and commitments depend on what people sense to be the values of others. Riesman believed that modern American society and western Europe were moving from an inner- to an other-directed environment.[12] It appears, however, that the sequence should be reversed: Western society is moving in the opposite direction. But we are not experiencing a return to rugged individualism. Instead, growing numbers of people are becoming more anxious about their mental and emotional health. Graham and the health reformers were very modern in this sense; they attempted to privatize their lives because they perceived the community and public life as dangerous and unrewarding. This bifurcation, however, did not alleviate the health reformers' anxieties but rather intensified them.

Americans in Graham's generation apparently suffered a punishing psychic blow caused by the modernization process. The decline in deference, authority, and stability, which was symbolized by rootless rural male migrants in burgeoning commercial centers, destroyed the middle class's sense of assurance in a stable social and moral order. Revivalism and social reforms tried to cope with these problems, but they were insufficient. The result was a massive psychic withdrawal from public life through the medium of Victorian sexuality, which was a misguided attempt to make the body self-sufficient. Nineteenth-century sexual ethics have almost disappeared, but our problems with a solipsistic individualism remain, and now sexual performance has replaced abstinence as a way of authenticating the self. The modern narcissistic American expresses himself differently than his Victorian ancestors, but the lack of faith in community continues.

NOTES

1. Daniel Scott Smith and Michael S. Hindus, "Premarital Pregnancy in America, 1640–1971: An Overview and Interpretation," *Journal of Interdisciplinary History* 4 (1975):550–52, 557–58; Henry F. May, *The End of American Innocence* (New York: Oxford University Press, 1959), pp. 307–10, 340–47; Paul Robinson, *The Modernization of Sex* (New York: Harper and Row, 1976); James R. McGovern, "The American Woman's Pre-World War I Freedom in Marriage and Morals," *Journal of American History* 55 (1968):315–33; John C. Burnham, "The Progressive Era Revolution in American Attitudes Toward Sex," *Journal of American History* 59 (1973):885–908.

2. Lewis M. Terman, *Psychological Factors in Marital Happiness* (New York and London: McGraw-Hill Book Company, 1938), p. 320.

3. Alfred Kinsey, *Sexual Behavior in the Human Female* (Philadelphia: Saunders, 1953), p. 593.

4. Terman, *Psychological Factors*, p. 321; Kinsey, *Sexual Behavior*, p. 275.

5. *The Boston Quarterly Review* 3 (1840):266.

6. Paul S. Boyer, *Purity in Print: The Vice-Society Movement and Book Censorship in America* (New York: Scribner's, 1968); David J. Pivar, *Purity Crusade: Sexual Morality and Social Control, 1868–1900* (Westport, Conn.: Greenwood Press, 1973).

7. Thomas Bender, *Community and Social Change in America* (New Brunswick, N.J.: Rutgers University Press, 1978).

8. Stuart Blumin, *The Urban Threshold: Growth and Change in a Nineteenth Century American Community* (Chicago: University of Chicago Press, 1976); Richard Birdsall, *Berkshire County: A Cultural History* (New Haven, Conn.: Yale University Press, 1959).

9. Quentin Anderson, *The Imperial Self: An Essay in American Literary and Cultural History* (New York: Alfred A. Knopf, 1971); Christopher Lasch, *The Culture of Narcissism: American Life in an Age of Diminishing Expectations* (New York: W. W. Norton, 1978); Richard Sennett, *The Fall of Public Man: On the Social Psychology of Capitalism* (New York: Alfred A. Knopf, 1977).

10: Alexis de Tocqueville, *Democracy in America*, trans. Henry Reeve, 2 vols. (New York: Random House, 1945), 2:204. According to G. Barker-Benfield, Tocqueville recognized that antebellum males projected onto women a sense of order which they feared was missing in themselves. I would extend Tocqueville's argument: males not only feared women but the entire environment as a corrupting influence. The antebellum male's alienation from women was a microcosm of his alienation from public life. See Barker-Benfield, *The Horrors of the Half-Known Life: Male Attitudes Toward Women and Sexuality in Nineteenth Century America* (New York: Harper and Row, 1976), pp. 3–60.

11. Ralph Waldo Emerson, *The Complete Works of Ralph Waldo Emerson,* ed. Edward Waldo Emerson, 10 vols. (Boston and New York: Houghton Mifflin Co., 1903–1904), 7:62.

12. David Riesman, *The Lonely Crowd: A Study of the Changing American Character* (New Haven, Conn.: Yale University Press, 1950).

Bibliography

A. PRIMARY SOURCES

1. Newspapers, Journals

Advocate of Moral Reform
American Journal of Education
American Phrenological Journal
American Vegetarian and Health Journal
Boston Courier
Boston Medical and Surgical Journal
Boston Post
Boston Recorder
The Boston Quarterly Review
Cincinnati *Botanico-Medical Recorder*
Cincinnati *Dial*
Dansville Advertiser
Good Health
Graham Journal of Health and Longevity
Hampshire Gazette
The Harbinger
Harper's New Monthly Magazine
Health Journal and Advocate of Physiological Reform
Health Reformer
Journal of Foreign Medical Science & Literature
Journal of Health
Library of Health
Moral Reformer

Moral Reformer and Teacher on the Human Constitution
New Jersey Medical Reporter
New York Daily Advertiser
New York Evening Post
New York Review
Newark Journal
Nichols' Journal of Health, Water-Cure, and Human Progress
Nichols' Monthly
Oberlin Evangelist
Ohio Medical and Surgical Journal
The Oneida Circular
Palladium of Liberty
The Philadelphia Journal of the Medical and Physical Sciences
Poulson's American Daily Advertiser
Water-Cure Journal
The Witness

2. Books

Accum, Frederick. *A Treatise on Adulterations of Food and Culinary Poisons.* London: J. Mallett, 1820.

Alcott, William A. *Essay on the Construction of Schoolhouses.* Boston: Hilliard, Gray, Little and Wilkins, 1832.

———. *Familiar Letters to Young Men on Various Subjects.* Buffalo: Geo. H. Derby and Co., 1850.

———. *Forty Years in the Wilderness of Pills and Powders.* Boston: J. P. Jewett, 1859.

———. *The House I Live In.* Boston: G. W. Light, 1839.

———. *The Laws of Health.* Boston: J. P. Jewett, 1857.

———. *The Physiology of Marriage.* Boston: Dinsmoor and Co., 1866.

———. *Tea and Coffee.* Boston: G. W. Light, 1839.

———. *Vegetable Diet: As Sanctioned by Medical Men and by Experience in All Ages.* Boston: Marsh, Capon, & Lyon, 1838.

———. *The Young Housekeeper.* Boston: G. W. Light, 1838.

———. *The Young Husband.* Philadelphia: n.p., 1835.

———. *The Young Man's Guide.* Boston: Lilly, Wait, Coleman, & Holden, 1833.

———. *The Young Mother.* Boston: Light and Stearns, 1836.

Alliborne, S. Austin. *A Critical Dictionary of English Literature and British and American Authors.* 3 vols. Philadelphia: Childs & Peterson, 1859. Vols. 1, 2.

Beaumont, William. *Experiments and Observations on the Gastric Juice, and the Physiology of Digestion.* Plattsburgh, N.Y.: F. P. Allen, 1833.

Beecher, Lyman. *Six Sermons on Intemperance.* Boston: T. R. Marvin, 1827.

Bible Communism: A Compilation from the Annual Reports and Other Publications of the Oneida Association and Its Branches. Brooklyn, N.Y.: Oneida Community, 1853.

Bichat, Xavier. *General Anatomy, applied to Physiology and Medicine.* 2 vols. Boston: Richardson and Lord, 1822. Vol. 1.

———. *Physiological Researches upon Life and Death.* Philadelphia: Smith and Maxwell, 1809.

Bigelow, C. *Sexual Pathology; A Practical and Popular Review of the Principal Diseases of the Reproductive Organs.* Chicago: Ottaway and Colbert, 1875.

Broussais, François J. V. *A Treatise on Physiology Applied to Psychology.* Philadelphia: H. C. Carey and I. Lea, 1826.

Calhoun, George R. *Report of the Consulting Surgeon on Spermatorrhoea or Seminal Weakness.* Philadelphia: Howard Association, 1859.

Chapin, Charles V. *The Sources and Modes of Infection.* New York: J. Wiley and Sons, 1910.

Chipley, W. S. *A Warning to Fathers, Teachers and Young Men, in Relation to a Frightful Cause of Insanity and Other Serious Disorders of Youth.* Cincinnati: n.p., 1866.

Claflin, Tennessee. *The Ethics of Sexual Equality.* New York: Woodhull & Claflin, 1873.

Combe, George. *Notes on the United States of North America during a Phrenological Visit in 1838-9-40,* 3 vols. Edinburgh: Maclachlan, Stewart, 1841. Vol. 3.

Constitution of the American Physiological Society: with a Catalogue of its Members and Officers. Boston: Marsh, Capon & Lyon, 1837.

Conway, Moncure D. *Autobiography, Memories and Experiences.* 2 vols. Boston and New York: Houghton, Mifflin and Company, 1904. Vol. 2.

Cooke, Nicholas Francis. *Satan in Society. By a Physician.* Cincinnati and New York: C. F. Vent, 1872.

Cornaro, Lewis. *Discourses on a Sober and Temperate Life.* Edited by Sylvester Graham. New York: M. Day, 1832.

Cornaro, Luigi. *Discourses on a Sober and Temperate Life.* Edited by John Burdell. New York: Fowlers and Wells, 1842.

DeVoe, Thomas. *The Market Assistant.* New York: Hurd and Houghton, 1867.

Doggett, Lawrence L. *Life of Robert McBurney.* Cleveland: F. M. Barton, 1902.

Ellis, John. *Marriage and Its Violations. Licentiousness and Vice.* New York: John Ellis, 1860.

Finney, Charles G. *Lectures on Revivals of Religion,* 1835. Edited by William G. McLoughlin. Cambridge, Mass.: Harvard University Press, 1960.

———. *Views of Sanctification.* Oberlin, Ohio: Steele, 1840.

First Annual Report of the American Physiological Society. Boston: George W. Light, 1837.

Fowler, Lorenzo. *The Principles of Phrenology and Physiology Applied to Man's Social Relations; together with an Analysis of the Domestic Feelings.* New York: Fowler and Wells, 1842.

Fowler, Orson. *Amativeness: or Evils and Remedies of Excessive and Perverted Sexuality.* New York: Fowler and Wells, 1846.

———. *Love and Parentage.* New York: Fowler and Wells, 1844.

———. *Physiology, Animal and Mental: Applied to the Preservation and Restoration of Health and Body, and Power of Mind.* New York: Fowler and Wells, 1847.

Frothingham, Octavius Brooks. *Transcendentalism in New England,* 1876. New York: Harper and Row, 1959.

Graham, Sylvester. *Aesculapian Tablets of the Nineteenth Century.* Providence, R.I.: Weeden and Cory, 1834.

———. *A Lecture on Epidemic Diseases Generally, and particularly the Spasmodic Cholera.* New York: M. Day, 1833.

———. *A Lecture to Young Men.* Providence, R.I.: Weeden and Cory, 1834.

———. *Lectures on the Science of Human Life.* 2 vols. Boston: Marsh, Capon, Lyon, and Webb, 1837. Vols. 1, 2.

———. *Thy Kingdom Come; A Discourse, on the Importance of Infant and Sunday Schools, delivered at the Crown St. Church, Philadelphia.* Philadelphia: W. F. Geddes, 1831.

Griscom, John H. *Improvements of the Public Health and the Establishment of a Sanitary Police in the City of New York.* Albany, N.Y.: Van Benthuysen, 1857.

Hartley, Isaac Smithson. *Memorial of Robert Milham Hartley; Edited by His Son.* Utica, N.Y.: Curtiss & Childs, 1882.

Heywood, Ezra. *Cupid's Yokes: or, the Binding Forces of Conjugal Life.* Princeton, Mass.: Co-operative Publishing Co., 1876.

Higginson, Thomas Wentworth. *Out-Door Papers.* Boston: Lee and Shepard, 1863.

Jackson, James Caleb. *The Sexual Organism, and Its Healthful Management.* Boston: Leverett, 1862.

Jennings, Isaac. *Medical Reform: A Treatise on Man's Physical Being and Disorders.* Oberlin, Ohio: Fitch & Jennings, 1847.

———. *The Philosophy of Human Life.* Cleveland, Ohio: O. Jewett, Proctor & Worthington, 1852.

Kellogg, John Harvey. *Man, the Masterpiece, or Plain Truths Plainly Told, About Boyhood, Youth, and Manhood.* Battle Creek, Mich.: Modern Medicine Publication Co., 1884.

———. *Plain Facts for Old and Young.* Burlington, Iowa: I. F. Segner, 1882.

Knowlton, Charles. *Fruits of Philosophy. An Essay on the Population Question,* 1842. London: Freethought Publishing Co., 1877.

Leibig, Justus von. *Animal Chemistry.* Cambridge, Mass.: J. Owen, 1842.

Mann, Horace. *The Life and Works of Horace Mann.* Edited by Mary Mann. 5 vols. Boston: Walker, Fuller and Company, 1865–1868. Vols. 2, 3, 5.

Mather, Cotton. *The Pure Nazarite.* Boston: T. Fleet, 1723.

Mullaly, John. *The Milk Trade in New York and Vicinity.* New York: Fowlers and Wells, 1853.

New Experiments. Means Without Living. Boston: Weeks, Jordan, 1837.

Newman, John B. *Philosophy of Generations; its Abuses, with their Causes, Prevention and Cure.* New York: n.p., 1856.

New York City Board of Health, *Majority and Minority Reports of the Select Committee of the Board of Health, Appointed to Investigate the Character and Condition of the Sources from which Cow's Milk is Derived, for Sale in the City of New York.* New York: n.p., 1858.

(Nichols) Gove, Mary S. *Experience in Water-Cure.* New York: Fowlers and Wells, 1850.

———. *Lecture to Women on Anatomy and Physiology.* New York: Harper & Brothers, 1846.

———. *Mary Lyndon, or Revelations of a Life.* New York: Stringer and Townsend, 1855.

———. *Solitary Vice. An Address to Parents and those who have the care of Children.* Portland, Maine: Journal Office, 1839.

Nichols, Thomas. *The Curse Removed; A Statement of Facts respecting the Efficacy of Water-Cure in the Treatment of Uterine Disease and the Removal of the Pains and Perils of Pregnancy and Childbirth.* New York: The Water-Cure Journal, 1850.

———. *Esoteric Anthropology.* New York: Thomas L. Nichols, 1853.

———. *Forty Years of American Life.* London: J. Maxwell and Company, 1864.

Nichols, Thomas, and Mary Gove Nichols. *Marriage: Its History, Character and Results.* Cincinnati: V. Nicholson & Co., 1854.

———. *Nichols' Medical Miscellanies; a Familiar Guide to the Preservation of Health, and the Hydropathic Home Treatment of the Most Formidable Diseases.* Cincinnati: T. L. Nichols, 1856.

Nicholson, Asenath. *Nature's Own Book.* New York: Wilbur and Whipple, 1835.

Noyes, John Humphrey. *John Humphrey Noyes: The Putney Community.* Edited by George Wallingford Noyes. Oneida, N.Y.: n.p., 1931.

———. *Male Continence.* Oneida, N.Y.: Office of the Oneida Circular, 1872.

Rohleder, Hermann. *Die Masturbation: Eine Monographie für Aerzte und Pädagogen.* Berlin: Kornfeld, 1899.

Roorbach, Orville A. *Supplement to the Bibliotheca Americana, A Catalogue of American Publications.* New York: D. A. Roorbach, 1855.

Rush, Benjamin. *Medical Inquiries and Observations.* 5 vols. Philadelphia: Thomas Dobson, 1794–1798. Vol. 4.

Second Annual Report of the American Physiological Society. Boston: George W. Light, 1838.

Shattuck, Lemuel. *Report of the Sanitary Commission of Massachusetts, 1850.* Cambridge, Mass.: Harvard University Press, 1948.

Shew, Joel. *Hydropathy; or, The Water-Cure: Its Principles, Modes of Treatment, & c.* New York: Wiley and Putnam, 1844.

Sims, J. Marion. *The Story of My Life.* New York: D. A. Appleton and Company, 1884.

State Lunatic Hospital at Worcester. *Annual Report of the Trustees,* 5th. Boston: n.p., 1837.

———. *Annual Report of the Trustees,* 9th. Boston: n.p., 1841.

Third Annual Report of the American Physiological Society. Boston: George W. Light, 1839.

Tissot, Samuel. *Onanism: Or, a Treatise upon the Disorders Produced by Masturbation; or, the Dangerous Effects of Secret and Excessive Venery.* London: D. Bell, R. Gray, and W. Thompson, 1781.

Tocqueville, Alexis de. *Democracy in America.* Translated by Henry Reeve. 2 vols. New York: Random House, 1945. Vol. 2.

Trall, Russell T. *Fruits and Farinacea the Proper Food of Man.* New York: Fowler and Wells, 1854.

————. *Home-Treatment for Sexual Abuses. A Practical Treatise.* New York: Fowler and Wells, 1853.

————. *The Hydropathic Encyclopedia.* 2 vols. New York: Fowlers and Wells, 1852. Vols. 1, 2.

————. *Nervous Debility; The Nature, Causes, Consequences, and Hygienic Treatment of Invalids Suffering from Prematurely Exhausted Vitality.* New York: Davies & Kent, 1861.

————. *Pathology of the Reproductive Organs; Embracing All Forms of Sexual Disorders.* Boston: B. Emerson, 1863.

————. *Sexual Physiology: A Scientific and Popular Exposition of the Fundamental Problems in Sociology.* New York: Miller, Wood, 1866.

Willard, Elizabeth O. G. *Sexology as the Philosophy of Life.* Chicago: J. R. Walsh, 1867.

Wise, Daniel. *The Young Man's Counsellor.* New York: Carlton and Phillips, 1853.

Woodward, Samuel B. *Hints for the Young in Relation to the Health of Body and Mind.* Boston: Light, 1856.

Wright, Henry Clarke. *Marriage and Parentage.* Boston: B. Marsh, 1855.

3. Later Edited Works

Barnes, Gilbert H., and Dwight L. Dumond, eds. *Letters of Theodore Dwight Weld, Angelina Grimké, and Sarah Grimké, 1822–1844.* 2 vols. New York: D. Appleton-Century Company, 1934. Vol. 2.

Emerson, Ralph Waldo. *The Complete Works of Ralph Waldo Emerson.* Edited by Edward Waldo Emerson. 10 vols. Boston and New York: Houghton Mifflin Co., 1903–1904. Vols. 1, 3, 7, 10.

————. *The Journals and Miscellaneous Notebooks of Ralph Waldo Emerson.* Edited by William H. Gilman et.al. 14 vols. Cambridge, Mass.: Harvard University Press, 1960. Vol. 7.

Rossiter, W. S. *A Century of Population Growth: From the First Census of the United States to the Twelfth, 1790–1900.* Washington D.C.: Government Printing Office, 1909.

Spiller, Robert E., and Alfred R. Ferguson, eds. *Collected Works of Ralph Waldo Emerson.* 3 vols. Cambridge, Mass.: Harvard University Press, 1971. Vol. 1.

U.S. Bureau of the Census. *Historical Statistics of the United States: Colonial Times to 1957.* Washington, D.C.: Government Printing Office, 1960.

B. SECONDARY WORKS

1. Articles

Ackerknecht, Erwin H. "Anticontagionism Between 1821 and 1867." *Bulletin of the History of Medicine* 22 (1948):562–93.

Alexander, John K. "Poverty, Fear and Continuity: An Analysis of the Poor in Late Eighteenth-Century Philadelphia." In *The Peoples of Philadelphia: A History of Ethnic Groups and Lower-Class Life, 1790–1940,* edited by Allen F. Davis and Mark H. Haller, pp. 13–36. Philadelphia: Temple University Press, 1973.

Allen, Phyllis. "Etiological Theory in America Prior to the Civil War." *Journal of the History of Medicine and Allied Sciences* 2 (1947):489–520.

Allmendinger, David F. "The Dangers of Ante-Bellum Student Life." *Journal of Social History* 7 (1973):78–85.

Ariès, Philippe, "Interpretation pour une histoire des mentalitès." In *La Prévention des naissances dans la famille: ses origines dans les temps moderne,* edited by Hélène Bergues, pp. 311–27. Paris: INED, 1970.

―――. "Sur les origines de la contraception en France." *Population* 3 (1953):465–72.

Baker, Luther G. "Changing Religious Norms and Family Values." *Journal of Marriage and Family* 27 (1965):6–12.

Barker-Benfield, Ben. "The Spermatic Economy: A Nineteenth Century View of Sexuality." *Feminist Studies* 1 (1972):45–74.

Basavarajappa, K. G. "Pre-marital Pregnancies and Ex-Nuptial Births in Australia, 1911–1966." *Australian and New Zealand Journal of Sociology* 4 (1968):126–45.

Beall, Otho T. "Aristotle's Master Piece in America: A Landmark in the Folklore of Medicine." *William and Mary Quarterly* 20 (1963):207–22.

Bell, Robert, and Leonard Blumberg. "Courtship Intimacy and Religious Background." *Marriage and Family Living* 21 (1959):356–60.

Berman, Alex. "Neo-Thomsonianism in the United States." *Journal of the History of Medicine and Allied Sciences* 9 (1956):133–55.

―――. "A Striving for Scientific Respectability: Some American Botanics and the Nineteenth Century Plant Materia Medica." *Bulletin of the History of Medicine* 30 (1956):7–31.

Blackburn, George, and Sherman L. Richards, Jr. "A Demographic History of the West: Manistee County, Michigan, 1850." *Journal of American History* 57 (1970):600–618.

Blumin, Stuart Mark. "Mobility and Change in Ante-Bellum Philadelphia." In *Nineteenth Century Cities: Essays in the New Urban History*, edited by Stephen Thernstrom and Richard Sennett, pp. 165–208. New Haven, Conn.: Yale University Press, 1969.

Bridenbaugh, Carl. "Baths and Watering Places of Colonial America." *William and Mary Quarterly* 3 (1946):151–81.

Brown, Norman O. "Apocalypse: The Place of Mystery in the Life of the Mind." *Harper's* 222 (May 1961):47–49.

Brown, Richard D. "Modernization and the Modern Personality in Early America, 1600–1865: A Sketch of a Synthesis." *Journal of Interdisciplinary History* 2 (1972):201–28.

———. "Modernization: A Victorian Climax." In *Victorian America*, edited by Daniel Walker Howe, pp. 29–46. Philadelphia: University of Pennsylvania Press, 1976.

Bullough, Vern. "An Early American Sex Manual, Or, Aristotle Who?" *Early American Literature* 8 (1973):236–46.

Burnham, John C. "The Progressive Era Revolution in American Attitudes Toward Sex." *Journal of American History* 59 (1973):885–908.

Butz, William P., and Jean-Pierre Habicht. "The Effect of Nutrition and Health on Fertility: Hypotheses, Evidence, and Interventions." In *Population and Development*, edited by Ronald G. Ridker, pp. 210–38. Baltimore: Johns Hopkins University Press, 1976.

Carmer, Carl. "That Was New York: The Fowlers, Practical Phrenologists," *New Yorker* 12 (February 13, 1937):22–27.

Cominos, Peter. "Late-Victorian Sexual Respectability and the Social System." *International Review of Social History* 8 (1963):18–48, 216–50.

Conway, Jill. "Perspectives on the History of Women's Education in the United States." *History of Education Quarterly* 14 (1974):1–12.

Cott, Nancy. "Passionlessness: An Interpretation of Victorian Sexual Ideology, 1790–1850." *Signs* 4 (1978–79):219–36.

Crouthamel, James C. "The Newspaper Revolution in New York, 1830–1840." *New York History* 45 (1964):91–113.

Cutright, Phillips. "Illegitimacy in the United States, 1920–1968." In *Demographic and Social Aspects of Population Growth*, edited by Charles F. Westoff and Robert Parke, Jr., pp. 381–438. Washington, D.C.: Government Printing Office, 1972.

———. "Illegitimacy: Myths, Causes and Cures." *Family Planning Perspectives* 3 (1971):26–47.

Davis, Kingsley, and Judith Blake. "Social Structure and Fertility: An Analytic Framework." *Economic Development and Cultural Change* 4 (1956):211–35.

Dedman, Jean. "The Relationship Between Religious Attitude and Attitude Toward Premarital Sexual Relations." *Marriage and Family Living* 21 (1959):171–76.

Degler, Carl N. "What Ought To Be and What Was: Women's Sexuality in the Nineteenth Century." *American Historical Review* 79 (1974):1467–90.

Demos, John, and Virginia Demos. "Adolescence in Historical Perspective." *Journal of Marriage and the Family* 31 (1969):632–38.

Deniel, Raymond. "La Population d'un village du Nord de la France: Sainghn-en-Mélantois, de 1665 à 1851." *Population* 20 (1965)563–602.

Depres, P. "The Demographic Development of Flanders in the Eighteenth Century." In *Population in History: Essays in Historical Demography*, edited by D. V. Glass and D. E. C. Eversley, pp. 608–30. London: Arnold, 1965.

Duffy, John. "Medical Practice in the Antebellum South." *Journal of Southern History* 25 (1959):53–72.

Eisenstadt, Samuel N. "Studies of Modernization and Sociological Theory." *History and Theory* 13 (1974):225–52.

Entralgo, Pedro Lain. "Sensualism and Vitalism in Bichat's 'Anatomie Générale.'" *Journal of the History of Medicine and Allied Sciences* 3 (1948):47–64.

Fishman, Sterling. "Suicide, Sex, and the Discovery of the German Adolescent." *History of Education Quarterly* 10 (1970):170–88.

Flandrin, Jean-Louis. "Contraception, mariage, et relations amoureuses dans l'Occident chrétian." *Annales: E.S.C.* 34 (1969):1370–90.

Fletcher, Robert Samuel. "Bread and Doctrine at Oberlin." *Ohio State Archeological and Historical Quarterly* 49 (1940):59–65.

Forman, Jonathan. "Alva Curtis." *Bulletin of the History of Medicine* 21 (1947):772–87.

Gallman, Robert E. "Trends in the Size Distribution of Wealth in the Nineteenth Century." In *Six Papers on the Size Distribution of Wealth and Income*, edited by Lee Soltow, pp. 1–25. New York: Columbia University Press, 1969.

Goldstein, Sidney,. "Premarital Pregnancies and Out-of-Wedlock Births in Denmark, 1950–1965." *Demography* 4 (1967):925–36.

Gordon, Michael, and M. Charles Bernstein. "Mate Choice and Domestic Life in 19th Century Marriage Manuals." *Journal of Marriage and the Family* 32 (1970):665–74.

Greven, Philip, Jr. "Historical Demography and Colonial America." *William and Mary Quarterly* 24 (1967):438–54.

Hair, P. E. H. "Bridal Pregnancy in Rural England in Earlier Centuries." *Population Studies* 20 (1966–1967):233–43.

———. "Bridal Pregnancy in Earlier Rural England, Further Examined." *Population Studies* 24 (1970):59–70.

Hare, E. H. "Masturbatory Insanity: The History of an Idea." *Journal of Mental Science* 108 (1962):1–25.

Hartley, Shirley M. "The Amazing Rise of Illegitimacy in Great Britain." *Social Forces* 44 (1966):533–45.

Henretta, James. "Economic Development and Social Structure in Colonial Boston." *William and Mary Quarterly* 22 (1965):75–92.

———. "Modernization: Toward a False Synthesis." *Reviews in American History* 5 (1977):445–52.

Horlick, Allan S. "Phrenology and the Social Education of Young Men." *History of Education Quarterly* 11 (1971):23–39.

Houdaille, Jacques. "Quelques résultats sur la démographie de trois villages d'Allemagne de 1750 à 1879." *Population* 25 (1970):649–54.

Inkeles, Alex. "Making Men Modern: On the Causes and Consequences of Individual Change in Six Developing Countries." *American Journal of Sociology* 75 (1969):208–25.

Jacobson, Paul H. "Cohort Survival for Generations since 1840." *Millbank Memorial Fund Quarterly* 42 (1964):36–53.

Jones, Russell. "American Doctors and the Parisian Medical World, 1830–1840." *Bulletin of the History of Medicine* 47 (1973):40–65, 177–204.

Jordan, Philip D. "The Secret Six, An Inquiry Into the Basic Materia Medica of the Thomsonian System of Botanic Medicine." *Ohio State Archeological and Historical Quarterly* 52 (1943):347–55.

Kanin, Eugene J., and David H. Howard. "Postmarital Consequences of Premarital Sex Adjustments." *American Sociological Review* 23 (1958):556–61.

Katner, John F., and Melvin Zelnik. "Contraception and Pregnancy: Experience of Young Unmarried Women in the United States." *Family Planning Perspectives* 5 (1973):21–35.

Kenniston, Kenneth. "Social Change and Youth in America." *Daedalus* 91 (1962):145–71.

Kerber, Linda. "Daughters of Columbia: Educating Woman for the Republic, 1787–1805." In *The Hofstader Aegis*, edited by Stanley Elkins and Eric McKitrick, pp. 39–59. New York: Columbia University Press, 1974.

Kett, Joseph F. "Adolescence and Youth in Nineteenth-Century America." *Journal of Interdisciplinary History* 2 (1971):283–98.

Kulikoff, Allan. "The Progress of Inequality in Revolutionary Boston." *William and Mary Quarterly* 28 (1971):375–412.

Ladurie, Emmanuel LeRoy. "Huguenots Contre Papistes." In *Histoire du Languedoc,* edited by Philippe Wolff, pp. 313–25. Toulouse: Edouard Privat, 1967.

Langer, William L. "The Origins of the Birth Control Movement in the Early Nineteenth Century." *Journal of Interdisciplinary History* 5 (1975):669–86.

Laslett, Peter. "Age at Menarche in Europe since the 18th Century." *Journal of Interdisciplinary History* 2 (1971):221–36.

LeDuc, Thomas H. "Grahamites and Garrisonians." *New York History* 20 (1939):189–91.

Legan, Marshall Scott. "Hydropathy in America: A Nineteenth Century Panacea." *Bulletin of the History of Medicine* 45 (1971):267–80.

Lemon, James T., and Gary B. Nash. "The Distribution of Wealth in Eighteenth Century America: A Century of Changes in Chester County, Pennsylvania, 1693–1802." *Journal of Social History* 2 (1968):1–24.

Lerner, Gerda. "The Lady and the Mill Girl: Changes in the Status of Women in the Age of Jackson." *American Studies* 10 (1969):5–15.

Levermore, Charles A. "Rise of Metropolitan Journalism." *American Historical Review* 6 (1901):446–65.

Lockridge, Kenneth. "Social Change and the Meaning of the American Revolution." *Journal of Social History* 6 (1973):403–39.

MacDonald, Robert H. "The Frightful Consequences of Onanism: Notes on the History of Delusion." *Journal of the History of Ideas* 28 (1967):423–41.

McGovern, James R. "The American Woman's Pre–World War I Freedom in Marriage and Morals." *Journal of American History* 55 (1968):315–33.

McGrew, R. E. "The First Cholera Epidemic and Social History." *Bulletin of the History of Medicine* 34 (1960):61–73.

Main, Gloria L. "Inequality in Early America: The Evidence from Probate Records of Massachusetts and Maryland." *Journal of Interdisciplinary History* 7 (1977):559–82.

Marcuse, Herbert. "A Reply to Erich Fromm." *Dissent* 3 (1956):79–81.

Martin, Asa Earl. "The Temperance Movement in Pennsylvania Prior to the Civil War." *Pennsylvania Magazine of History and Biography* 49 (1925):195–230.

Mechling, Jay. "Advice to Historians on Advice to Mothers." *Journal of Social History* 9 (1975):44–63.

Meeker, Edward. "The Improving Health of the United States, 1850–1915." *Explorations in Economic History* 9 (1972): 353–75.

Morantz, Regina. "The Lady and Her Physician." In *Clio's Consciousness Raised: New Perspectives on the History of Women*, edited by Mary Hartman and Lois W. Banner, pp. 38–53. New York: Harper and Row, 1974.

———. "Making Women Modern: Middle Class Women and Health Reform in 19th Century America." *Journal of Social History* 10 (1977):490–507.

———. "Nineteenth Century Reform and Women: A Program of Self-Help." In *Medicine without Doctors: Home Care in American History*, edited by Guenter B. Risse, Ronald L. Numbers, and Judith W. Leavitt, pp. 73–93. New York: Science History Publication, 1977.

Morgan, Edmund S. "The Puritans and Sex." *New England Quarterly* 15 (1942):591–607.

Moynihan, Daniel Patrick. "The Negro Family: The Case for National Action." In *The Moynihan Report and the Politics of Controversy*, edited by Lee Rainwater and William L. Yancey, pp. 47–124. Cambridge, Mass.: MIT Press, 1967.

Naylor, Mildred V. "Sylvester Graham, 1794–1851." *Annals of Medical History* 4 (1942):236–40.

Neuman, Robert P. "Masturbation, Madness, and the Modern Concepts of Childhood and Adolescence." *Journal of Social History* 8 (1975):1–27.

Parsons, Gail Pat. "Equal Treatment for All: American Medical Remem-dies for Male Sexual Problems, 1850–1900." *Journal of the History of Medicine and Allied Sciences* 32 (1977):55–71.

Pessen, Edward. "The Egalitarian Myth and the American Social Reality: Wealth, Mobility, and Equality in the 'Era of the Common Man.'" *American Historical Review* 79 (1971):989–1034.

Potter, J. "The Growth of Population in America, 1700–1860." In *Population in History: Essays in Historical Demography*, edited by D. V. Glass and D. E. C. Eversley, pp. 631–88. Chicago: University of Chicago Press, 1965.

Quay, Eugene. "Justifiable Abortion—Medical and Legal Foundations." *The Georgetown Law Journal* 49 (1961):395–526.

Reigel, Robert E. "Early Phrenology in the United States." *Medical Life* 37 (1930):361–76.

Reiss, Ira. "Premarital Sexual Permissiveness among Negroes and Whites." *American Sociological Review* 29 (1964):688–98.

Riley, Glenda. "The Subtle Subversion: Change in the Traditionalist Image of American Woman." *The Historian* 32 (1970):210–27.

Rodman, Hyman. "Illegitimacy in the Carribbean Social Structure: A Reconsideration." *American Sociological Review* 31 (1966):673–86.

——. "The Lower-Class Value Stretch." *Social Forces* 42 (1963):205–15.

Rogin, Michael Paul. "Nature as Politics and Nature as Romance in America." *Political Theory* 5 (1977):5–30.

Rolleston, J. D. "F. J. V. Broussais: His Life and Doctrines." *Proceedings of the Royal Society of Medicine* 32 (1939):405–13.

Rorabaugh, W. J. "Estimated U.S. Alcoholic Beverage Consumption, 1790–1850." *Journal of Studies on Alcohol* 37 (1976):357–64.

Rosen, George. "Approaches to a Concept of Social Medicine, A Historical Survey." *Millbank Memorial Fund Quarterly* 26 (1948):7–21.

——— "The Philosophy of Ideology and the Emergence of Modern Medicine in France." *Bulletin of the History of Medicine* 20 (1946):328–39.

——. "Public Health Problems in New York City During the Nineteenth Century." *New York State Journal of Medicine* 50 (1950):73–79.

——. "What is Social Medicine? A Genetic Analysis of the Concept." *Bulletin of the History of Medicine* 21 (1947):674–733.

Rosenberg, Carroll Smith, and Charles A. Rosenberg. "The Female Animal: Medical and Biological Views of Woman and Her Role in Nineteenth Century America." *Journal of American History* 60 (1973):332–56.

Rosenberg, Charles. "The Bitter Fruit: Heredity, Disease, and Social Thought." *Perspectives in American History* 8 (1974):189–235.

——— "The Cause of Cholera: Aspects of Etiological Thought in Nineteenth Century America." *Bulletin of the History of Medicine* 34 (1960):331–54.

——. "Sexuality, Class and Role in 19th Century America." *American Quarterly* 25 (1973):131–53.

Rosenkrantz, Barbara Gutmann, "Cart Before Horse: Theory, Practice and Professional Image in American Public Health, 1870–1920." *Journal of the History of Medicine and Allied Sciences* 24 (1974):55–73.

Salmon, Louis B. "The Least-Remembered Alcott." *New England Quarterly* 34 (1961):87–93.

Shorter, Edwards. "Capitalism, Culture, and Sexuality: Some Competing Models." *Social Science Quarterly* 53 (1972–1973):341–56.

——. "Female Emancipation, Birth Control, and Fertility in European History." *American Historical Review* 78 (1973):605–40.

———— "Illegitimacy, Sexual Revolution and Social Change in Modern Europe." *Journal of Interdisciplinary History* 2 (1971):237–72.

————. "Sexual Change and Illegitimacy: The European Experience." in *Modern European Social History,* edited by Robert J. Bezucha, pp. 231–69. Lexington, Mass.: D. C. Heath, 1972.

Shorter, Edward, John Knodel, and Etiene van de Walle. "The Decline of Non-Marital Fertility in Europe, 1880–1940." *Population Studies* 24 (1971):375–93.

Sigerist, Harry E. "American Spas in Historical Perspective." *Bulletin of the History of Medicine* 2 (1942):133–47.

Smith, Daniel Scott. "The Dating of the American Sexual Revolution: Evidence and Interpretation." In *The American Family in Social-Historical Perspective,* edited by Michael Gordon, pp. 321–35. New York: St. Martin's Press, 1973.

Smith, Daniel Scott, and Michael S. Hindus. "Premarital Pregnancy in America, 1640–1971: An Overview and Interpretation." *Journal of Interdisciplinary History* 5 (1975):537–70.

Soltow, Lee, "Economic Inequality in the United States in the Period from 1790 to 1860." *Journal of Economic History* 31 (1971):822–39.

Spitz, René. "Authority and Masturbation: Some Remarks on a Bibliographical Investigation." *Psychoanalytic Quarterly* 21 (1952):490–527.

Stewart, Charles T., Jr. "Allocation of Resources to Health." *Journal of Human Resources* 6 (1971):103–21.

Sutter, J. "Sur la diffusion des méthodes contraceptives." In *La Prévention des naissances dans la famille: ses origines dans les temps moderne,* edited by Hélène Berques, pp. 341–59. Paris: INED, 1960.

Tanner, J. M. "Sequence, Tempo, and Individual Variation in the Growth and Development of Boys and Girls Aged Twelve to Sixteen." *Daedalus* 100 (1971): 907–30.

Temkin, Owsei. "The Role of Surgery in the Rise of Modern Medical Thought." *Bulletin of the History of Medicine* 25 (1951): 248–59.

Thernstrom, Stephen, and Peter R. Knights. "Men in Motion: Some Data and Speculations about Urban Population Mobility in Nineteenth-Century America." *Journal of Interdisciplinary History* 1 (1970):7–36.

Thomas, John L. "Romantic Reform in America, 1815–1865." *American Quarterly* 17 (1965):656–81.

Thoms, H. "William Andrus Alcott: Physician, educator, writer." *Bulletin of the Society of Medical History* 4 (1928):123–30.

Walker, William B. "Luigi Cornaro; A Renaissance Writer on Personal Hygiene." *Bulletin of the History of Medicine* 28 (1954):525–34.

Walters, Ronald. "The Erotic South: Civilization and Sexuality in American Abolitionism." *American Quarterly* 25 (1973):177–201.

Wood, Anne D. "The Fashionable Diseases: Women's Complaints and Their Treatment in Nineteenth-Century America." *Journal of Interdisciplinary History* 4 (1973):25–52.

Woude, A. M. van der, and G. J. Mentink. "La Population de Rotterdam au XVIIe et au XVIIIe siècle." *Population* 21 (1966):1165–90.

Wright, Gavin. " 'Economic Democracy' and the Concentration of Agricultural Wealth in the Cotton South, 1850–1860." *Agricultural History* 44 (1970):63–94.

Wrigley, E. A. "The Process of Modernization and the Industrial Revolution." *Journal of Interdisciplinary History* 3 (1972):225–60.

Young, James Harvey. "American Medical Quakery in the Age of the Common Man." *Mississippi Valley Historical Review* 47 (1961):579–93.

Zirkle, Conway. "The Early History of the Inheritance of Acquired Characters and Pangenesis." *Transactions of the American Philosophical Society* 35 (1946):141–46.

2. Books

Ackerknecht, Erwin H. *Medicine at the Paris Hospital, 1794–1848.* Baltimore: Johns Hopkins University Press, 1967.

Almond, Gabriel A. and Sidney Verba. *The Civic Culture: Political Attitudes and Democracy in Five Nations.* Princeton, N.J.: Princeton University Press, 1963.

Anderson, Quentin. *The Imperial Self: An Essay in American Literary and Cultural History.* New York: Alfred A. Knopf, 1971.

Bacci, Massimo Livi. *A Century of Portugese Fertility.* Princeton, N.J.: Princeton University Press, 1971.

———. *A History of Italian Fertility During the Last Two Centuries.* Princeton, N.J.: Princeton University Press, 1977.

Banks, J. A. *Prosperity and Parenthood, A Study of Family Planning Among the Victorian Middle Classes.* New York: Schocken Books, 1954.

Barker-Benfield, Ben. *The Horrors of the Half-Known Life: Male Attitudes Toward Women and Sexuality in 19th Century America.* New York: Harper and Row, 1976.

Bathe, Greville, and Dorothy Bathe. *Oliver Evans.* Philadelphia: The Historical Society of Philadelphia, 1935.

Bender, Thomas. *Community and Social Change in America.* New Brunswick, N.J.: Rutgers University Press, 1978.

Berkovitch, Sacvan. *The American Jermiad.* Madison, Wisc.: University of Wisconsin Press, 1978.

Birdsall, Richard. *Berkshire County: A Cultural History.* New Haven, Conn.: Yale University Press, 1959.

Black, Cyril E. *The Dynamics of Modernization.* Princeton, N.J.: Princeton University Press, 1966.

Blake, Rev. Mortimer. *Centennial History of the Mendon Association of Congregational Ministers.* Boston: S. Harding, 1853.

Blumin, Stuart. *The Urban Threshold: Growth and Change in a Nineteenth Century American Community.* Chicago: University of Chicago Press, 1976.

Bode, Carl. *The American Lyceum: Town Meeting of the Mind.* New York: Oxford University Press, 1956.

———. *Antebellum Culture.* Berkeley and Los Angeles: University of California Press, 1959.

Boyer, Paul S. *Purity in Print: The Vice-Society Movement and Book Censorship in America.* New York: Scribners, 1968.

Braun, Rudolf. *Industrialisierung und Volksleben: Die Veranderungen der Lebensformen in einem ländlichen Industriegebiet vor 1800 (Züricher Oberland).* Erlenbach—Zurich: Eugen Rentsch, 1960.

Brown, Norman O. *Life Against Death: The Psychoanalytic Meaning of History.* Middletown, Conn.: Wesleyan University Press, 1959.

———. *Love's Body.* New York: Random House, 1966.

Brown, Richard. *Modernization: The Transformation of American Life, 1600–1865.* New York: Hill and Wang, 1976.

Bullough, Vern, and Bonnie Bullough. *Sin, Sickness, and Sanity: A History of Sexual Attitudes.* New York: Garland Publishing, 1977.

Burgess, Ernest, and Paul Wallin. *Engagement and Marriage.* Philadelphia: J. B. Lippincott, 1953.

Burrow, James O. *AMA: Voice of American Medicine.* Baltimore: Johns Hopkins University Press, 1963.

Bury, J. A. *The Idea of Progress: An Inquiry into its Origins and Growth.* London: Macmillan, 1924.

Bushman, Richard L. *From Puritan to Yankee: Character and Social Order in Connecticut, 1690–1765.* Cambridge, Mass.: Harvard University Press, 1967.

Calhoun, Arthur W. *A Social History of the American Family from Colonial Times to the Present.* 3 vols. Cleveland, Ohio: Arthur H. Clark Co., 1917–1919. vols. 2, 3.

Campbell, Randolph B. and Richard G. Lowe. *Wealth and Power in Antebellum Texas.* College Station, Tex.: Texas A & M Press, 1977.

Carlson, Rick J. *The End of Medicine.* New York: Wiley, 1975.

Carpenter, Helen Graham. *The Rev. John Graham of Woodbury, Connecticut and His Descendants*. Chicago: The Monastery Hill Press, 1942.

Carson, Gerald. *Cornflake Crusade*. New York: Holt, Rinehart and Winston, 1957.

Chalfant, Harry M. *Father Penn and John Barleycorn*. Harrisburg, Pa.: The Evangelical Press, 1920.

Chambers, J. S. *The Conquest of Cholera: America's Greatest Scourge*. New York: Macmillan, 1938.

Coale, Ansley J. and Melvin Zelnik. *New Estimates of Fertility and Population in the United States*. Princeton, N.J.: Princeton University Press, 1963.

Cole, Edith. "Sylvester Graham, Lecturer on the Science of Human Life: The Rhetoric of a Dietary Reformer." Ph.D. diss., Indiana University, 1975.

Comfort, Alex. *The Anxiety Makers*. London: Nelson, 1967.

Cott, Nancy F. *The Bonds of Womanhood: "Woman's Sphere" in New England, 1780–1835*. New Haven: Yale University Press, 1977.

Cummings, Richard Osborn. *The American and His Food*. Chicago: University of Chicago Press, 1941.

Davies, John D. *Phrenology Fad and Science: A Nineteenth Century American Crusade*. New Haven, Conn.: Yale University Press, 1955.

Degler, Carl. *At Odds: Women and the Family in America from the Revolution to the Present*. New York: Oxford University Press, 1980.

Doherty, Robert. *Society and Power: Five New England Towns, 1800–1860*. Amherst, Mass.: University of Massachusetts Press, 1977.

Douglas, Mary. *Natural Symbols: Explorations in Cosmology*. London: Barrie and Jenkins, 1973.

———. *Purity and Danger: An Analysis of Concepts of Pollution and Taboo*. New York: Basic Books, 1966.

Dubos, René. *The Mirage of Health: Utopian Progress and Biological Change*. New York: Harper and Row, 1959.

Ed. Duffy, John. *History of Medicine in Louisiana*. 2 vols. Baton Rouge, La.: Louisiana State University Press, 1962. Vol. 2.

Eisenstadt, Samuel N. *Modernization: Protest and Change*. Englewood Cliffs, N.J.: Prentice-Hall, 1966.

Ellis, Havelock. *Sex in Relation to Society*. Philadelphia: F. A. Davis Company, 1911.

Erikson, Erik. *Young Man Luther*. New York: W. W. Norton, 1958.

Fass, Paula S. *The Damned and the Beautiful: American Youth in the 1920's*. New York: Oxford University Press, 1977.

Fehlandt, August F. *A Century of Drink Reform in the United States.* Cincinnati: Jennings and Graham, 1904.

Flandrin, Jean-Louise. *Familles: parenté, maison, sexualité, dans l'ancien société.* Paris: Hachette, 1976.

Fletcher, Robert Samuel. *A History of Oberlin College from its Foundation Through the Civil War.* 2 vols. Oberlin, Ohio: Oberlin College, 1943. Vol. 1.

Forward, Charles W. *Fifty Years of Food Reform: A History of the Vegetarian Movement in England.* London: The Ideal Publishing Union, Ltd., 1898.

Foucault, Michel. *The History of Sexuality. Vol. I: An Introduction.* Translated by Robert Hurley. New York: Random House, 1978.

———. *Naissance de clinique.* Paris: Presses Universitaires de France, 1963.

Freud, Sigmund. *Civilization and Its Discontents.* Translated by James Strachey. New York: W. W. Norton, 1962.

Fryer, Peter. *The Birth Controllers.* New York: Stein and Day, 1966.

Gasking, Elizabeth. *Investigations into Generation, 1651–1828.* Baltimore: Johns Hopkins University Press, 1966.

Gaustad, Edwin Scott. *Historical Atlas of Religion in America.* New York: Harper and Row, 1976.

Giedion, Siegfried. *Mechanization Takes Command.* New York: W. W. Norton, 1969.

Gillis, John R. *Youth and History: Tradition and Change in European Age Relations, 1770–Present.* New York: Academic Press, 1974.

Gordon, Linda. *Woman's Body, Woman's Right: A Social History of Birth Control in America.* New York: Viking, 1977.

Gove, William Henry. *The Gove Book.* Salem, Mass.: S. Perley, 1922.

Greven, Philip, Jr. *Four Generations: Population, Land and Family in Colonial Andover, Massachusetts.* Ithaca, N.Y.: Cornell University Press, 1970.

Gusfield, Joseph R. *Symbolic Crusade: Status Politics and the American Temperance Movement.* Urbana, Ill.: University of Illinois Press, 1963.

Hageman, John F. *History of Burlington and Mercer Counties, New Jersey.* Philadelphia: Everts & Peck, 1883.

Haller, John S., and Robin Haller. *The Physician and Sexuality in Victorian America.* University of Illinois Press, 1973.

Handlin, Oscar. *The Americans.* Boston: Little, Brown and Co., 1963.

———. *Race and Nationality in American Life.* Boston: Little, Brown and Co., 1957.

Henretta, James. *The Evolution of American Society, 1700–1815: An Interdisciplinary Analysis.* Lexington, Mass.: D. C. Heath, 1973.

Herbert, Will. *Protestant, Catholic, Jew.* Garden City, N.Y.: Doubleday, 1955.

Hill, Christopher. *Society and Puritanism in Pre-Revolutionary England.* New York: Schocken Books, 1964.

Himes, Norman E. *Medical History of Contraception.* Baltimore: The Williams and Wilkins Co., 1936.

Horlick, Allen Stanley. *Country Boys and Merchant Princes: The Social Control of Young Men in New York.* Lewisburg, Pa.: Bucknell University Press, 1975.

Illich, Ivan. *Medical Nemesis: The Expropriation of Health.* New York: Pantheon Books, 1976.

Inkeles, Alex, and David H. Smith. *Becoming Modern: Individual Changes in Six Developing Countries.* Cambridge, Mass.: Harvard University Press, 1974.

James, Henry. *Partial Portraits.* London: Macmillan, 1911.

Jay, Martin. *The Dialectical Imagination: A History of the Frankfort School and the Institute of Social Research, 1923–1950.* Boston: Little, Brown and Co., 1973.

Jones, Richard F. *Ancients and Moderns: A Study of the Rise of the Scientific Movement in Seventeenth-Century England.* Berkeley and Los Angeles: University of California Press, 1965.

Katz, Michael B. *The Irony of Early School Reform: Educational Innovation in Mid-Nineteenth Century Massachusetts.* Cambridge, Mass.: Harvard University Press, 1968.

Kaufman, Martin. *Homeopathy in America: the Rise and Fall of a Medical Heresy.* Baltimore: Johns Hopkins University Press, 1971.

Kennedy, David M. *Birth Control in America: The Career of Margret Sanger.* New Haven, Conn.: Yale University Press, 1970.

Kett, Joseph F. *The Formation of the American Medical Profession.* New Haven, Conn.: Yale University Press, 1968.

————. *Rites of Passage: Adolescence in America, 1790 to the Present.* New York: Basic Books, 1977.

Kinsey, Alfred. *Sexual Behavior in the Human Female.* Philadelphia: Saunders, 1953.

Kler, Joseph H. *God's Happy Cluster: 1688–1963, History of the Bound Brook Presbyterian Church.* N.p., 1963.

Knights, Peter R. *The Plain People of Boston, 1830–1860: A Study of City Growth.* New York: Oxford University Press, 1971.

Knodel, John E. *The Decline of Fertility in Germany, 1871–1939.* Princeton, N.J.: Princeton University Press, 1974.

Kobler, John. *Ardent Spirits: The Rise and Fall of Prohibition.* New York: Putnam, 1973.

Krout, John A. *The Origins of Prohibition.* New York: Alfred A. Knopf, 1925.

Kuhlmann, Charles Byron. *The Development of the Flour-Milling Industry in the United States.* Boston: Houghton Mifflin Co., 1929.

Lader, Lawrence. *Abortion.* Boston: Bobbs-Merrill, 1966.

Ladurie, Emmanuel LeRoy. *Les Paysans de Languedoc.* Paris: S.E.V.-P.E.N., 1966.

Lasch, Christopher. *The Culture of Narcissism: American Life in an Age of Diminishing Expectations.* New York: W. W. Norton, 1978.

Leonard, Delavan Levant. *The Story of Oberlin; the Institution, the Community, the Idea, the Movement.* Boston: The Pilgrim Press, 1898.

Lerner, Daniel. *The Passing of Traditional Society: Modernizing the Middle East.* Glencoe, Ill.: Free Press, 1958.

Lesthaeghe, Ron J. *The Decline of Belgian Fertility, 1800–1900.* Princeton, N.J.: Princeton University Press, 1977.

Levin, Harry. *The Power of Blackness.* New York: Alfred A. Knopf, 1958.

Lewis, R. W. B. *The American Adam.* Chicago: University of Chicago Press, 1955.

McKeown, Thomas. *The Modern Rise of Population.* London: Arnold, 1976.

McWilliams, Wilson Carey. *The Idea of Fraternity in America.* Berkeley and Los Angeles: University of California Press, 1973.

Main, Jackson Turner. *The Social Structure of Revolutionary America.* Princeton, N.J.: Princeton University Press, 1965.

Marcus, Steven. *The Other Victorians: A Study of Sexuality and Pornography in Mid–Nineteenth-Century England.* New York: Basic Books, 1966.

Marcuse, Herbert. *Eros and Civilization.* Boston: Beacon Press, 1965.

———. *Five Lectures.* Boston: Beacon Press, 1970.

———. *Negations.* Boston: Beacon Press, 1968.

Marx, Leo. *The Machine in the Garden.* New York: Oxford University Press, 1964.

Masters, William, and Virginia Johnson. *Human Sexual Inadequacy.* Boston: Little, Brown and Co., 1970.

May, Henry F. *The End of American Innocence.* New York: Oxford University Press, 1959.

Melder, Keith. *Beginnings of Sisterhood: The American Woman's Rights Movement, 1800–1850.* New York: Schocken Books, 1977.

Miller, Perry. *The Life of the Mind in America: From the Revolution to the Civil War.* New York: Harcourt Brace and Jovanovich, 1965.

Mohr, James C. *Abortion in America: the Origins and Evolution of National Policy.* New York: Oxford University Press, 1978.

Molinier, Alain. *Une Paroisse du bas Languedoc: Serignan, 1650–1792.* Montpellier: Imp. Déhan, 1968.

Möller, Helmut. *Die Kleinbürgerliche Familie im 18 Jahrhundret: Verhalten und Gruppenkultur.* Berlin: de Gruyter, 1969.

Morgan, Edmund. *The Puritan Family: Religious and Domestic Relations in Seventeenth-Century New England, 1944.* Westport, Conn.: Greenwood Press, 1966.

Mott, Frank Luther. *American Journalism: A History, 1690–1960.* New York: Macmillan, 1962.

———. *A History of American Magazines, 1741–1850.* New York: D. Appleton, 1930.

Nissenbaum, Stephen W. "Careful Love: Sylvester Graham and the Emergence of Victorian Sexual Theory in America, 1830–1840." Ph.D. diss., University of Wisconsin, 1968.

———. *Sex, Diet, and Debility in Jacksonian America: Sylvester Graham and Health Reform.* Westport, Conn.: Greenwood Press, 1980.

Noonan, John T. *Contraception.* Cambridge, Mass.: Harvard University Press, 1966.

The Northampton Book. Northampton, Mass.: Tercentenary Committee, 1954.

Olmsted, James M.D. *François Magendie: Pioneer in Experimental Physiology and Scientific Medicine in XIX Century France.* New York: Schuman's, 1944.

Passmore, John Arthur. *The Perfectability of Man.* London: Scribners, 1970.

Pessen, Edward. *Riches, Class and Power before the Civil War.* Lexington, Mass.: D. C. Heath, 1973.

Phayer, J. Michael. *Sexual Liberation and Religion in Nineteenth Century Europe.* London: Rowman and Littlefield, 1977.

Pivar, David J. *Purity Crusade: Sexual Morality and Social Control, 1868–1900.* Westport, Conn.: Greenwood Press, 1973.

Pollitzer, R. *Cholera.* Geneva, Switzerland: UNESCO, 1959.

Purcell, Richard J. *Connecticut in Transition, 1775–1818.* Washington, D.C.: American Historical Association, 1918.

Ranum, Orest and Patricia Ranum, eds. *Popular Attitudes Toward Birth Control in Pre-Industrial France and England.* New York: Harper and Row, 1972.

Reed, James. *From Private Vice to Public Virtue: The Birth Control Movement and American Society since 1830.* New York: Basic Books, 1978.

Riesman, David. *The Lonely Crowd: A Study of the Changing American Character.* New Haven, Conn.: Yale University Press, 1950.

Robertson, Constance Noyes. *Oneida Community: The Breakup, 1876–1881.* Syracuse, N.Y.: Syracuse University Press, 1972.

Robinson, Dores E. *The Story of Our Health Message: The Origin, Character, and Development of Health Education in the Seventh-Day Adventist Church.* Nashville, Tenn.: Southern Publishing Association, 1955.

Robinson, Paul A. *The Freudian Left.* New York: Harper and Row, 1969.

———. *The Modernization of Sex.* Harper and Row, 1976.

Rodman, Hyman. *Lower-Class Families: The Culture of Poverty in Negro Trinidad.* New York: Oxford University Press, 1971.

Root, Waverly, and Richard de Rochement. *Eating in America.* New York: William Morrow, 1976.

Rosenberg, Charles E. *The Cholera Years.* Chicago: University of Chicago Press, 1962.

Rostow, W. W. *The Stages of Economic Growth.* Cambridge, England: Cambridge University Press, 1960.

Rothman, David J. *The Discovery of the Asylum: Social Order and Disorder in the New Republic.* Boston: Little, Brown and Co., 1971.

Rothstein, William G. *American Physicians in the Nineteenth Century.* Baltimore: Johns Hopkins University Press, 1972.

Rugoff, Milton. *Prudery and Passion: Sexuality in Victorian America.* New York: Putnam, 1971.

Sanborn, Franklin B. *Bronson Alcott at Alcott House, England, and Fruitlands, New England (1842–1844)* Cedar Rapids, Iowa: The Torch Press, 1908.

Savvy, Alfred. *Le prévention des naissances.* Paris: Presses Universitaires de France, 1965.

Schlebecker, John T. *Cattle Raising on the Plains, 1900–1961.* Lincoln, Neb.: University of Nebraska Press, 1963.

Schmidt, Gunter, and Volkmar Sigusch. *Arbeiter-Sexualität: Eine empirische Untersuchung an jungen Industriearbeiten.* Neuwied: Luchterland, 1971.

Schwartz, Richard W. *John Harvey Kellogg.* Nashville, Tenn.: Southern Pub. Association, 1970.

Sears, Hal D. *The Sex Radicals: Free Love in High Victorian America.* Lawrence, Kansas: Regents Press of Kansas, 1977.

Sennett, Richard. *The Fall of Public Man: On the Social Psychology of Capitalism.* New York: Alfred A. Knopf, 1977.

Shorter, Edward. *The Making of the Modern Family.* New York: Basic Books, 1975.

Shyrock, Richard H. *Medicine and Society in America: 1660–1860.* Ithaca, N.Y.: Cornell University Press, 1960.

———. *Medicine in America: Historical Essays.* Baltimore: Johns Hopkins University Press, 1966.

Sterns, Madeleine. *Heads & Headlines: The Phrenological Fowlers.* Norman, Okla.: University of Oklahoma Press, 1971.

Stevens, Rosemary. *American Medicine and the Public Interest.* New Haven, Conn.: Yale University Press, 1971.

Stiles, Henry Reed. *Bundling: Its Origins, Progress and Decline in America.* Albany, N.Y.: Knickerbocker, 1871.

Stone, Lawrence. *The Family, Sex and Marriage in England, 1500–1800.* New York: Harper and Row, 1977.

Szasz, Thomas. *The Manufacture of Madness.* New York: Harper and Row, 1970.

Terman, Lewis M. *Psychological Factors in Marital Happiness.* New York and London: McGraw-Hill Book Company, 1938.

Thompson, Warren S. and P. K. Whelpton. *Population Trends in the United States.* New York and London: McGraw-Hill Book Company, 1933.

Turner, Victor. *The Forest of Symbols.* Ithaca, N.Y.: Cornell University Press, 1967.

Villard, Henry. *Memoirs of Henry Villard, Journalist, and Financier: 1835–1900.* 2 vols. Boston: Houghton, Mifflin and Company, 1904. Vol. 2.

Walker, Mack. *German Home Towns: Community, State, and General Estate, 1648–1871.* Ithaca, N.Y.: Cornell University Press, 1971.

Walker, William B. "The Health Reform Movement in the United States, 1830–1870." Ph.D. diss., Johns Hopkins University, 1955.

Walters, Ronald. *The Antislavery Appeal: American Abolitionism After 1830*. Baltimore: Johns Hopkins University Press, 1976.

Warner, Sam Bass, Jr. *The Urban Wilderness: A History of the American City*. New York: Harper and Row, 1972.

Weber, Max. *The Protestant Ethic and the Spirit of Capitalism*. Translated by Talcott Parsons. New York: Scribners, 1947.

Weinstein, Fred and Gerald M. Platt. *The Wish To Be Free: Society, Psyche, and Value Change*. Berkeley and Los Angeles: University of California Press, 1969.

Weiss, Harry B., and Howard R. Kemble. *The Great American Water-Cure Craze: A History of Hydropathy in the United States*. Trenton, N.J.: The Past Times Press, 1967.

Welter, Rush. *The Mind of America, 1820–1860*. New York: Columbia University Press, 1975.

Werner, Oscar Helmuth. *The Unmarried Mother in German Literature with Special Reference to the Period 1770–1800*. New York: Columbia University Press, 1917.

White, Morton, and Lucia White. *The Intellectual Versus the City*. Cambridge, Mass.: Harvard University Press, 1962.

Young, James Harvey. *The Toadstool Millionaires*. Princeton, N.J.: Princeton University Press, 1961.

Zuckerman, Michael. *Peaceable Kingdoms: New England Towns in the Eighteenth Century*. New York: Alfred A. Knopf, 1970.

Index

Abolitionists, 150; conflicts among, 12; and hydropathy, 160
Abortion, 30
Accum, Frederick, 116
Adolescence, 81; Graham on, 88. *See also* Youths
Adulteration of foods, 115–16
Alcohol: Bell and Condie on, 64; consumption of, 119; Graham on, 61
Alcott, Bronson, 130
Alcott, William A., 145, 158; and American Physiological Society, 151; career of, 153–55; on exercise, 168; and Graham, 154–55; on heredity, 90; on masturbation, 88–90; on medicine, 113–14; at Oberlin, 148; popularity of, 143, 167; quoted briefly, 13, 118; regimen of, 154–55; on vegetarianism, 101, 102, 108, 109; on women, 163
American Anti-Slavery Society: foundation of, 12, 147; mentioned, 160
American Colonization Society, 12
American Health Convention, 150
American Hydropathic Institute, 131
American Hygienic and Hydropathic Association of Physicians and Surgeons, 129
American Medical Association, 166
American Peace Society, 12
American Phrenological Journal, 157
American Physiological Society: and Beaumont, 108; and Cambell, 151; and Mary Gove [Nichols], 130; and Mahan, 148; on women, 163
American Purity Alliance, 177

American Vegetarian Society, 118, 129
Amherst Academy, 57
Anderson, Quentin, 180–82
Andrews, Stephen Pearl, 128, 132, 134; on free love, 140 n. 4
Animal magnetism, 145
Antioch College, 134
Ariès, Philippe, 28–29

Baker, Luther, 51
Balzac, Honoré de, 23
Barr, R. N., 80
Battle Creek Sanitarium, 162–63
Beaumont, William, 108–09
Beecher, Lyman, 60–61
Bell, John, 64–65; on Graham, 75 n. 25
Bell, Luther V., 152
Bender, Thomas, 179–80
Benson, John, 151
Bichat, Xavier, 62–63, 90, 107; influence of, on Graham, 65, 67, 105
Birth control: health reformers and, 128, 137–39, 164–65; history of, 28–30. *See also* Male continence; Voluntary motherhood
Black family life, 46–47
Boston Watch and Ward Society, 177
Botanical medicine, 110–11, 146; number of practitioners of, 124 n. 49
Bouillard, Jean Baptiste, 62
Bread, 116–17
Breakfast cereal, 162–63
Brisbane, Albert, 131
Brook Farm, 123 n. 17
Broussais, François J. V., 62–63; in-

fluence of, on and through Graham, 65, 67, 90, 107
Brown, Norman O., 43–45
Brownson, Orestes, 177
Buffon, Georges, 90
Burdell, John, 102–03
Burgess, Ernest, 50

Cabot, Godfrey Lowell, 177
Calvinism: in childrearing, 88; Weber on, 42
Cambell, David, 147–49, 151, 160
Capitalism, 41
Celibacy, 135, 138
Censorship and vigilance campaigns, 150, 163, 177
Cereal, breakfast, 162–63
Chapin, Charles V., 166
Childrearing: advice and practice for, 34; Graham on, 87–88
Children, masturbation by, 86–88
Cholera, 65–69
Claflin, Tennessee, 139
Coeducation: at American Hydropathic Institute, 131; at Antioch, 134; at Oberlin, 147
Combe, George, 156
Comfort, Alex, 80
Community, concept of, 179–80, 183
Comstock, Anthony, 177
Condie, Charles, 64–65
Contagion, 69
Contraception, 139. *See also* Birth control; Voluntary motherhood
Conway, Moncure, 136
Cornaro, Luigi, 102–03
Criticism: of Graham, 69, 152–53; of Nicholses, 130, 134–35
Cultural disorganization model of sexual liberalization, 45–47
Culture of sexuality, 41
Curtis, Alva, 112

Darwin, Charles, 90
Davis, Andrew Jackson, 157
Death instinct, 44
Decline: of American Physiological Society, 151–52; of Graham, 144; of health reform movement, 169; of hydropathy, 161; of Memnonia, 136;

of Oberlin Grahamism, 148; of Oneida, 138; of orthodox Grahamism, 152, 155, 160
Degler, Carl, 32–34
Diet and sexuality. *See* Sexuality and diet
Diet: of nineteenth-century Americans, 114–17, 119, 167–68; primacy of in history, 104. *See also* Gastrointestinal system, primacy of
Diet of reformers. *See* Regimens
Disintegration of traditional life. *See* Modernization
Dress reform: at Battle Creek, 162; Mary Gove [Nichols] on, 148; at Oberlin, 148; *Water Cure Journal* on, 164

Educational reform by Alcott, 154–55. *See also* Coeducation
Ellis, Havelock, 40
Ellis, John, 86
Emerson, Ralph Waldo, 121, 157; on city vs. country, 83, 120; and health reformers, 104; on the individual, 182; on lecturing, 70; on reform movements, 11; on youth, 77
Enlightenment: and betterment, 11; and revolution, 48; and sexuality, 12
Erikson, Erik, 56
European sexual ethics, 19–20, 23–25, 46, 49–50
Evans, Oliver, 117
Exercise, 168. *See also* Regimens

Family: traditional, 82; modernized, 48–49, 84; Victorian, 179
Fertility, 29
Finney, Charles G., 147, 148
Fish in vegetarian diet, 118
Fishman, Sterling, 81
Food industry, 116–17, 119
Foucault, Michel, 95
Fowler, Lorenzo, 87, 146, 156–59
Fowler, Lydia, 146
Fowler, Orson S., 86, 90, 156–59
Franklin, Benjamin, 42
Free love: Nicholses' doctrine of, 128, 131–34, 139; Townerites' doctrine of, 142 n. 61

Free market, 41, 49–50
Freud, Sigmund, 40
Freudians, leftist, 41–45
Friendly Botanic Societies, 111
Frothingham, Octavius Brooks, 12

Gall, Franz Joseph, 155–56
Gardner, Augustus K., 116
Garrison, William Lloyd, 121, 150
Gastrointestinal system, primacy of: to Broussais, 63; to Cornaro, 102; to Graham, 67–68, 105; to Jackson, 161; to Noyes, 137; to Thomson, 111
Genitalia, primacy of, 94
Gillis, John R., 81
Goodell, William, 150
Government's role: as seen by health reformers, 100, 167; as seen by vigilance societies, 177. See also Public health movement
Graham boardinghouses, 149, 150; and Kellogg sanitarium, 163
Graham Clubs, 147
Graham Journal of Health and Longevity, 147, 151
Graham, Sylvester, 13–14, 64, 120–22, 145; compared to other reformers, 121; family and youth of, 55–59; influence of, 13, 14, 128, 144, 155, 157–58, 161; medical studies of, 59–62; nervous breakdowns by, 58, 143; old age of, 143–44; personality of, 152–53, 155; and phrenology, 156; poetry of, 73 n. 6, 143–44; speaking style of, 71, 152. See also Health reformers
Grahamite schools and institutions. See Schools and institutions on Grahamite principles
Grimké, Angelina, 171 n. 30
Grimké, Sarah, 150
Griscom, John H., 103, 145

Hahnemann, Samuel, 111
Handlin, Oscar, 25
Hare, E. H., 80
Hartley, Robert M., 107, 145
Hauser, Casper, 106
Hawthorne, Nathaniel, 120
Health and nutrition: fertility and, 27, 30; improvement of, 168

Health Reformer, 162, 167
Health reformers, 13, 40, 93–94, 177–78; influence of, 95, 119–20, 146–69; personality type of, 72–73; and public health movement, 145–46; Brownson on, 177. See also Popularity; Schools and other institutions on Grahamite principles
Heidegger, Martin, 44
Herberg, Will, 51
Heredity, 89–90
Heywood, Ezra, 139
Higginson, Thomas Wentworth, 150
Himes, Norman E., 28–29
History, Graham's view of, 104
Homeopathy, 110, 111–13; number of practitioners of, 124 n. 49; mentioned, 145
Horlick, Allan S., 159
Huguenots, 42
Hydropathy, 145, 159–63; Fowlers and, 159; Nicholses and, 129, 131, 134

Ideology, Erikson on, 56
Immigrants, 169
Individual, 11–12, 181–82; Graham on, 121; Nichols on, 131
Inkeles, Alex, 21
Insane asylums, 89
Insanity: copulatory, 162; masturbatory, 80, 88–89
Instability and insecurity. See Modernization
Institutions and schools on Grahamite principles. See Schools and institutions on Grahamite principles

Jackson, James Caleb, 146, 160, 161–62; on immigrants, 169; on women, 164
James, Henry, 83
Jennings, Dr. Isaac, 114
Johnson, Virginia, 51
Journal of Foreign Medical Science and Literature, 64
Journal of Health, 64, 151

Kellogg, John Harvey, 162–63
Kinsey, Alfred, 51, 176

Knowlton, Charles, 89
Koch, Robert, 66

Laennec, R. T. H., 62
Lane, Charles, 130
Lane Seminary, 147
Lasch, Christopher, 180–82
Lecture and sermon compared, 70–71
Lecture tours: by Graham, 71, 143; by Mary Gove [Nichols], 130
Leibig, Justus von, 108, 117
Lévi-Strauss, Claude, 104
Life: length *vs.* intensity of, 115–16; purpose of, 107. *See also* Graham, Sylvester, old age of
Life expectancy, 168
Lyell, Charles, 90

MacDonald, Robert, 80
Magendie, François, 108
Mahan, Asa, 147–48
Male continence, 137
Mann, Horace: and Alcott's school reform, 155; and Memnonia, 134–36
Marcuse, Herbert, 43–45
Market economy, 41, 49–50
Marriage: age at, 31; Lorenzo Fowler on, 157; Graham on, 86, 132; A. Grimké on, 171 n. 30; Nichols on, 131–34
Marx, Karl, 21.
Marxists. *See* Freudians, leftist
Masters, William, 51
Masturbation, 78–81, 86–91; controversy about discussing, 100, 130; prevalence of, 23, 86–87, 96 n. 13
Masturbatory insanity, 80, 88–89
Mather, Cotton, 12
Meat consumption, 119
Meat in Grahamite diet, 116, 118
Mechling, Jay, 34
Medical profession: Alcott on, 112–13; attitude to patients of, 94, 96 n. 12, 138; challenges of, 166; Graham on, 113, 152; heroic treatments by, 109–10, in public health, 145, 166–67, 168; Trall on, 114. *See also* Paris school of medicine; Sectarian medicine
Melville, Herman, 120

Memnonia, 134–36
Menarche, age of, 27–28
Mendon Association, 58
Metcalfe, William, 101–02
Middle class, 25, 179
Milk: in vegetarian diet, 118; wholesomeness of, 115, 116
Millennialism, 120–21
Millerites, 120
Modernization, 21–24, 55, 178–80, 183; authority and, 48–49; health reformers and, 146, 165; jeremiads against, 103; models of sexuality in, 41–52
Modern personality type, 21, 24, 180–83; development of, facilitated by health reformers, 14, 93, 122; development of, in New England, 55; Tocqueville on, 181
Mosher, Clelia Duel, 33
Moynihan, Daniel, 46–47
Mullaby, John, 116

National Anti-Slavery Standard, 160
Natural physiological laws, 91, 145, 165
Nature, state of, 104; Hauser exemplifying, 106
Negro family life, 46–47
Neuman, John B., 86, 88
Neuman, Robert P., 81
New England Non-Resistance Society, 12
New York Hygeio-Therapeutic College, 146
Nichols, Mary Sargaent Neal Gove, 129–31, 158; on physiological laws, 165; popularity of, 167; on women, 163
Nichols, Thomas L., and Mary, 127–39; on heredity, 90
Nietzsche, Friedrich Wilhelm, 44
Northampton, Mass., 143
Noyes, John Humphrey, 128, 137–38
Nutritional value of foods: Graham on, 117–18; traditional beliefs on, 102, 114

Oberlin College, 147–150
Onan, 95 n. 6

Oneida, 137–38, 142 n. 61
Orgasm: female, 33, 51; male, 85–86, 137; Nichols on, 128
Owen, Robert Dale, 128, 132, 157

Pacifists, 12
Paine, Emerson, 58
Pangenesis, 90
Paris school of medicine, 62–64; influence of on health reformers, 107
Parker, Theodore, 121
Patent medicines, 110, 112
Pennsylvania Society for Discouraging the Use of Ardent Spirits, 58, 64
Perfectionism, 11
Performance principle, 43–44
Philadelphia Medical Institute, 64
Philadelphia school of medicine, 59–62; and Paris school, 63–64; and temperance movement, 60–61, 64
Phrenology, 146, 155–59; and Mann, 155; and Trall, 161
Physical culture, 145
Physicians. See Medical profession
Physio-Medical College, 112
Pinel, Philippe, 62
Platt, Gerald M., 48–49
Poe, Edgar Allan, 120, 131
Popularity: of Alcott, 143, 167; of Mary Gove [Nichols], 130; of Graham, 65, 71–72, Lecture to Young Men, 78, 143, 167; of Trall, 167. See also Testimonials to Graham
Population growth, 82–83
Pornography, 23
Premarital pregnancy and illegitimacy: concurrent trends in, 25–26, 30–31, 37 n. 23; as evidence of sexual behavior, 20, 24, 27–32; trends in, 13, 23–25, 31–32, 50
Premarital sexual relations around World War I, 176–77
Priessnitz, Vincenz, 159–61
Proletarian subculture, 49
Prostitution: campaign against, 150, 163; in Europe, 23
Puberty, onset of, 81, 88. See also Menarche, age of
Public health movement, 144–46; and purity advocates, 165–66, 169

Public indecency, 163
Publications and lectures: increase of, 69–71, 167; influence of, 34; about masturbation, 78; about sexuality, 20, 32
Puritans: and sexuality, 12, 42; personality type of, 55
Purity advocates. See Health reformers

Quakers, 130

Reform movements: affinity of, 11–12, 113, 121, 146, 149–50; Emerson on, 11
Regimens: of Alcott, 154–55; of Fowlers, 157; of Mary Gove [Nichols], 130; of Graham, 61, 101, 153; at Graham boardinghouses, 149; of Hahnemann's homeopathy, 111; of health reformers generally, 146, 168; of hydropathy, 159–61; of Kellogg, 162–63; at Memnonia, 135; at Oberlin, 148; of Thomson's botanical medicine, 110–12. See also Fish in vegetarian diet; Meat in Grahamite diet; Milk; Vegetarianism
Reich, Wilhelm, 43
Reiss, Ira, 51
Religion, effect of on sexuality, 50–52. See also Lecture and sermon compared
Revivalism, 121, 145
Riesman, David, 182
Ripley, George, 103. See also Brook Farm
Rodman, Hyman, 47
Rogers, Nathaniel P., 160
Roheim, Geza, 43
Rohleder, Hermann, 87
Rousseau, Jean Jacques, 104
Ruggles, David, 160
Rural life, 92, 120. See also Urbanization
Rush, Benjamin: cited by Graham, 67; medical principles of, 61–63; on temperance, 60, 61

Sartre, Jean-Paul, 44
School for Life. See Memnonia
School of Integral Education, 131

Schools: Alcott's reform of, 154–55; masturbation in, 87. *See also* Coeducation

Schools and institutions on Grahamite principles, 144, 146–52; of Nicholses, 129–31, 134–36

Scientific evidence for vegetarianism, 101, 107–09

Sectarian medicine, 146; growth of, 109–10, 124 n. 49. *See also* Botanical medicine; Homeopathy; Hydropathy; Patent Medicines, Phrenology

Semen, 80, 85; Graham on, 90; Tissot on, 79, 90

Sennett, Richard, 180–82

Seventh Day Adventists, 162–63

Sexual culture and subculture, 41

Sexual heterodoxy, 40, 127

Sexual intercourse: Kellogg on, 162; Nichols on, 127–28. *See also* Orgasm

Sexual intercourse, frequency of, recommended: by Graham, 86, 132; by Nichols, 128, 131–32, 135; by Trall, 32

Sexual intercourse, purpose of, according to: Judeo-Christian tradition, 79; Nichols, 138–39; Noyes, 137; women, 33; Wright, 165

Sexual revolution around World War I, 176–77

Sexuality, controversy about discussion of, 78, 100, 131, 152–53

Sexuality and diet, 114; in cholera, 68; Finney on, 147; Fowlers on, 157–58; Graham on, 77–78, 115, 153; Trall on, 161

Sexuality and hunger, 105

Shattuck, Lemuel, 110

Shew, Joel, 159–61

Shorter, Edward, 49–50

Sims, J. Marion, 110

Smell, sense of, 106–07

Smith, David M., 21

Society of Friends, 130

Spencer, Herbert, 90

Spiritualism, 134–36

Spitz, René, 80

Spurzheim, Johan Casper, 155–56

Stanton, Henry B., 150

Stomach. *See* Gastrointestinal system, primacy of

Subculture of gratification, 48–50

Subculture of sexuality, 41, 47

Sublimation of sexuality in modernization, 41–45

Sunderland, LaRoy, 150

Surplus repression, 43–44

Symbolic significance of body and its functions, 91–92

Szasz, Thomas, 80

Tappen, Lewis, 150

Temperance movement, 60–61; influence of, 119

Terman, Lewis M., 176

Testimonials to Graham, 69, 118

Thomson, Samuel, 110–11, 145

Tissot, Samuel, 79, 90, 132; on children's masturbation, 87

Tocqueville, Alexis de: on American character, 181; quoted briefly, 12; on upward mobility, 83; on women, 183–84 n. 10

Townerites, 142 n. 61

Trall, Russell T., 146, 160, 161; at Battle Creek, 162; on diet and sexuality, 161; on frequency of intercourse, 32; on masturbation, 88; on medicine, 114; on Nichols, 131; popularity of, 167; on swimming, 168; on vitalism and diet, 107; on voluntary motherhood, 138

Trinidad, sexual mores in, 47

Urbanization, 82–85, 120; Kellogg on, 163

Vegetarianism: Alcott on, 109; Metcalfe on, 102; physiological defense of, 101; religious defense of, 101; scientific evidence for, 101, 107–09. *See also* Fish in vegetarian diet; Meat in Grahamite diet; Milk; Regimens

Victorian sexual ethics, 19, 179

Vitalism, 62–63; Graham and, 67, 105, 109; health reformers and, 107; and sexuality, 90

Voluntary motherhood, 128, 134, 138–39, 142 n. 55

Walker, Amasa, 150

Walker, Mack, 46

Wallin, Paul, 50
Warren, Josiah, 134
Watch and Ward Campaigns, 150, 163, 177
Water cure. *See* Hydropathy
Water Cure Journal, 129, 167
Wealth, concentration of, 82–83
Weber, Max, 41–42
Weinstein, Fred, 48–49
Weld, Theodore, 150
Wesleyan College, 147
Western Health Reform Institute, 162
White, Ellen G., 162
Whitman, Walt, 157
Willard, Elizabeth, 86
Williams College, 147
Women: Mary Gove [Nichols] and, 129–30; Graham on, 165; health reformers and, 92, 163–65; marriage and, 133; primacy of reproductive system in, 94, 138; sexual attitudes of, 33, 51, 133–34, 137, 142 n. 55; slogan of, 157; Tocqueville on, 183–84 n. 10. *See also* Coeducation; Dress reform; Voluntary motherhood
Women's Christian Temperance Union, 163
Woodhull, Victoria, 40
Woodward, Samuel B.; 158; on masturbation, 88, 89, 92;
Wright, Henry Clarke, 165

Yellow Springs, Ohio, 134–35
Youths: compared to health reformers, 72–73; in cities, 77, 82–85, 92; increase of, 81–82. *See also* Adolescence